MASTERS OF WORLD LITERATURE

PUBLISHED

IN PREPARATION

Jane Austen

MASTERS OF WORLD LITERATURE SERIES

LOUIS KRONENBERGER, GENERAL EDITOR

Jane Austen

by Douglas Bush

M

First published in the U.S.A. 1975
First published in the United Kingdom 1975

Published by
THE MACMILLAN PRESS LTD
London and Basingstoke
Associated companies in New York
Dublin Melbourne Johannesburg and Madras

SBN 333 14207 1

Printed and bound in Great Britain by
REDWOOD BURN LIMITED
Trowbridge & Esher

To Hazel, once more

Contents

Preface

FOUR OF JANE AUSTEN's novels were published anonymously during 1811-15, the other two together at the end of 1817, after her death. The reception of the first four, in the few years before she died, was highly encouraging (though sales were nowhere near those of Scott, Maria Edgeworth, or Hannah More); but she might have been astonished if she could have known that the years 1923-73 (to take an arbitrary round number) would yield some sixty-seven books about her and her work, some thirty-one of them in the last decade—not to mention editions, parts of critical books, and hundreds of essays and articles. Jane Austen has benefited from the general advance of modern criticism from loose impressionism to precise analysis, and many modern studies have promoted knowledge and greatly sharpened and sensitized understanding, at least among specialists, of the literary and ideological background of her fiction, the growing subtlety of her ironic art, and the larger and deeper significance of her supposedly small themes. But her ever-widening popularity, from her own time to ours, has been due less to interest in her finely unobtrusive craftsmanship or her view of society than to her humorous and serious insight into the character and the personal relations, the happy and unhappy experience, of ordinary people of the upper middle class. Intimate association with such people, whose feelings and thoughts, problems and actions, are set forth by a sane imagination at once realistic and detached, moral and comic, satirical and sympathetic—this is what the multitude of readers, from cosy "Janeites" to austere highbrows, have in their various ways enjoyed. And such enjoyment does not appear to have been made pallid by the strong spices required in most recent fiction.

To speak of the number of modern books about Jane Austen is to suggest that there is no urgent reason for another one, since neither lifelong devotion nor her bicentenary is enough. A better reason is that many recent critics have addressed experts in her work or in the history or technique of fiction and that this book, as the first two chapters imply, is only a general account, a sort of "companion" to Jane Austen, on a modest scale, addressed to general readers. Hence, while it has profited from the mass of books and essays (scores of which could not be cited), both the author's aim and his limitations forbid elaborate, ultra-sophisticated analysis of either technique or ideas. But something can be shown of Jane Austen's increasing mastery of dramatic situation, dialogue, characterization, and atmosphere, of form and theme, of her active awareness of a principle enunciated by Henry James: that "the art of the novel," "only to a less extent" than that of the drama, "is above all the art of preparations."[1] It is assumed here that the best way to appreciate Jane Austen's mastery of form and other virtues is the simplest way: to follow her development of a story, with varying degrees of brevity, as a basis for comment. It may be hoped that enough evidence is given to illustrate the long-accepted fact that the retiring spinster, while no Dickens, and rarely a "poet," is one of the finest of English novelists and that in both her art and her moral and social outlook she is the only, or the supreme, "classical" writer in that rich domain.

There are other reasons for adding one's small testimony to the long shelf. At times in modern criticism what one may think philosophical over-reading translates Jane Austen's instinctive

[1] Preface to *The Tragic Muse* (New York Edition), 7, xii; *The Art of the Novel: Critical Prefaces by Henry James*, ed. R. P. Blackmur (New York: Scribner, 1950), 86.

concreteness into large abstractions or social parables which she would hardly have recognized: we hear, for instance, of her epistemology and ontology and, more commonly, of that master-key to all social phenomena of the past twenty-five centuries, the rise of the middle class. She does of course use, with precise awareness of their established meaning, the abstract terms of the moral vocabulary, but that is another matter. Then some emancipated critics have been moved to denounce Jane Austen's moral principles and attitudes, especially as embodied in *Mansfield Park*. Although such libertarians have been so severe, even violent, it may be remembered that their and our age of undisciplined sensibility and defective ethical reason had already been judged by her. Further, some more or less sympathetic critics have assumed or argued that Jane Austen's view of life was thoroughly secular and that early tributes to her religious seriousness only came from perfunctory familial piety. Without subscribing to the legend of "gentle Jane," one may have a different opinion on these important points.

Several kinds of "sources" have been used, acutely or erratically, by some modern critics to illustrate Jane Austen's materials and methods, but these are in general slighted here. One kind of speculation began in her own lifetime, the "recognition" of originals of characters among her connections or even among strangers. This was an indirect testimony to her power of lifelike character-drawing, but her relations themselves did not discern such resemblances (apart from a few minute items), and we may stand on the author's firm principle that she wished "to create not to reproduce": "I am much too proud of my own gentlemen ever to admit that they are only Mr. A. or Major C."[2]

Two more fruitful areas of exploration have been Jane Austen's own early writings (made fully available only in 1922 f.) and the relation of all her work to the novels of her predecessors,

[2] The witness quoted—who will be quoted again on occasion—was a Mrs. Barrett, who had been a friend and correspondent of Jane Austen and who died in 1865. Her recollections were recorded in a letter of 1869 from a clergyman friend which R. W. Chapman printed in part in *Nineteenth-Century Fiction* 4 (1949–50), 171–74. This text was presumably more accurate than that given in the *Memoir* (1870 f.; ed. R. W. Chapman, 1926, p. 157) and quoted therefrom in Chapman's *Jane Austen: Facts and Problems* (Oxford, 1950), 126.

Richardson, Fanny Burney, and many minor writers, and to eighteenth-century literature in general. It seems clear—and it was
altogether natural—that she took up and developed, satirically or
seriously, some themes, incidents, and types of character already
treated or touched by her youthful self and by other novelists. In
both cases what is significant is not mere "borrowing" but the
manner of re-creation. Fanny Burney, for instance, provided a
model, more up to date than Richardson, for the presentation of
young women encountering the world; yet Fanny, with all her
vigor, is a paddle-wheel steamer that churns and splashes on its
zigzag course and Jane Austen is a streamlined yacht—or, at
times, a submarine. But examples of re-creation need space, and
this book cannot go beyond occasional brief references (some of
them new, I hope).

Quotations from the text of the novels are taken from R. W.
Chapman's standard edition (1923; 3rd edition, 1932–34), but not
the numbering of chapters by the volume, in which he followed
the original editions of three or two volumes. (Those original
divisions, we may note, tended, in careful planning, to parallel the
acts of a play; one example of a dramatic climax is cited below in
the chapter on *Mansfield Park*.) But most readers presumably do
not have Chapman's edition, and in this book references to chapters (in roman numerals) follow the consecutive numbering
normally used in modern editions.

Readers will regret that the general editor, Louis Kronenberger, who had already written about Jane Austen, did not see
his way to doing this volume, which was originally to be his, and
passed on the assignment to me, who had already written too
many books in this series.

The dedication recalls much helpful domestic debate.

D.B.

Abbreviations

Letters = *Jane Austen's Letters to her sister Cassandra and others, collected and edited by R. W. Chapman*. London and New York: Oxford University Press, 1964. (First published 1932; 2nd edition, 1952; reprinted with slight corrections, 1959, 1964). Quoted by permission of the publishers.

Life = William and R. A. Austen-Leigh, *Jane Austen: Her Life and Letters: A Family Record*. London and New York, 1913; New York, 1965.

Memoir = *Memoir of Jane Austen by her nephew James Edward Austen-Leigh*, ed. R. W. Chapman. Oxford: Clarendon Press, 1926. The *Memoir* was first published in 1870.

M. W. = *Minor Works Now first collected and edited from the manuscripts by R. W. Chapman*. London and New York: Oxford University Press, 1954; reprinted 1958. (Volume VI of Chapman's edition of the novels)

Southam = B. C. Southam, *Jane Austen's Literary Manuscripts: A study of the novelist's development through the surviving papers*. London and New York: Oxford University Press, 1964.

1

Jane Austen's England

THE SPACIOUS HEADING promises no more than a glance at some facts, traditions, and attitudes which are part of the fabric of Jane Austen's novels because they were part of the social fabric of her age.[1] Such a reminder of ways of life that have more or less changed or vanished only separates some temporal elements from the timeless truth of the novelist's insight into human nature. And one general limitation of scope is of course her wise choice of the milieu in which she was thoroughly at home. To quote her much-quoted words about the novel her niece Anna Austen was writing, "You are now collecting your People delightfully, getting them exactly into such a spot as is the delight of my life; —3 or 4 Families in a Country Village is the very thing to work on" (Letter 100: September 9, 1814). We should not, though, assume that Jane Austen was retreating from normal life: a large proportion of people still lived in the country and country towns and villages,

---

[1] One may question the view sometimes encountered in modern criticism, that the England of the novels was far from the historical reality. Both contemporary reviewers and the numerous relatives and friends whose opinions of her books Jane Austen recorded (*M. W.*, 431–39) evidently accepted the novels as slices of the life they knew. Of course "realism" and kindred words are used of Jane Austen in the limited sense applicable to her selective and stylized pictures.

traditionally a more conservative scene than London and the smaller cities.

One elementary and conspicuous fact, which had many centuries of history behind it, was the division of social classes—though it is well to remember that, with all the social mobility of modern times, the class structure is still a fact of life in England and, with differences, in the supposedly egalitarian United States. Jane Austen is obviously not a rebel, but, as an instinctive realist, she depicts her chosen world as it is. At the same time, like other satirists, she is too clear-eyed and rational to be content with the existing world and subjects many attitudes prevalent in her stratified society to humorous ridicule or moral condemnation. Yet there have been readers—readers as different as D. H. Lawrence and Sir Harold Nicolson—who have so far failed to understand her dramatic and ironic manner of presentation (and much else) as to call her a snob. It should be transparently clear that throughout the novels Jane Austen steadily satirizes snobbery, not merely in Lady Catherine de Bourgh and the toady Mr. Collins or in Sir Walter and Elizabeth Elliot but in her heroine Emma Woodhouse, whose snobbery is one main cause of the harm she does to other people, and in the otherwise excellent Lady Russell, whose prejudice keeps Anne Elliot and her worthy suitor apart for eight unhappy years. Elizabeth Bennet's acute embarrassment over her ill-bred mother's inanities hardly comes under the head of snobbery.

Jane Austen always distinguishes between true and spurious gentility, between internal worth and external rank or possessions. Conventional gentility is founded on land and money (which can largely atone for inferior birth), and the rich, like General Tilney or Mrs. Ferrars or Mrs. Churchill, are seldom examples of real worth and good-breeding. The supercilious Darcy, brought up with a wrong kind of pride, falls short in goodwill and civility until he learns his lesson from Elizabeth Bennet. And many people lower in the financial and social scale are guided by false values and self-interest rather than by a sound head and unselfish heart. There is no essential difference, apart from a veneer of manners and style, between, say, Miss Bingley and the vulgar Isabella Thorpe and Lucy Steele. In a positive way, characters are distinguished in accordance with the rightness and fineness of their feelings and taste, and taste is a moral quality. The novels have very few characters who enjoy the author's or the reader's entire approval, and her comedies of manners have far more edged satire than unalloyed humor.

In this connection it may be observed that a prime necessity for readers of Jane Austen is to learn her language and not to be misled by its smooth surface (or, it should be added, by changes in the meaning and connotation of words). She has relatively little interest in her characters' physical appearance, but the language they use is a continual revelation of their cultural and moral standing. Characters who unthinkingly reflect the common or meretricious values of their world use words, especially such general terms as "elegant," "genteel," "gentleman," with a looseness or wrongness that indicates their more or less serious deficiencies. But the author, and the characters she presents as thoughtful and right-minded, use such terms, simple or complex, with conscious, intelligent correctness, and they carry the weight of moral, cultural, and social tradition and taste. The author could rely with some confidence on the right response from sensitive readers who shared her scale of values; and, because those values were recognized, she could use established terms not only with positive assurance but, in satirical contexts, with ironic ambiguity. One notable exemplar of linguistic and moral discrimination is Henry Tilney, who lectures Catherine Morland on her lack of verbal—that is, critical—precision; and he is only the first of the heroes who show such a concern.[2]

There is no need to comment on small matters of etiquette which belong to a society more formalized than ours, but some usages are significant for situation or character and some appear

[2] Interest in this aspect of Jane Austen has of late years amounted almost to a movement and it has refined our understanding of both her art and her cultural outlook. Some stages in the movement are: an appendix in the first volume of Chapman's edition of the novels; the chapter on style in Mary Lascelles' *Jane Austen and Her Art* (Oxford, 1939); and some larger and later studies of varying scope: H. S. Babb, *Jane Austen's Novels: The Fabric of Dialogue* (Columbus, 1962); K. C. Phillipps, *Jane Austen's English* (London, 1970); K. Kroeber (below, c. 10, n. 2); Norman Page, *The Language of Jane Austen* (London and New York, 1972), with a bibliography on style; Lloyd W. Brown, *Bits of Ivory: Narrative Techniques in Jane Austen's Fiction* (Baton Rouge, 1973); S. M. Tave, *Some Words of Jane Austen* (Chicago and London, 1973).

to change during the course of Jane Austen's writing. One thing that strikes us as surprisingly informal is that such women as Mrs. Dashwood and Marianne can speak of or even address a man by his surname only, but this seems to be a mark of established friendship; Emma Woodhouse, in her angry catalogue of Mrs. Elton's vulgarities, exclaims first over her referring to "Knightley" (xxii). Willoughby's calling Marianne by her first name is good evidence for their being engaged. At formal parties the order of precedence for women depends on rank, marital status, and age: Lydia Bennet Wickham, quite unabashed by her belated marriage, complacently asserts her priority over her oldest sister, even at a family meal; and Elizabeth Elliot, as a baronet's daughter, has for thirteen years been "walking immediately after Lady Russell out of all the drawing-rooms and dining-rooms in the country." Her sister, Mrs. Charles Musgrove, for the same reason is always pushing ahead of her mother-in-law.

Class divisions are solidified by the fact that most genteel families have fixed roots; they live in the house where their forebears lived and represent a relatively unchanging level of civility and culture, high or low. Jane Austen, with her deep attachment to rural Hampshire, makes her strong sense of place an increasingly substantial and functional element in the novels. The title *Mansfield Park* carries full significance as the name of Sir Thomas Bertram's kingdom, which undergoes some shocks. In *Pride and Prejudice* Netherfield, Bingley's rented place, and Pemberley, Darcy's ancestral estate, are the appropriate setting for and image of their possessors. Bingley is the first "gentleman" in his line because his father left him a fortune, though very few books, and he has not yet settled down, whereas Darcy has at Pemberley a splendid library which "has been the work of many generations" (viii). Thus the mobility of the newly rich is contrasted with traditional stability. The village of Longbourn stands less for the bookish Mr. Bennet than for his foolish wife and youngest daughters, and Darcy, shortly before he proposes to Elizabeth, assumes that she has moved beyond such limitations: "*You* cannot have been always at Longbourn" (xxxii). It is significant that all the heroines except Elizabeth and Emma Woodhouse are uprooted from their homes so that they can encounter new scenes and people—and Elizabeth's two important meetings with Darcy take place in Mrs. Collins' house and at Pemberley. In the social structure of the age and the novels places of abode are fixed points of cultural reference. This is one part, though only a part, of what Henry James called "the supreme virtue of a novel," namely, "solidity of specification."[3]

The craving to augment family wealth, power, and prestige is a prime motive among the rich or well-to-do—"They're all on the make, in a quiet way, in Jane," says a character in Kipling's *The Janeites*—and, in novels about young women, the prime field of activity is marriage. While the novels do depict happy marriages, among most of the characters the commercial view of marriage, however qualified by other considerations, is largely a matter of course. It is presented, with the author's usual irony and subtle overtones, in the opening sentences of *Mansfield Park*:

About thirty years ago, Miss Maria Ward, of Huntingdon, with only seven thousand pounds, had the good luck to captivate Sir Thomas Bertram, of Mansfield Park, in the county of Northampton, and to be thereby raised to the rank of a baronet's lady, with all the comforts and consequences of an handsome house and large income. All Huntingdon exclaimed on the greatness of the match, and her uncle, the lawyer, himself, allowed her to be at least three thousand pounds short of any equitable claim to it.

In the course of the story the Bertrams' daughter Maria—not without some abortive qualms on her father's part—escapes from home by marrying the stupid Mr. Rushworth, whose only attraction is his wealth; and that does not hold her very long.

In Jane Austen's England, although on the higher social levels parents were still active operators in the marriage market, daughters had gained far more freedom of choice than had been open to the persecuted Clarissa Harlowe. And in Jane Austen's novels, while we are kept aware of the commercial view, heroines and heroes marry for love and parents, with some exceptions, are acquiescent. Some young women—Penelope Watson, Isabella Thorpe, the Steele sisters, Mrs. Clay—have to carry on their own predatory campaigns, and they are quite ready to abandon one prey if a better one appears. But the Austen heroines, who have

[3] "The Art of Fiction," *Henry James: The Future of the Novel*, ed. Leon Edel (New York: Vintage Books, 1956), 14.

higher motives, are also on their own, and they do not need to sit like Patience on a monument—as Fanny Price does—but may, like Elizabeth Bennet, bring their loving suitors to scratch or, like even the gentle Jane Bennet, go in quest of them.

For young men, the army and navy and—not on the lowest rungs—the church and the law offer socially respectable openings to those who seek them, but young men of actual or prospective wealth do not commonly embrace a profession or settled occupation of any kind. Most "gentlemen," living on their incomes or hopes, spend their abundant leisure in the diversions prescribed by their tastes and means or debts. All the novels have examples. It is taken for granted that young men of expensive habits, like Willoughby or Wickham or William Elliot, or younger sons of good family, like Henry Tilney or Colonel Fitzwilliam (an earl's son), must marry for money or at least permit themselves to love only a well-endowed girl. On the other hand, it is assumed that young men of fortune, like Darcy and Bingley, must not marry beneath them but find wives of assured position, preferably with money too. Even Mr. Collins, a clergyman on the make who will receive the Bennet estate by entail, takes pains to learn the precise amount of money that goes with Elizabeth Bennet; refused by her, he promptly turns to Charlotte Lucas, who has no fortune but is the daughter of a knight.

All this commercialism is of course repugnant to Jane Austen, but she presents the world she knows from observation and reading, and—as in the sentences quoted from *Mansfield Park*—she can turn its own language to satirical account. But while her heroes and heroines break the accepted rules of the market, we should not expect a clear-headed realist to glorify love in a cottage—that is left to the hypocritical Isabella Thorpe and Lucy Steele. Even that romantic idealist, Marianne Dashwood, assumes that a "competence" means eighteen hundred or two thousand pounds a year; her rational sister rates one thousand as wealth. Critics have quoted Lord David Cecil's saying, that in Jane Austen's moral-realistic view it is wrong to marry for money but silly to marry without it.[4] Yet, though the first half of this dictum has abundant support in the novels, the second half, while

[4] *Jane Austen* (Cambridge and New York, 1935), 33.

in accord with our general notion of Jane Austen's common sense, gets much less illustration. At any rate the last completed novel, *Persuasion*, might (with qualifications) be called a moving plea for love and risk against worldly prudence.

The case of Charlotte Lucas is a reminder that for the multitude of genteel young women there were only three prospects: marriage, aging spinsterhood at home, or becoming a governess or teacher in a school. Charlotte, to be sure, is much less sensitive than her friend Elizabeth Bennet, but she is twenty-seven, she has never been "romantic," and she asks "only a comfortable home" (xxii); and she finds a tolerable degree of happiness, if not in the companionship of her husband and the patronage of Lady Catherine, at least in her house and parish and poultry. But the life of a governess means ill-paid drudgery and social subservience, with no hope of amelioration or escape—unless perhaps one is a Jane Eyre or Becky Sharp. In *The Watsons* Emma and Elizabeth view the lot of a teacher with horror. Emma Woodhouse's Miss Taylor, who becomes a loved companion and friend and then a happy wife and a figure in Highbury, is a unique exception to the rule. In the same novel, Jane Fairfax has hitherto had a similarly happy life in the Campbell family, but her imminent entry into the governess market arouses deep commiseration: she herself speaks of looking up "Offices for the sale—not quite of human flesh— but of human intellect."

Of the kinds and degrees of poverty and misery in the new manufacturing towns, or even among agricultural laborers, Jane Austen was not in a position to acquire first-hand knowledge. But, as the daughter of a village clergyman, she was aware of the poor around her, and she seems to have done her share of parish visiting and charitable giving. She had little money to give, but "Her needlework was nearly always a garment for the poor" (*Life*, 242). Public agitation and legislation on behalf of the submerged nine-tenths had for the most part to wait for the Victorian age; earlier, what help was supplied came largely from private charity. Emma Woodhouse, however snobbish on higher levels, is generous in giving time and aid to the poor of her neighborhood. Before the Elliot family's enforced departure from Kellynch, Anne alone pays visits to the small tenants. One of Darcy's many virtues, according to his housekeeper, is his

bountiful kindness to the poor. On the other hand, his aunt Lady
Catherine, an ancestress of Dickens' Mrs. Pardiggle, inspires a
paragraph of tart satire (xxx):

Elizabeth soon perceived that though this great lady was not in the
commission of the peace for the county, she was a most active
magistrate in her own parish, the minutest concerns of which were
carried to her by Mr. Collins; and whenever any of the cottagers were
disposed to be quarrelsome, discontented or too poor, she sallied
forth into the village to settle their differences, silence their complaints, and scold them into harmony and plenty.

The subject of money brings in a marginal fact which at first
surprises readers of all nineteenth-century fiction: that even poor
families, if not the very poorest, have some domestic help. Mrs.
Dashwood and her three daughters, who live simply on five hundred pounds a year, and the five Watsons, whose income is apparently about the same or less, have two maids and a man. The
slatternly Mrs. Price has two servants, who help, after a fashion,
to cope with her large family. But we remember that even a small
household required much work and that throughout the century
there was a "servant class," an abundant supply of cheap labor.
To mention a different item by way of contrast, the taking of a
newspaper was commonly limited to the well-to-do: Sir John
Middleton passed on his paper to the Dashwoods—as at Steventon
the Austens received the same favor from a more affluent friend.
Jane Austen leaves us in no doubt of the mental vacancy of
most members of the squirearchy and the upper middle class of
country and town—Mrs. Allen (Catherine Morland's chaperone
in Bath), Sir John and Lady Middleton ("He hunted and shot,
and she humoured her children; and these were their only resources"), Mrs. Bennet, Mr. Hurst, Lady Catherine de Bourgh,
Lady Bertram, Mr. Rushworth, Mr. Woodhouse, Sir Walter Elliot, and others. That is not to say, of course, that these characters lack individual flavor and functional value: for instance, if
we see Lady Bertram forever on her sofa with her needlework
and her dog, on occasion uttering memorable phrases ("I sent
Chapman to her"), she can on occasion penetrate Mrs. Norris'
hide and, when she has actually seen her sick son, she can change

from unfelt words to "the language of real feeling and alarm."
On a level above the mentally retarded, things are not much
better: at a grand dinner given by the John Dashwoods for Mrs.
Ferrars, "no poverty of any kind, except of conversation, appeared" (xxxiv). On the other hand, when Darcy, who has seen
and heard Elizabeth's mother, meets her uncle, Mr. Gardiner,
who is in "trade," she can rejoice in his intelligence, taste, and
good manners. The unfamiliar world of the nobility Jane Austen
does not really enter, but that, we imagine—on the strength of
nearly all of its few representatives, from Lord Osborne in *The
Watsons* to Viscountess Dalrymple in *Persuasion*—would not be
very different.

We should not expect Jane Austen's village and county gentry
to be notably or even tolerably cultivated and intellectual. The
novels often show amateur musicians performing, since piano-
playing and singing were standard accomplishments for young
ladies (Mary Crawford plays the harp). But novels cannot show
people reading, and generally we do not think of much reading
being done by women or by most of the men. Mr. Hurst considers it "rather singular" that Elizabeth Bennet prefers reading to
cards. Mary Bennet is an unhappy example of complacently
bookish banality; the highly intelligent Mr. Bennet takes refuge
from his wife and family in bookish irresponsibility. The Bertram
girls are astonished by the ignorance of their poor relation, Fanny
Price, when she comes to Mansfield Park (ii):

"How long ago it is, aunt, since we used to repeat the chronologi-
cal order of the kings of England, with the dates of their accession,
and most of the principal events of their reigns!"
"Yes," added the other; "and of the Roman emperors as low as
Severus; besides a great deal of the Heathen Mythology, and all the
Metals, Semi-metals, Planets, and distinguished philosophers."

That is doubtless not far from the intellectual furniture of upper-
class girls in general.

Marianne Dashwood, Fanny Price, and Anne Elliot are hero-
ines whose serious reading is concretely illustrated. Emma
Woodhouse's pretensions are contrasted, by the candid George
Knightley, with the real cultivation of Jane Fairfax. The one

novel that can be called bookish—in a mainly satirical sense—is of course *Northanger Abbey*: apart from the author's defense of novels (v), we have remarks from Isabella Thorpe and her uncouth brother, from the naive Catherine Morland and the cultivated Tilneys, chiefly on *The Mysteries of Udolpho* and its kind, with glances at *Camilla* and *Sir Charles Grandison* (vi, vii, xiv; cf. xxv). Elsewhere books come into conversation in various ways: in the debate over the propriety of the play *Lovers' Vows* and the response to Henry Crawford's highly dramatic reading from Shakespeare (*Mansfield Park*, xiv f., xxxiv); in Harriet Smith's endeavor to get her farmer lover to read Gothic romances as well as his Agricultural Reports (*Emma*, iv); in the brief accounts of talk about poems of Scott and Byron between Captain Benwick and Anne Elliot (*Persuasion*, xi, xii); and in Sir Edward Denham's rhapsodies on both poetry and novels, which have warmed his inflammable sensibility and taught him the arts of seduction (*Sanditon*). All these passages are given as evidence of the speakers' character and temperament, not as literary discussion *per se*, which the author would exclude as extraneous and irrelevant: witness her famous ironical comment on things that would add respectable solidity to *Pride and Prejudice*, such as "a critique on Walter Scott."

As a daughter, sister, and acquaintance of clergymen, Jane Austen was especially qualified to deal with that branch of mankind, and she gives more or less full accounts of five and glimpses of others. Henry Tilney, Edward Ferrars, and Edmund Bertram are of course the heroes of three novels; Mr. Collins and Mr. Elton are satirized in broad and delicate ways respectively. Mr. Howard, in *The Watsons*, has a "quietly-chearful, gentlemanlike air" and attracts Emma, who was destined to marry him, but he has not space enough to come to life. Catherine Morland's father, "a very respectable man," remains in the background. Dr. Grant, in *Mansfield Park*, is a self-centered gourmet who dies of apoplexy brought on "by three great institutionary dinners in one week." And Charles Hayter, in *Persuasion*, is a young curate who, says his fiancée, Henrietta Musgrove, could be well placed at home if the aged and over-conscientious Dr. Shirley would only retire.

Writing in the 1860's, the author of the *Memoir*, himself a clergyman and the son of Jane Austen's clerical brother James, remarked that

no one in these days can think that either Edmund Bertram or Henry Tilney had adequate ideas of the duties of a parish minister. Such, however, were the opinions and practice then prevalent among respectable and conscientious clergymen before their minds had been stirred, first by the Evangelical, and afterwards by the High Church movement which this century has witnessed (c. x, p. 154).

That statement, by the way, is not at all fair to Edmund Bertram. It must be granted that in the eighteenth and the early nineteenth century the Church of England, if not altogether "Wrapt in the old miasmal mist," was less notable for spiritual zeal than for lethargy and worldliness. It was an age in which it could be said (if I remember some satirist correctly) that bishops "Revere their maker and respect their God," and in which plural livings, lay impropriations, and acceptance of the church as a natural haven for younger sons were still a matter of course. As Cowper said, "The parson knows enough who knows a duke" (*Tirocinium* 404). But, in regard to both actual life and Jane Austen's novels, we should bear several things in mind: that the novelist is well aware of the difference between what the clergy often are and what they should be; that, even under the old bad system, not all clergymen were bad, that many might be, like the Austens, highly creditable parish ministers; that it was part of the Anglican temper to shun Methodistical "enthusiasm" and practise reticence concerning the inner life (when there was an inner life); and that seeds widely sown by John Wesley and others grew rapidly in what must have been fertile soil, within as well as outside the Church of England. During and after Jane Austen's lifetime the Evangelical movement achieved something like a second Reformation in religion, morals, and manners—not, to be sure, without much Puritan and Philistine extremism.[5]

Of the depth of Jane Austen's own religious faith there can be no question (though it has been not only questioned but denied),

[5] A full account is Ford K. Brown's *Fathers of the Victorians: The Age of Wilberforce* (Cambridge University Press, 1961). See also Maurice J. Quinlan, *Victorian Prelude: A History of English Manners 1700–1830* (New York, 1941; Hamden, Conn., 1965).

and—as the end of the next chapter indicates—she developed
some Evangelical sympathies.[6] (Her favorite brother, the gay
and buoyant Henry, who was ordained in 1816, became an
earnest preacher of that school.) But, as a person in her world,
Jane Austen had her full share of Anglican reserve; and, as novelist, especially a novelist writing before problems of belief came to
be a theme for fiction, she normally and naturally treated her
young clergymen in their social and secular roles as lovers.
(Trollope, that worshiper of Jane, avowedly confined his portraits of clergymen to their ecclesiastical, social, and domestic
lives, without going far into their personal religious concerns.)
Jane Austen presents her young clerics as they appear to other
characters who do not come under their ministerial care, and she
treats them in different ways. General Tilney, as we might expect, speaks of his younger son's needing a profession in the same
terms as if he were a lawyer; and, in such a book as *Northanger
Abbey*, the engaging Henry himself would be stepping out of
character if he talked of having embraced a sacred calling. It is
much to the credit of Edward Ferrars, the son and presumed heir
of a rich mother, that he has, against his family's wishes, decided
to take orders, although he gives no reason. Edmund Bertram is
the younger son of a baronet, but he has made a sober commitment (with which his father sympathizes), and, in his efforts to
win over the worldly Mary Crawford, he speaks seriously of a
clergyman's duties. We can well believe that all three would do
good well beyond the church's modest desire to have an educated
gentleman in every parish; we doubt if the odious Mr. Elton
would, and anyhow he is scarcely a gentleman. Macaulay has
been criticized for fixing—in his essay on Madame D'Arblay
(Fanny Burney)—on Jane Austen's three clerical heroes and Mr.
Elton to illustrate her faculty for creating distinct and lifelike
individuals, in this case young men of the same profession; but
Macaulay was quite right in noting how different they are.

---

[6] Earlier, in 1809, Jane told Cassandra of her disinclination to read
Hannah More's didactic novel, *Coelebs in Search of a Wife*: "I do not like
the Evangelicals"—though she added that, when she reads it, she will be
delighted, like other people (Letter 65). The young heroine of the very
popular *Coelebs* did much to establish the ideal of religion, active virtue,
and propriety (Quinlan, 148 f.; Brown, *passim*).

In the sphere of sexual morality people of the upper and lower classes have always assumed more or less freedom to do as they please, and strictness has been mainly a middle-class concern. In modern fiction, if any traditional moral values are in active operation, they are seldom readily discernible. And even if our novelists do not themselves share current notions of untrammeled freedom, they can hardly count on generally accepted standards among readers; such standards, we read on all sides, belong to "bourgeois values," "Victorian morality," "the WASP tradition." In fact, of course, those standards were recognized for many centuries, even by those who broke through them; and, so far as rebels have abolished "the guilt business," they have undermined the ground for a good deal of both tragedy and comedy.

Jane Austen's period carried on traditional upper-class laxity or license: a conspicuous example was set by the Prince Regent. And nothing was more natural than natural children: the offspring of one of Byron's mistresses, the Countess of Oxford, were called, in a scholarly pun, "the Harleian Miscellany." Jane Austen, living for the most part in a secluded world, could record in her letters this or that local or public scandal, such as the acquisition of a mistress by the noble patron of her sister's fiancé, Rev. Thomas Fowle. In the novels there are half a dozen incidents or facts in keeping with actual or fictional transgressions. Willoughby seduces Colonel Brandon's young ward; Mrs. Jennings assumes, wrongly, that the girl is the Colonel's "love-child" and thinks none the worse of him for having one. Wickham—who at two periods in his life was resolved on ordination!—after attempting to carry off Darcy's sister, elopes with Lydia Bennet, driven by debts and her urgency, and is bribed, with Darcy's money, to marry her. Harriet Smith is the natural daughter of a prosperous tradesman (not of a gentleman, as Emma Woodhouse fondly believed). Mary Crawford comes to Mansfield to live with her sister because her uncle and guardian, a widowed admiral, has established his mistress in his house. Henry Crawford elopes, not very happily, with Mrs. Rushworth. Mrs. Clay, after angling for Sir Walter Elliot, lapses into the "protection" of his nephew and heir, with some hope of still becoming Lady Elliot. Such acceptance of the facts of life does not, to be sure, make Jane Austen's novels modern; if her heroes and heroines can hardly be imagined in bed, characters in our fiction of narrower scope can hardly be seen anywhere else.

What matters of course is the author's handling of these data and her moral reactions as expressed through approved characters or, sometimes, through the reactions of characters who are not approved. It is needless to say that Jane Austen's standards of sexual morality are sincerely and steadfastly orthodox, but she does not see misconduct in terms of mere black and white. Willoughby's action is severely condemned by Elinor Dashwood not simply as a violation of the moral code but as the result of a life of unprincipled selfishness. Members of the Bennet family are horrified by Lydia's behavior and the consequent family disgrace, but Mrs. Bennet, who has no more moral sense than Lydia, is restored to entire happiness by her marriage—as Elizabeth is not. To Mr. Bennet the episode brings not only a consciousness of his own guilty evasion of paternal responsibility but a further piece of self-knowledge: "I am not afraid of being overpowered by the impression. It will pass away soon enough." Sir Thomas Bertram's consciousness of guilt in not having dissuaded Maria from a loveless marriage weighs much more heavily upon him, and even the apathetic Lady Bertram is saddened; Edmund Bertram and Fanny Price are deeply upset, Edmund especially because he has loved Mary Crawford, who now easily condones what she calls her brother's "folly." Mrs. Norris, who had made a favorite of Maria and labored to promote the marriage, feels a great shock, not to any moral principles but to her ego. Thus the episodes of Lydia and Maria—which lead to the union of hero and heroine in each book—are a test of character for the members of both families.

If Jane Austen mainly avoids the "guilt and misery" of overt immorality, the novels are full of the guilt of what may be more corrosive and injurious, the common human faults of selfishness, insensitivity, insincerity, and the like. One special kind of misery, which afflicts the innocent, is a young woman's living with the thought of a loved man lost to her—the experience, brief or prolonged, of all the heroines. And although Jane Austen does not philosophize about sex, her decorous heroines are more or less intense embodiments of forces more fully and truly human than, say, the primitive female daemons of D. H. Lawrence could understand.

Modern criticism has only confirmed and enhanced the greatness of an author whose most famous comment on her work would seem to be a modest disclaimer of any large and timeless themes or virtues. Writing to a nephew about the novel he was working on, and observing that she could not have purloined a missing slice of his manuscript, she said (Letter 134: December 16, 1816):

What should I do with your strong, manly, spirited Sketches, full of Variety and Glow?—How could I possibly join them on to the little bit (two Inches wide) of Ivory on which I work with so fine a Brush, as produces little effect after much labour?

As one of the great "classical" artists, Jane Austen strives for and usually achieves an ordered pattern and a smooth surface, but, as Rebecca West remarked, "To believe her limited in range because she was harmonious in method is as sensible as to imagine that when the Atlantic Ocean is as smooth as a mill-pond it shrinks to the size of a mill-pond."[7]

[7] *The Strange Necessity* (London: Cape, 1928), 264.

2

Life

JANE AUSTEN WAS BORN on December 16, 1775, at Steventon, a hamlet in north Hampshire near the main road from London to Basingstoke and Salisbury.[1] Steventon was her home for her first twenty-five years. Her life brought few dramatic events, but from the start there were many actors on the small domestic stage. Jane was the seventh child and second daughter of the Rev. George Austen (1731–1805), the son of a Tonbridge surgeon (the Austens had deep roots in Kent) who became a Scholar and Fellow of St. John's College, Oxford. From 1761 until his retirement in 1801 Mr. Austen was rector of the parish of Steventon. He had received the living from a relative, Thomas Knight, and the additional living of nearby Deane was bought for him about 1773 by

[1] Several standard authorities are cited above under "Abbreviations." Some additional books are: Caroline Austen, *My Aunt Jane Austen* (written *c.* 1867; printed for the Jane Austen Society, 1952); Elizabeth Jenkins, *Jane Austen* (London, 1938; revised, 1948; New York, 1949, 1959), and Jane A. Hodge, *The Double Life of Jane Austen* (London: Hodder and Stoughton, 1972), biographies with some critical comment; two lavishly illustrated books, Marghanita Laski's *Jane Austen and her world* (London and New York, 1969), a good compendious biography, and W. A. Craik's *Jane Austen in Her Time* (London and New York, 1969), a survey of life and manners based on the novels; and a *tour de force* in verse, Mary Corringham's *I, Jane Austen* (London, 1971).

an uncle. In 1764 Mr. Austen had married Cassandra Leigh (1739–1827), the daughter of a Fellow of All Souls and the niece of a witty, long-lived Master of Balliol, Theophilus Leigh. She had spirit and wit that survived the birth of eight children and sundry vicissitudes; one proof is some verses she wrote after a serious illness of 1801, *A Dialogue between Death and Mrs. A.*

If we are to see Jane Austen in the setting in which she grew up and did her first writing, we must be aware not only of her parents but of her sister and brothers, and later—at least in a wholesale way—of her brothers' multiplying progeny.

The eldest son James (1765–1819), like his father an Oxonian and a clergyman, succeeded his father at Steventon. The second son George (1766–1838), who is not mentioned in Jane's letters, had some disability which apparently allowed him no place in family life. Edward, the third son (1768–1852), was adopted as the heir of the second Thomas Knight (d. 1794) and in 1812 took the name of Knight for himself and his family. Henry Austen (1771–1850), Jane's favorite brother, her closest adviser and helper in literary matters, had an odd career: Oxford University, the Oxford Militia, London banking (which declined from prosperity to bankruptcy), and finally thirty-four years as a country clergyman. He was—like Henry Tilney in *Northanger Abbey*—clever, amusing, imperturbably cheerful: "his Mind is not a Mind for affliction," said Jane, who also remarked, with the authority of an amateur connoisseur, on the high quality of his sermons. To postpone Cassandra for a moment, the fifth son, Francis (1774–1865), had a career in the navy and was one of the most devout worshipers of Nelson; he rose to be an Admiral of the Fleet and was knighted in 1837. The sixth son, Charles (1779–1852), Jane's and Cassandra's "own particular little brother,"[2] also became an admiral; he died on duty in India.

Cassandra (1773–1845), the older sister to whom Jane wrote the great bulk of her letters when they were separated by visit-

[2] Letter 18 (January 21, 1799). The phrase echoed Sir Hugh Tyrold's about Camilla, "my own particular little niece" (Fanny Burney, *Camilla*, ed. 1802, vol. 3, bk. vi, c. x, p. 297). Jane Austen had been one of the subscribers for *Camilla* in 1796. The phrase is a reminder of the language of allusion natural in a family of readers. The words "particular little friend" are used of Harriet Smith in *Emma* (xxvi).

ing, was, according to a family opinion upheld and perhaps started by Jane, in all important respects the superior of the two—an opinion that we, who lack evidence, are not likely to share. But they may have been equal at least in a lifelong mutual affection that was unusually close and implies some temperamental affinity. The scholarly father—like Tennyson's father later— taught his sons (and those of some friends) at home, preparing two of them for Oxford; but the two girls were sent away to school, first at Oxford, then at Southampton—where they caught a "putrid fever" (typhoid?) nearly fatal to Jane—and at Reading. These several sojourns were brief; Jane's formal schooling apparently ended in 1786–87, when she was ten or eleven. We have few external facts about the next eight or nine years, but the outward texture of her life may be inferred from the letters, which begin in January 1796; and her extant juvenilia, which began when she was eleven or twelve, make it clear not only that she read and wrote abundantly but that she already viewed popular romantic and sentimental fiction with the critical eye of a satirist. In her youth her parents and the numerous children, most of them rather vigorous personalities, made something of a crowd under one roof—a roof the father had to extend at intervals. And in time five brothers, out in the world, had wives—nine among the five—and more or less large families, so that Jane became the adored Aunt Jane of a swarm of nieces and nephews. The children we remember in the novels are mainly spoiled brats.

A catalogue of the immediate family invites some further data on its social status and background. Henry was for a time a captain and adjutant in the militia (not the regular army, for which he had hankerings); and the well-bred naval officers in *Persuasion* were more akin to Francis and Charles Austen than, say, to Smollett's seamen of an earlier generation (or to Fanny Price's father). Jane had much more intimate knowledge of the character and ways of the rural clergy through her father and brother James, Henry again (though only at the end of her life), and some less close relatives. Also, Cassandra was engaged to a young man, Rev. Thomas Fowle, who went as a chaplain to the West Indies with his kinsman and prospective patron, Lord Craven, and died there. Whatever the common torpor of the church in the period, the clergymen of the Austen tribe seem to have been conscientious as well as cultivated men.

There were higher connections in the family or in its genealogy. Jane's brother Edward, as the adopted heir of Thomas Knight, became a rich country gentleman and married the daughter of Sir Brook Bridges. His chief residence, Godmersham Park in Kent, was visited by his sisters, especially Cassandra; his daughter Fanny—Fanny Knight after 1812—grew to be Jane's favorite niece (and in 1820 married Sir Edward Knatchbull). Henry Austen married his cousin Eliza, the glamorous widow of a French count who was guillotined in 1794; she had been born in India and had as her godfather no less a personage than Warren Hastings (who was to be a warm admirer of *Pride and Prejudice*). To go further back, Jane's maternal great-grandfather had become a brother-in-law of the first Duke of Chandos, and her brother James's first wife was a granddaughter of the second Duke of Ancaster; and other noble names might be added.

If the preceding paragraph awakens thoughts of Lady Catherine de Bourgh or Sir Walter Elliot, we may come down to earth and Steventon. In spite of such aristocratic connections in the past and some "county" connections in the present, the Austen family must be seen as relatively normal members of the upper middle class, above ordinary parish clergy, living with frugal comfort, visiting and being visited by relations and friends old and young, enjoying themselves with reading, talking, letter-writing, dancing, acting charades and plays by Sheridan, Garrick, and others—all the common resources of a lively, bookish, self-sufficient, and closely knit household of the period. Next to her family, Jane Austen's great object of devotion was of course writing. But that impulse was also manifest, in a small way, in others of the clan: Cassandra, apparently, though her interest was in drawing and painting; James and Henry, who, at Oxford, produced a periodical; and, much later, ambitious nieces and a nephew, who received from Aunt Jane wise and generous counsel, counsel which has long done service in the criticism of her own work. At the end of her life she advised young Caroline Austen to give up writing until she was sixteen: "she herself often wished she had *read* more, and written less, in the corresponding years of her own life" (*My Aunt Jane Austen*, 10). Jane had grown up, like Elizabeth Bennet, with no governess but with books at hand and encouragement to read (*Pride and Prejudice*, xxix).

Two special friends must be mentioned. A close friend of both sisters was Martha Lloyd, whose sister Mary in 1797 became James Austen's second wife; Martha was in later years to live with Mrs. Austen, Cassandra, and Jane and, in 1828, to become Francis Austen's second wife. Another close friendship, of shorter duration, developed between Jane and a Mrs. Lefroy, wife of the rector of Ashe, although she was twenty-five years older. In 1804, on Jane's birthday, Mrs. Lefroy was killed by a fall from her horse; in 1808 the anniversary of that accident drew from Jane the only serious poem she is known to have composed, a fervent tribute to an ideal woman and friend (*M. W.*, 440–42).

Other troubles had already touched her in various ways and degrees. There would be continuous anxiety about her brothers in the navy during the long war, especially in an age in which news traveled slowly. In view of the special bond between Jane and Cassandra, she must have suffered acutely through the death of her sister's fiancé in 1797. In 1798 their cousin Lady Williams (Jane Cooper), a frequent visitor at Steventon rectory (where her wedding had taken place), to whom Jane had dedicated two of her juvenilia, was killed in a carriage accident. In 1799–1800 Jane was on the edge of a queer, painful, and prolonged situation. Her mother's sister-in-law, wife of the wealthy James Leigh Perrot, was charged (apparently in the hope of blackmail) with a theft from a Bath shop for which the legal penalty was death or transportation, and, with her husband, she was held in unpleasant custody for eight months. Mrs. Austen suggested that Cassandra and Jane (the latter liked her uncle but not her aunt) should stay with her during the trial, but Mrs. Leigh Perrot declined such a sacrifice from "those elegant young women." Acquittal did not blot out what had already been endured.

Jane's twenty-five years at Steventon ended in 1801, when her father gave up his parish and the now diminished family moved to Bath. She was "greatly distressed," her niece Caroline wrote later, by having to leave the familiar scene; Steventon was for her what Norland was for Marianne Dashwood or, more aptly, what Kellynch was for the older and more sober Anne Elliot, who had to move to Bath with her father and sister. Apart from occasional absences, Jane lived in Bath from the autumn of 1801 until the summer of 1806. Along with the fact of exile and her dislike of towns in general, many things combined to cloud these years: Mrs. Austen's serious illness and Mr. Austen's decline and death; the lack of any relatives except the Leigh Perrots and of any real friends; the long shadows cast by the death of Cassandra's fiancé and the death of Mrs. Lefroy, and another, more indistinct shadow to be recorded later. From uncongenial existence in Bath there was relief in visits paid to relatives in the country and to seaside resorts in Dorset and Devon. But it seems clear that un-settling and depressing experiences—including two publishers' lack of interest—did much to check the flow of Jane's mature writing. During 1795–99 she had done the early versions of *Sense and Sensibility*, *Pride and Prejudice*, and *Northanger Abbey*, but the years 1800–08—so far as we know—yielded only some revi-sion of *Northanger Abbey* ("finished in the year 1803," Jane said) and composition of the fragment her nephew called *The Watsons* (1804–05).

Since good portraits of Jane Austen are lacking, her readers must fall back on descriptions from those who knew her. In November 1791, when Jane was nearly sixteen, her cousin Eliza, the Comtesse de Feuillide, heard—from the family—that Jane and Cassandra were "two of the prettiest girls in England." Ac-cording to the Biographical Notice that Henry Austen prefixed to *Northanger Abbey* and *Persuasion*,[3] Jane was of upper middle height, quiet and graceful, possessed of true elegance; her fea-tures, separately good, together "produced an unrivalled expres-sion of that cheerfulness, sensibility, and benevolence, which were her real characteristics. Her complexion was of the finest texture. It might with truth be said, that her eloquent blood spoke through her modest cheek." (The echo of Donne is inter-esting, though the lines on Elizabeth Drury had become common

[3] Reprinted in Chapman's volume 5: Southam, *Jane Austen: The Critical Heritage* (London: Routledge; New York: Barnes & Noble, 1968); and the Kinsley–Davie edition of the two novels (London and New York, 1971).

property.) Jane's nephew and biographer, James Edward Austen (later Austen-Leigh) was more specific in his memory of her as she looked in her later thirties (*Memoir*, c. v, p. 87):

In person she was very attractive; her figure was rather tall and slender, her step light and firm, and her whole appearance expressive of health and animation. In complexion she was a clear brunette with a rich colour; she had full round cheeks, with mouth and nose small and well formed, bright hazel eyes, and brown hair forming natural curls close round her face. If not so regularly handsome as her sister, yet her countenance had a peculiar charm of its own to the eyes of most beholders.

In spirit, and partly in appearance, probably most readers see the Jane Austen of nineteen or twenty in her own early favorite among her heroines, Elizabeth Bennet (some of her nephew's items recall Emma Woodhouse), and the older Jane in Anne Elliot, even though her creator thought Anne almost too good and though in some essential ways she is very different.

Jane's extant letters run from January 9, 1796, shortly after her twentieth birthday, until late May 1817, about six weeks before her death. Though some of the best went to nieces and the congenial Martha Lloyd, most of the letters were written to Cassandra, who, we should remember, destroyed very many—"the greater part," she told Caroline Austen—and excised parts of others. Thus, allowing for large and small lacunae, we can see Jane, throughout her mature life, amid the settings and activities she so minutely described. The letters have been severely damned, for instance by such notable persons as E. M. Forster and Sir Harold Nicolson, as a desert of trivia recorded by a compound of Lydia Bennet and a harpy.[4] Such lofty indignation seems unimaginative and out of place. It may be granted that, apart from religious utterances (which do not appeal to some critics), the writer seldom reveals her inner self; her chief com-

[4] Forster, "Miss Austen and Jane Austen," *Times Literary Supplement*, November 10, 1932 (reprinted, with other pieces on Jane Austen, in *Abinger Harvest*, London: Arnold, 1936); Nicolson, *New Statesman and Nation*, November 26, 1932. Sir Harold let himself go on the novels, with some obtuseness, in *Good Behaviour* (1955). One of Jane Austen's recent biographers, Miss M. Laski, speaks of "letters of a bitchiness and coarseness not inferrable from the 'impeccable sense of human values' in her books" (*TLS*, July 27, 1973).

ments on novelistic art are quoted elsewhere in this book. We would not expect to find estimates of the state of letters or of Europe. Space is largely given to family and local news and gossip, some to dances, clothes, bonnets, all the commonplace concerns of living. But Cassandra and Jane were fairly well acquainted with each other's inner life and each other's views of the great world, and the letters we have—perhaps often intended to be read aloud or passed around—are what might be expected from a young or youngish woman, even a genius, writing to a sister when they are separated. The letters are at least the most authentic picture there is of the everyday life of young women of Jane's class in the period.

The letters are spiced with abundant items which, though written with unpolished spontaneity, suggest the satirical and ironical wit as well as the material of the novels:

Charles Powlett gave a dance on Thursday, to the great disturbance of all his neighbours, of course, who, you know, take a most lively interest in the state of his finances, and live in hopes of his being soon ruined. (Letter 13: December 1, 1798)

They [the Lances] live in a handsome style and are rich, and she seemed to like to be rich, and we gave her to understand that we were far from being so; she will soon feel therefore that we are not worth her acquaintance. (Letter 48: January 7, 1807)

Tender-minded readers fasten on one quite untypical bit: "Mrs. Hall, of Sherborne, was brought to bed yesterday of a dead child, some weeks before she expected, owing to a fright. I suppose she happened unawares to look at her husband." (Letter 10: October 27, 1798). But is there anyone who has never yielded to the temptation of a witticism in momentary disregard of human feeling? We remember how Emma is condemned for addressing a cruel gibe directly to Miss Bates. In general, to emphasize what is not altogether a truism, the persons who are unfavorably ticked off in the letters link themselves with the fictional characters, the self-seeking, insincere, and ill-bred, who are justly satirized, not with the major or minor ones whom the author and her readers like and respect. Jane might have said, as Elizabeth Bennet said to Darcy, that she hoped she never ridiculed what was wise and good, but that she was diverted by follies and nonsense, whims and inconsistencies. In her abundant letter-writing Jane Austen unwittingly gave herself a practical course in some areas of the novelist's art; and in some juvenile and later fiction she used the epistolary form so popular in the eighteenth century. Although she abandoned that form, the novels of her maturity contained numerous letters as expressive of their various authors in substance and style as their spoken words, and sometimes more dramatically arresting.

In such a family of readers, given especially to novels, literary allusions were a matter of course. In Jane's letters—to cite a few names in the order of their first or only appearance (all are indexed by Chapman)—we meet *Tom Jones*; Fanny Burney's *Camilla* (several references); Cowper (several); "my dear Dr. Johnson" (several); *Evelina* (several); Mrs. Piozzi (two); Shakespeare (seven, mainly to plays as performed); William Godwin ("He [a Mr. Pickford] is as raffish in his appearance as I would wish every Disciple of Godwin to be"); *Tristram Shandy*; Scott (a dozen, to poems and two novels: September 28, 1814 was an early date for a relative outsider to be aware of Scott's authorship of *Waverley*); Madame de Staël's *Corinne*; Fanny Burney's *Cecilia*; Maria Edgeworth (several); George Crabbe (several); *Sir Charles Grandison* (two); Fanny Burney's *The Wanderer*; Byron ("I have read the Corsair, mended my petticoat, & have nothing else to do" [but write another letter]). As these samples suggest, Jane was quite well-read in eighteenth-century and some contemporary literature; and along with her special interest in novels went perhaps more than the usual feminine knowledge of books of sermons. She "read French with facility"—although, like other people, she read translations that came her way—and "knew something of Italian" (*Memoir*, c. v, p. 88).

Although Jane regretted the appearance of unwonted indelicacies in a novel by Madame de Genlis (Letter 48: January 7, 1807), she could write from London, after witnessing *Don Juan, or the Libertine Destroyed*, that she had never seen on the stage "a more interesting character than that compound of cruelty and lust" (Letter 82: September 15, 1813). And the letter-writer—who alluded so casually to *Tom Jones* and *Tristram Shandy*—was not disturbed in telling Cassandra of the indelicate behavior of persons conspicuous in real life, such as noble lords' acquisition of mistresses (Letters 36 and 49). Such comments reflect neither sophisticated acquiescence nor unsophisticated outrage; the writer's serious attitude is expressed briefly in Letter 52 and more amply in several of the novels.

In this connection we might observe how the innocent author could have the charge of prudery lodged against her even by notable devotees. The usually careful R. W. Chapman said that in the second edition of *Sense and Sensibility* Mrs. Jennings' mention of a "natural son" was expunged (*Jane Austen*, 119, 219); the phrase, which was "natural daughter" (xiii), was not expunged (as Chapman later acknowledged). Further, in his edition of the novel (p. xiv) Chapman remarked on the omission, "in the interests of propriety," of a sentence which followed the item just cited: "Lady Middleton's delicacy was shocked; and in order to banish so improper a subject as the mention of a natural daughter, she actually took the trouble of saying something herself about the weather." This led E. M. Forster to exclaim ". . . what a light is thrown on Jane Austen's own character" by such deference to propriety: the "prude" "is moving away from the eighteenth century into the nineteenth, from *Love and Freindship* towards *Persuasion*" (*Abinger Harvest*, 146, 155). The sentence —which of course was making fun of Lady Middleton's prudery —was deleted perhaps because, near the end of the preceding chapter, the same speaker had used the weather to break off Mrs. Jennings' inelegant raillery about Edward Ferrars (in chapter xix she changes the subject to get away from the same offender's reference to an approaching confinement). At a later time Jane Austen's favorite niece, Fanny Knight, now Lady Knatchbull, looked back with apologetic distaste upon her aunt's lack of refinement.[5]

Since all the novels are concerned with love, love that leads to

[5] An undated letter printed in the *Cornhill Magazine*, No. 973 (1947–48), 72–73, and quoted in the biographies of M. Laski (126–27) and J. A. Hodge (93).
Tony Tanner, I find, offers another explanation for the deleting of the sentence cited just above: that, since Mrs. Jennings had lowered her voice, Lady Middleton might be expected not to have heard her remark (*Sense and Sensibility*, Penguin, 1969, p. 370—an edition with a freshly suggestive introduction).

marriage, we may wonder about the degree of Jane Austen's personal experience. Although we hear of four suitors, there is nothing in the surviving letters about the two with whom she was seriously concerned. In the two earliest extant letters, to Cassandra (January 9 and 14–15, 1796), her ironic humor plays about Tom Lefroy, nephew of her beloved Mrs. Lefroy, "a very gentlemanlike, good-looking, pleasant young man." Jane is almost afraid to tell her sister of their shocking profligacy "in the way of dancing and sitting down together." They have met only at the last three balls, and he will probably propose at the next one; she is about to flirt her last with the young man, for whom she does not care sixpence. According to Jane's niece, Caroline Austen, whose mother was near at the time, "Mrs. Lefroy sent the gentleman off at the end of a *very* few weeks, that no more mischief might be done." (He later went to Ireland, married an Irishwoman with money, and eventually became Lord Chief Justice of Ireland.) Neither his heart nor Jane's seems to have been much, if at all, involved. But nearly three years afterward he is still in her consciousness: she has just seen Mrs. Lefroy, who did not once mention his name to her, and her own pride forbade any inquiries (Letter 11: November 17, 1798).

That same letter touches a more shadowy admirer. Mrs. Lefroy showed Jane a letter she had received from a "friend" (apparently a Rev. Samuel Blackall, a Cambridge don), regretting that he could not now improve his acquaintance with the Austens; he has "a hope of creating to myself a nearer interest." Jane thinks his letter expresses "less love and more sense . . . than sometimes appeared before," and she expects that indifference will soon be mutual. Evidently Mr. Blackall did not pursue his interest. Much later Jane told her brother Francis of his having got a College living and now a wife, who should be of a silent turn: "He was a piece of Perfection, noisy Perfection," whom she always recollects with regard (Letter 81: July 3, 1813).

A third and nameless suitor is even more shadowy but is the most important of all. Accounts written later by members of the family are more or less vague and sometimes confused but they seem to yield some main points: that Jane and the man met during a seaside visit (in 1801 or possibly 1802); that both fell deeply in love; that Cassandra, an exacting judge, warmly approved of him as worthy of Jane; that he intended to follow up their brief intimacy with a visit; and that the family soon received, not the visitor, but news of his death. If the story is true, as it seems to be, we can only guess at the measure of Jane's shock and subsequent suffering. (There are no surviving letters between May 26, 1801 and September 14, 1804.) Her prospects in life were now radically altered in the same way as Cassandra's had been a few years before. Jane had then testified to Cassandra's uncommon fortitude and we may believe that she herself would be no less strong; we remember how the rational and self-disciplined Elinor Dashwood concealed her anguish of heart from her sister and mother.

The next crisis in Jane's life came with the fourth and last episode of the kind that we hear of; this was in every way different from the first three. While staying with James Austen and his wife at Steventon in November 1802, Cassandra and Jane visited old friends at Manydown Park, the estate of a Mr. Bigg-Wither, a widower who had a twenty-one-year-old son Harris and three also grown-up daughters. But the sisters returned to Steventon before they were expected, in a very agitated state, and, giving no explanation, insisted that James drive them back to Bath the next day. Jane had accepted a proposal from Harris Bigg-Wither and the next morning, having realized that she did not really love him, had withdrawn her acceptance. We may wonder if the blighting of her one true love had left her with less than her normal clarity of feeling and judgment—though she had quickly summoned up enough to resist the attractions of friendship and security as a basis for marriage.

A summary of facts and probabilities about Jane Austen's own experience confirms, so far as it goes, what the novels declare or imply: that she had a very high ideal of the love that should unite a husband and wife, and that she understood more than enough to depict its growth and its complexities. All her heroines—even if they have more sense and less sensibility than Marianne Dashwood—know, in proportion to their maturity, the meaning of ardent love.

Mr. Austen's death in 1805, along with the personal loss, entailed a sharp reduction in income (soon relieved by the sons) and a year and a half of anxious uncertainties. But late in 1806

Mrs. Austen, Cassandra, and Jane, with their old friend and relative, Martha Lloyd, were established in Southampton. Life here
was more pleasant than it had been in Bath, and there were, as
usual, visits with relations, especially with Edward Austen
(whose wife died in October 1808, leaving him with a large
family). The problem of a fixed abode was solved by Edward's
offering them one of his properties, and in the summer of 1809
the four women were settled in the commodious "Cottage" (its
later name) at Chawton. The place was less than fifty miles from
London and about a mile from the town of Alton; in front of the
Austen house the road to Gosport joined the main road from
London to Winchester—but traffic, though busy, was not gas-
eous. Here, in a small village in her beloved county, Jane and her
mother and sister—and Martha Lloyd—lived more happily than
they had since the departure from Steventon. From 1812 onward
the Great House, less than half a mile from the Cottage, was
often occupied by Edward or Francis and their families. At
Chawton Jane practised daily on the piano before breakfast, a
meal it was now her task to prepare. We might note that persons
who knew her attested the elegant neatness of her handwriting
and needlework and her dexterity in manual games—modest talents which we may if we like relate to the quality of her novelistic craftsmanship and to her concern for accuracy of reference to
everything from hedgerows to the names of ships.

In this settled state, with many if not all troubles behind her,
Jane evidently had a renewal of her literary energies, now in
their maturity. In the six years 1811–16 two of her three early
novels were published, in revised form, and the three later novels
were written and two of them published—all anonymously and
in the customary three volumes. The first—published on commission at the author's risk—was *Sense and Sensibility: A Novel* . . .
By a Lady (November 1811). *Pride and Prejudice: A Novel* . . .
By the Author of "Sense and Sensibility" appeared in January
1813. There were second editions of both works in November
1813; the author paid for that of *Sense and Sensibility*. *Mansfield
Park*, begun about February 1811 and finished in the summer of
1813, was published on commission at the author's expense in
May 1814; a second edition, published in the same way by John
Murray, came in 1816 and incurred a considerable loss. Jane's

first publisher, Thomas Egerton, had paid £110 for *Pride and Prejudice*, less than the sales of the first book warranted, since it had brought her £140; and he profited a good deal from the two books published on commission. With *Emma* Jane shifted from Egerton to the more illustrious John Murray ("a rogue of course, but a civil one": Letter 111, October 17, 1815). *Emma*, begun in January 1814 and finished in March 1815, was published (dated 1816) in December 1815; it too was published on commission. *Persuasion* was begun in August 1815 and completed in the following August; it and the early *Northanger Abbey* were issued together, with a biographical sketch by Henry Austen, in December 1817 (dated 1818), after Jane's death. In the early months of 1817 she was working on *Sanditon*. It is of interest to note French translations: *Sense and Sensibility*, 1815; *Mansfield Park* and *Emma*, 1816; *Persuasion*, 1821; *Pride and Prejudice*, 1822—oddly late for what had been the English favorite; *Northanger Abbey*, 1824. In the United States, *Emma* was issued in Philadelphia in 1816 and all the novels were published by the same firm in 1832–33. In England they were reprinted from 1833 onward.

The printing of the books took Jane to London for proofreading and consultations with Henry, her faithful adviser. Remembering the rejected offer of *First Impressions* and the long burial of *Susan* (i.e. *Northanger Abbey*) in an uninterested publisher's office, which Jane had endured with such astonishing patience, we can readily imagine the excitements of actual—and rapidly successful—authorship. Like other writers, she thoroughly enjoyed all the fruits of success: "tho' I like praise as well as anybody, I like what Edward calls *Pewter* too" (Letter 106, to Fanny Knight, November 30, 1814). But her lifetime earnings, less than £700, were about a third of what the single book *Patronage* brought Maria Edgeworth—whose novels, by the way, Jane declared to her niece Anna, were the only ones, along with Anna's and her own, that she had made up her mind to like (Letter 101: September 28, 1814). It was in the letters of the Chawton period (1809 f.) that Jane made those fine and famous comments on her aims and methods which reflect a new degree of confidence.

We may recall the likewise famous picture, given by Edward's daughter Marianne, which shows composition going on in the

midst of her brother's family, probably in the Great House at
Chawton: "I also remember how Aunt Jane would sit quietly
working [i.e. sewing] beside the fire in the library, saying nothing for a good while, and then would suddenly burst out laughing, jump up and run across the room to a table where pens and
paper were lying, write something down, and then come back to
the fire and go on quietly working as before."[6] But most of the
fundamental brain-work must have been done in hours of concentration at home, although in the Chawton house she had no
work-room of her own. It was fortunate that Jane was such a
social being and so lovingly devoted to her family, since it would
appear that, after leaving Steventon, she never had much of the
peace and quiet needed by the professional writer (which, to be
sure, she was not, except in her creative, critical, and self-critical
genius). But even she, after the strain of company, could wonder
how Cassandra managed to do so much in addition to the care of
the house: "Composition seems to me Impossible, with a head full
of Joints of Mutton & doses of rhubarb" (Letter 133: September
8, 1816).

Henry James, in his American lecture on Balzac (1905), remarked that "Jane Austen, with all her light felicity, leaves us
hardly more curious of her process, or of the experience in her
that fed it, than the brown thrush who tells his story from the
garden bough."[7] It was a left-handed tribute from an artist whose
own labyrinthine process had come to involve his readers inex-
orably and inextricably. Jane Austen was of course no artless
thrush; she merely concealed what her nephew called a "mystic
process" (*Memoir*, c. vi, p. 103). Her sensitive artistic consciousness went along with good sense. For instance, she hopes that a
sister-in-law's acute criticism may not hurt her style by making
her too fussy: she finds herself weighing her words and sentences
more than she did and looking everywhere for sentiments and

---

[6] Constance Hill, *Jane Austen: Her Homes & Her Friends* (London and
New York, 1902), 202. Mrs. Hodge (133) thinks this picture "the happy
later embroidery" of Jane Austen's nieces. It may be, but embroidery
would seem to require a base.

[7] *Henry James: The Future of the Novel*, ed. Leon Edel, 99. Cf. Edel,
Henry James: The Master (Philadelphia, 1972), 282. James's rather patron-
izing praise of one of his artistic ancestors included some deprecation of
what he thought her exaggerated merit and interest.

metaphors; if her ideas flowed as fast as the rain in the store closet all would be well (Letter 65: January 24, 1809).

With all Jane's satisfaction in her work and considerable success, she shrank—unlike most authors—from publicity. Even her nephew James Edward had read the first two novels before he knew who wrote them, and members of the family who knew kept the pledge of secrecy she had exacted. But such a pledge was too much for Henry. Writing to her brother Francis on September 25, 1813 (Letter 85), Jane reports one occasion—by no means the first—on which Henry was overcome by "the warmth of his Brotherly vanity & Love," when, in Scotland, he heard Lady Robert Kerr and another woman praising *Pride and Prejudice*; the secret has in fact spread so far that it is hardly any longer a secret. Yet Jane still shunned any approach to a public role as novelist. In 1816, when she was in London dealing with *Emma* and the dedication, a nobleman told Henry that he was giving a party at which Madame de Staël was to be present and that she, and he himself, would greatly enjoy meeting Miss Austen; but Jane promptly declined.[8]

The dedication of *Emma* entailed a series of letters (113–26: November 15, 1815–April 1, 1816) which, as a slice of high comedy, one would like to reproduce in full. In the autumn of 1815, when Henry was seriously ill and Jane was in London nursing him, one of the Prince Regent's physicians, who was attending Henry, told Jane that the Prince greatly admired her novels and kept a set in each of his residences. (This is one of the few creditable things on record about His Royal Highness; Leigh Hunt had lately spent two years in prison for printing a candid account of him.) The physician had also informed the Prince of Miss Austen's being in London. Under the Prince's instructions,

[8] When Sir James Mackintosh, the noted philosopher, recommended one of the novels, Mme de Staël found it uninteresting and pronounced it *"vulgaire,"* to which he replied that "there is no book which that word would suit so little" (*Memoirs*, by R. J. Mackintosh, 1835, 2, 471). The word takes us up to Emerson. In 1861 he, mystified by Jane Austen's reputation, described her as "vulgar in tone, sterile in artistic invention, imprisoned in the wretched conventions of English society, without genius, wit, or knowledge of the world. Never was life so pinched and narrow." *Journals*, ed. E. W. Emerson and W. E. Forbes (Boston: Houghton Mifflin), 9 (1913) 336–37; Southam, *Jane Austen: The Critical Heritage*, 28.

his chaplain-librarian, Rev. J. S. Clarke, then called on her, conducted her on a tour of Carlton House, and hinted that a dedication would be agreeable to its royal occupant. Jane—who hated
the husband of the ill-used Princess—wrote to ask about the degree of obligation implied in the hint ("permission," friends
advised, must be taken as "a command"). In explaining, Mr.
Clarke expressed his own admiration and proposed that she "de-
lineate in some future Work the Habits of Life and Character
and enthusiasm of a Clergyman—who should pass his time between the metropolis & the Country. . . ." In her reply, apropos
of dedicating *Emma* (an honor she could not well escape), Jane
declared her inability to present any side of a clergyman except
the comic (though the predecessor of the newly created Mr.
Elton had been Edmund Bertram), "but not the good, the en-
thusiastic, the literary," because of her total ignorance of science,
philosophy, the classics, or even the full range of English literature; in short, she is "the most unlearned and uninformed female
who ever dared to be an authoress." This large assertion failed to
squelch her pushing patron. In acknowledging a copy of *Emma*
Mr. Clarke repeated his plea for a clerical hero, offering some
quaint specific suggestions that come still closer to a picture of
himself; he is sending her a copy of his sermons (composed and
preached at sea) and his edition of Falconer's poem *The Ship-
wreck.*

Later, in conveying the Prince's formal thanks, Mr. Clarke
reported his new appointment in the service of the Prince of
Cobourg and suggested a dedication to him: "any historical romance, illustrative of the history of the august House of Cobourg, would just now be very interesting." Jane replied that she
knew the difference in "profit or popularity" between a romance
and her "pictures of domestic life in country villages," but she
could write such a book only to save her life, and, if she had to
keep it up and never relax into laughter at herself or other people,
she would be hung before she had finished the first chapter. Mr.
Clarke was evidently a simple-minded, good-hearted man, but, if
chronology did not forbid, we might think that in some respects
he had been a model for Mr. Collins. At any rate he was the main
inspiration for the diverting burlesque, *Plan of a Novel, accord-*

ing to hints from various quarters (1816: *M. W.*, 428–30), in
which the maturely critical author, returning to her youthful
vein, made fun of the melodramatic and incoherent plots, the
cardboard characters good and bad, and the extravagant style of
romantic fiction.[9]

If, on the strength of the works mentioned, the egregious Mr.
Clarke can be counted as an author, he appears to have been the
only one Jane Austen ever met—unless we add Sir Egerton
Brydges, the antiquarian bibliographer (and brother of Mrs.
Lefroy), who spoke briefly of her appearance in his *Autobiography* (1834: 2, 41). The high repute the novels won in her lifetime
and her epistolary acquaintance with the eminent publisher John
Murray would have made it easy enough, if she had been so
minded, to become a literary figure. In place of that role there
was only a family joke about George Crabbe, the realistic poet of
village life. Jane's nephew said, with both critical justice and due
regard to decorum (*Memoir*, c. v, p. 89):

She thoroughly enjoyed Crabbe; perhaps on account of a certain
resemblance to herself in minute and highly finished detail; and
would sometimes say, in jest, that, if she ever married at all, she
could fancy being Mrs. Crabbe; looking on the author quite as an
abstract idea, and ignorant and regardless what manner of man he
might be.

[9] Thinking of Jane Austen's early burlesques, and of *Northanger Abbey*,
we might recall the first chapter of Scott's first novel, *Waverley* (1814),
in which he listed four types of current fiction: romances like *The
Mysteries of Udolpho*; romances "from the German," with a profligate
abbot, an oppressive duke, Rosicrucians, caverns, etc.; the sentimental
tale, of a heroine who moves, with her harp, from castle to cottage,
guided by an unintelligible peasant girl; and accounts of fashionable life
and scandal in London. His own material, he said, would be drawn from
"the great book of Nature," "those passions common to men in all stages
of society." He said some similar things in his review of *Emma*, the first
important critique of Jane Austen (*Quarterly Review* 14, 1815[–16], pp.
188–201; reprinted in Southam, *Jane Austen: The Critical Heritage*). More
familiar than the review is one of the comments in Scott's *Journal* (March
14, 1826; Southam, 106): "The Big Bow-wow strain I can do myself like
any now going, but the exquisite touch which renders ordinary commonplace things and characters interesting from the truth of the description
and the sentiment is denied to me." This generous praise was quite unjust
to Scott's own rendering of Scotch life, character, and dialogue.

In pursuance of the joke, Jane could speak of hearing "some *bad news* lately, namely that *Mr. Crabbe* is going to be married."[10]

Of the world at large, as of the literary world, Jane Austen's knowledge came chiefly from reading. There can have been very few of the world's novelists who remained throughout life so close to their native place. Not only was Jane Austen never abroad; she had firsthand knowledge of only limited parts of England. For roughly four fifths of her life her home was in Hampshire, at Steventon and at Chawton; one fifth was spent in Bath and Southampton; she visited in Kent and elsewhere, stayed at some seaside resorts, and on occasion was in London—and that was all. At any rate her lack of a traveler's acquaintance with much of England and with all the world outside England did not make her parochial or provincial; she knew very fully what she needed to know. Her prime interest in people, preferably people in villages, did not exclude a genuine love of the countryside. Her brother Henry, in his biographical sketch, remarked: "She was a warm and judicious admirer of landscape, both in nature and on canvass. At a very early age she was enamoured of Gilpin on the Picturesque. . . ."[11] Such authentic feeling, which found varied expression in the novels, from *Northanger Abbey* and *Sense and Sensibility* to *Sanditon*, did not preclude satirical treatment of affected raptures.

To return to the biographical chronicle, Jane Austen was working on *Sanditon* from January 27, 1817 until March 18, but it remained a fragment because of what was to prove a fatal illness. Analyzing the symptoms recorded in the letters, with some further data from Caroline and Cassandra Austen, Sir Zachary Cope was able to diagnose Jane's trouble as "Addison's disease of the suprarenal capsules"—a disease Thomas Addison first identified years after her death.[12] She seems, in something over a year, to have slowly wasted away, although, as we just

[10] Geoffrey Grigson, "New Letters from Jane Austen's Home," *Times Literary Supplement*, August 19, 1955. Cf. Fanny Lefroy, "Is it Just?", *Temple Bar* 67 (1883), 275.

[11] During 1782–1809 William Gilpin published eight accounts of scenic landscapes in various regions which had "Picturesque Beauty" in their titles. A reference in *Love and Friendship* is noticed in the next chapter, and the novels have more or less talk about the picturesque.

[12] "Jane Austen's Last Illness," *British Medical Journal*, July 18, 1964.

observed, she had enough spirit and energy, in the first months of
1817, to begin a new novel in a new vein. Her decline in health
may have begun with her anxious care of Henry during his serious illness in the autumn of 1815; and the next eighteen months
brought other family anxieties in which she shared. Henry's
bankruptcy in March 1816—from which he quickly bounced
back—entailed heavy losses for his uncle, Mr. Leigh Perrot, and
his brother Edward (Jane lost only £13). Also, Edward was in
prolonged danger of losing his Chawton estates—that is, two-
thirds of his property and income—which he succeeded in retain-
ing only by the payment in 1817 of a large sum of money (there
had been a technical error in the deed transferring the property
to Edward and a suit had been brought by some of the original
Knight family). Thus Edward, the father of eleven children, was
not in the best position to assist Mrs. Austen and her daughters.
Finally, the rich and childless Mr. Leigh Perrot died in March
1817, leaving nothing to his sister, Mrs. Austen (who said, very
charitably, that he had probably expected to outlive her). Writing to her brother Charles on April 6, Jane was ashamed to confess that the "shock" of her uncle's will had brought on a relapse;
she added, with reason, that "a weak Body must excuse weak
Nerves." We may suppose that she was thinking more of her
mother and Cassandra than of herself, since there are various
hints of her feeling that she would not recover.[13]

In the letters of her last months Jane refers to her invalid state,
of which her correspondents would wish to know, but she tries
to keep up her old gossipy and satirical verve. In a letter to Fanny
Knight (140: February 20, 1817) she would like to recommend
to Mr. and Mrs. Deedes, who are having another child (they
seem to have had eleven by 1808), that they adopt "the simple

13 When she visited the Fowles in Berkshire in the spring of 1816, they
thought (or later imagined they had) "that her health was somewhat
impaired" and that, going about her old haunts, she recalled old associations
"in a particular manner, as if she did not expect ever to see them again"
(*Memoir*, c. xi, p. 159; cf. Caroline Austen, 14). Caroline (13) recorded a
memory of her aunt's period of illness. Since the one sofa was often used
by Mrs. Austen at any hour of the day, Jane would never lie down on
it but contrived a "comfortless" substitute with three chairs, which it
seemed understood that she preferred. The young niece, puzzled, badgered
her aunt with questions until she said that if she ever used the sofa her
mother would never lie down but leave it for her.

regimen of separate rooms"—an idea she had presumably not suggested to her brother Edward, the father of Fanny and ten other offspring. On March 14, encouraging her niece Caroline and her nephew James Edward in their efforts at fiction, Aunt Jane accounted for her "fine flow of Literary Ardour" by her having just received nearly £20 on the second edition of *Sense and Sensibility* (Letter 141.1). To Fanny Knight she wrote on March 23: "I must not depend upon being ever very blooming again. Sickness is a dangerous Indulgence at my time of Life" (Letter 142). But the same letter shows that her critical faculty can still be pungent: her condemnation of perfect heroines and her unjust disparagement of Anne Elliot in particular are quoted below in the chapter on *Persuasion*.

On April 27 Jane made a brief will, in which she left everything to Cassandra except £50 each to Henry and Henry's housekeeper, Mme Bigeon, who had lost her savings through his bankruptcy. As weeks went on, at times she reported what seemed to be an improvement: "I am now really a very genteel, portable sort of an Invalid" (Letter 145: May 22, to Anne Sharp, the former governess at Godmersham). On May 24 Cassandra and Jane moved to lodgings in Winchester to secure better medical treatment. Perhaps a few days later, to an unidentified person she wrote, as she had written in earlier letters, of Cassandra's loving, indefatigable care. She lives chiefly on the sofa, "But I am getting too near complaint. It has been the appointment of God, however secondary causes may have operated. . . ." (Letter 147). She died at Winchester on July 18, 1817, just beyond the middle of her forty-second year; after a private funeral she was buried in Winchester Cathedral (where she had Izaak Walton as a literary neighbor). Even the watchful Cassandra had not suspected how near the end was until it came. "When I asked her if there was any thing she wanted, her answer was she wanted nothing but death & some of her words were 'God grant me patience, Pray for me oh Pray for me'" (*Letters*, p. 514). Writing to Fanny Knight of Jane's death, the strong and usually reserved Cassandra poured out her grief and desolation in having lost a part of herself. And relations old and young lamented their loss in very personal and heartfelt terms. It would seem that Jane, daughter, sister, cousin, and aunt, was the best-loved member of the whole large Austen clan.

In one of her last letters (145: May 22, 1817) Jane wrote:

In short, if I live to be an old Woman, I must expect to wish I had died now; blessed in the tenderness of such a Family, & before I had survived either them or their affection. . . . But the Providence of God has restored me—& may I be more fit to appear before him when I *am* summoned, than I sh^d have been now!

This and other utterances of these months of stress are in full accord with her several written prayers (*M. W.*, 453–57) and her earlier and calmer words on religion and life, death, and immortality. In a letter to her brother Francis, apropos of Henry's having revealed her authorship of *Pride and Prejudice*, she said: "After all, what a trifle it is in all its Bearings, to the really important points of one's existence even in this World!"[14] (Letter 85: September 25, 1813). Another expression of Jane's everyday thinking and feeling appears in another unlikely context, a letter in which, with much diffidence, she is trying to give Fanny Knight the advice she has asked for in regard to a suitor. She cannot see any objection to his "*Goodness*," even if he were to become Evangelical: "I am by no means convinced that we ought not all to be Evangelicals, & am at least persuaded that they who are so from Reason and Feeling, must be happiest & safest." Fanny must not be alarmed by his uncommonly strict following of the precepts of the New Testament (Letter 103: November 18, 1814). Some days later, on the same question, Jane adds that she and Fanny cannot differ in their ideas of the Christian religion: they only attach "a different meaning to the Word *Evangelical*" (Letter 106).

 ⁻ To take Jane Austen's religious utterances at their face value may be to incur the charge of naiveté, but it may seem more than naive to explain away her manifestly earnest faith as conventional

---

[14] The remark may have been quite spontaneous, but it was at least in agreement with her favorite moralist (and Christians in general). Speaking of literary fame, Dr. Johnson said to Boswell: "Ah, Sir, that should make a man think of securing happiness in another world, which all who try sincerely for it may attain. In comparison of that, how little are all other things!" (*Boswell's Life of Johnson*, ed. G. B. Hill and L. F. Powell, Clarendon Press, 1934–50, 2, 358). Cf. *The Rambler*, No. 20, paragraph 13.

pietism or less than that. The problem, or supposed problem, concerns the novels. Such diverse interpreters as Marvin Mudrick, Graham Hough, Gilbert Ryle (the distinguished philosopher), Laurence Lerner, and Mrs. Hodge see the novelist treating moral issues without any recognition of religion.[15] Mr. Mudrick, while often subtly penetrating, wrenches or amputates Jane Austen's moral and religious ideas to suit his Procrustean prejudices. For Mr. Hough "Jane Austen's ethical system represents the best standards of the society that she actually knew; that is to say an English middle-class version of Christian morals—Christian morals with all the heroism, all the asceticism, all the *contemptus mundi* left out." Mr. Ryle says that her "heroines face their moral difficulties and solve their moral problems without recourse to religious faith or theological doctrines. Nor does it ever occur to them to seek the counsels of a clergyman"; her "moral system was a secular, Aristotelian ethic-cum-aesthetic." Mrs. Hodge, quoting Professor Ryle, sees one reason for Jane Austen's continuing readability in the fact that "her characters make their moral decisions in the same kind of climate of unknowing, or even of unbelief, that we are used to today" (14). Mr. Lerner's first chapter opens with the simple declaration: "Jane Austen, George Eliot and D. H. Lawrence had one important thing in common: they none of them believed in God."

Such views of Jane Austen's novelistic or personal attitude range from the misleading to the wild. Marianne Dashwood, the only unreticent heroine, is desperately eager "to have time for atonement to my God" (xlvi). Sir Thomas Bertram, brooding at the end on his daughters' behavior, sadly reflects that "They had

---

[15] M. Mudrick, *Jane Austen: Irony as Defense and Discovery* (Princeton: Princeton University Press; London: Oxford University Press, 1952; Berkeley: University of California Press; London: Cambridge University Press, 1968).

G. Hough, "Morality and the Novel," *The Dream and the Task* (London: Duckworth, 1963), 47.

G. Ryle, "Jane Austen and the Moralists," *Oxford Review* 1 (1966), 5–18; reprinted in *Critical Essays on Jane Austen*, ed. B. C. Southam (London: Routledge; New York: Barnes and Noble, 1968).

L. Lerner, *The Truthtellers: Jane Austen—George Eliot—D. H. Lawrence* (London: Chatto and Windus; New York: Schocken, 1967).

An earlier, sometimes good and sometimes sour critic, O. W. Firkins, found no trace of religious feeling in either the letters or the novels (*Jane Austen*, New York, 1920, pp. 204, 210).

been instructed theoretically in their religion, but never required to bring it into daily practice" (xlviii). But particulars must give place to general considerations. Such critics as those quoted seem to assume that the novels are non-religious because the novelist did not write like Hannah More. Two early witnesses, who lived in her spiritual climate, understood that Jane Austen, being what she was, would take religion for granted as the supreme guide and conditioning force, which one did not ordinarily talk about. Richard Whately (later an archbishop) in his important critique reprehended "any *direct* attempt at moral teaching" but praised Jane Austen for "being evidently a Christian writer," one who went as far as she could without alienating many readers by making "a religious principle . . . too palpably prominent."[16] What Richard Whately divined, Jane Austen's friend Mrs. Barrett reported from personal knowledge of her expressed views, but it is needless to repeat identical testimony.

Unprejudiced readers cannot doubt the large share Jane Austen's religious beliefs and convictions have in that moral poise which is so inseparable from her art; the passage just cited in Letter 141 is one corroboration. In an essay which inaugurated twentieth-century criticism A. C. Bradley declared that her "inmost mind lay in her religion—a religion powerful in her life and not difficult to trace in her novels, but quiet, untheoretical, and rarely openly expressed."[17] The novelist Angus Wilson, himself avowedly non-religious, affirms the opinion that "Jane Austen can only be understood as an intensely devout religious writer."[18]

[16] *Quarterly Review* 24 (1820–21), 352–76; reprinted in Southam's *Critical Heritage*. Jane Austen uses the phrase "Religious Principle," e.g., at the end of Letter 141, and, as a student of her language, K. C. Phillipps, says (55), in her vocabulary the noun alone "is a word with religious implications."

[17] "Jane Austen," *Essays and Studies by Members of the English Association* 2 (Clarendon Press, 1911), 9; p. 35 in Bradley's *A Miscellany* (London: Macmillan, 1929).

[18] "Evil in the English Novel," *The Listener* 68 (1962), 1079–80. See also, e.g., C. S. Lewis, "A Note on Jane Austen," *Essays in Criticism* 4 (1954), 359–71; reprinted in *Discussions of Jane Austen*, ed. William Heath (Boston, 1961) and *Jane Austen: A Collection of Critical Essays*, ed. Ian Watt (Englewood Cliffs, N.J., 1963); and M. Bradbury, "Jane Austen's *Emma*," *Critical Quarterly* 4 (1962), 335–46; reprinted in the author's *Possibilities* (London, 1973) and in *Critics on Jane Austen*, ed. Judith O'Neill (London and Coral Gables, 1970). This piece Mr. Hough (45) describes as "a Christian-existentialist introduction to the devout life."

He rightly links her with the tradition represented, in extreme form, by two of her favorite authors, Dr. Johnson and Cowper, who lived in intense apprehension of "the terrors of the next life." "Because there is a real threat, there is a real meaning in the next world for her," and time and quiet are needed for preparation. Remarks in Jane Austen's letters on death and "another World" are not perfunctory pietism.

Finally, if the evidence supplied by Jane Austen herself and the judgments quoted cannot stand against arbitrary modern skepticism, perhaps all but the most stubborn skeptics would accept the modest claim made for the novels by her nephew, even though he was a Victorian clergyman (*Memoir*, c. x, p. 153):

They certainly were not written to support any theory or inculcate any particular moral, except indeed the great moral which is to be equally gathered from an observation of the course of actual life— namely, the superiority of high over low principles, and of greatness over littleness of mind.

3

Early Writings

J ANE AUSTEN was only eleven or twelve when, with a satirical impulse inspired by her reading of popular fiction and by the talk of a family of novel-readers, she began to write short burlesque tales to amuse herself and her immediate relatives and a few close friends. These persons, old and young, were saluted in mock-formal dedications. She was interested enough, over a long time, to make transcripts of these and later and longer pieces in note-books which she called *Volume the First*, *Volume the Second*, and *Volume the Third*. These writings, regarded as family possessions, did not begin to be printed until 1871 and were not fully available until 1922 f.[1] They were products of the years 1787–93, and, as we might expect, they reflect the young author's considerable growth. In 1793–94 came a further advance in maturity,

[1] The contents of all three volumes were included, with *Lady Susan* and later fragments, in the *Minor Works* added in 1954 by R. W. Chapman to his edition of the novels. The few early writings discussed in this chapter are quoted from that collection, except *Love and Friendship*, which is quoted from B. C. Southam's scholarly edition of *Volume the Second* (1963). Although modern readers are familiar with the title as *Love and Freindship*, the editor (218) notes the MS. change, under "Contents," to the more orthodox *ie*. I am indebted, here and elsewhere, to Mr. Southam's valuable work, *Jane Austen's Literary Manuscripts* (1964: see "Abbreviations" above).

the much longer work which Jane Austen's nephew, printing it in his *Memoir* in 1871, called *Lady Susan*. And during 1795–99 she wrote the first versions of *Sense and Sensibility*, *Pride and Prejudice*, and *Northanger Abbey*. Thus, although it was once possible to think of Jane Austen as emerging, a full-fledged artist, in six novels produced in two short periods, in fact, as modern criticism has been enabled to recognize, she had a long apprenticeship. The satirical objectivity of these early writings does not make them a portrait of the artist as a young girl and young woman, but they reveal her nonetheless, and the process and evidence of her development are of compelling interest. In the present sketch it is better to let a few representative examples speak for themselves than through a much less lively commentary.

The chief contents of *Volume the First* are ten short tales (two of them in the epistolary form Richardson had made popular) and two short plays, all but one written during *c.* 1787–90, when the author's age advanced from eleven or twelve to fifteen. The tales are miniature novels, divided into chapters, which burlesque the loves and friendships, the misadventures and mysteries, and the high style of sentimental romances of the later eighteenth century. Such romances had already invited burlesque, as in Charlotte Lennox's famous *The Female Quixote* (1752), which Jane apparently read early; and there was stimulus nearer home, in attacks on the cult of sensibility in the Oxford periodical edited in 1789–90 by Jane's brothers, James and Henry. From the start, when pure farce predominates, the young author shows a remarkable command of language, a prime essential for a parodist. Absurdity is achieved through such means as inflated rhetoric, incongruity, pseudo-heroics, fantastic motives, sentiments, and actions. Jane could at times make use even of authors and books she admired: in the first chapter of the first "Novel," *Frederic & Elfrida*, a "picturesque" description seems to parody a bit of *Sir Charles Grandison* (Oxford, 1932: 2, Letter 49, p. 427)—a grove of poplars, a verdant lawn enamelled with variegated flowers, "watered by a purling Stream, brought from the Valley of Tempé by a passage under ground."

In this tale the hero and heroine are too eminently proper to reveal their love "either to the object beloved, or to any one else." On the other hand, Elfrida's amiable friend Charlotte, visiting in London, in half a page engages herself rapidly to two strange men, one aged and one young, and the next morning, overcome by guilty recollection, commits suicide. In the words of her *Epitaph*, she "Threw her sweet Body & her lovely face/ Into the Stream that runs thro' Portland Place." Yet the same tale has this sentence (possibly suggested by a bit in the third chapter of *The Female Quixote*), which, with slight changes, might have appeared in one of the mature novels: "Charlotte, who perfectly understood the meaning of her freind's speech, was too good-temper'd & obliging to refuse her, what she knew she wished,—a compliment; & they parted the best freinds in the world." Elfrida, who grows old in spinsterhood because she has too much delicacy to name a wedding day, is roused to jealousy of a new young flame of Frederic's: "she flew to Frederic & in a manner truly heroick, spluttered out to him her intention of being married the next Day." The unexpected everyday realism of "spluttered" is carried on in the courageous Frederic's reply: "Damme Elfrida *you* may be married tomorrow but *I* wont." However, Elfrida's continuous fainting fits worked on a heart in some respects "as soft as cotton," and he "was united to her Forever." This and the other earliest tales are in the vein of juvenile highjinks. They, and later pieces of "sense," are at the farthest pole from the Gothic "sensibility" the young Brontës expressed in their Angrian and Gondal imaginings. Both sets of writings foretold their authors' future; and Jane Austen's novels were as distasteful to Charlotte Brontë as Charlotte's would have been to Jane.

The most elaborate and amusing of the literary burlesques is *Love and Freindship a novel in a series of Letters*, dated in June 1790, when its author was fourteen and a half. Among the many provocative "sources" was, some critics have thought, the *Laura and Augustus* (1784) of Elizabeth Bromley. Jane Austen's tale of thirty-three pages was inscribed to her cousin Eliza, "Madame la Comtesse de Feuillide," who brought the electric air of Paris to the Steventon parsonage (1787 f.) and stimulated the acting of plays by members of the family.

Both for those who have read the "novel" and for those who have not, an outline—however much pregnant detail it must omit—will best recall or suggest its character. The first two short letters give us the implausible situation: at the request of her old friend Isabel, Laura, now a recluse of fifty-five, agrees to relate "the Misfortunes and Adventures" of her life to Isabel's daughter Marianne, as a lesson in fortitude. All the rest of the letters are written by Laura, so that they could have been a continuous narrative: but the letters tend—like instalments of soap operas—to end at a point that creates suspense, here mild and momentary; and autobiography greatly sharpens the satire, because we view everyone, and Laura herself, through her starry eyes or blinkers.

Looking back to her youth in Wales, Laura sees her only fault as excessive sensibility. Her friend Isabel, though agreeable, had not a hundredth part of her beauty and accomplishments, but she had worldly sophistication, the result of two years at a London school, a fortnight in Bath, and a supper in Southampton. But Isabel's warnings against the dangers of the world seemed needless to Laura, returned from a French convent to live in her parents' humble cottage in the Vale of Uske. A winter evening brought to their door and fireside a handsome young man, with his servant, who had lost their way, and Laura's sensibility was instantly ignited. He was, he said, the son of an English baronet who insisted that he marry a Lady Dorothea, but, lovely as she was, he refused: "Never shall it be said that I obliged my Father." His mood and rhetoric suggested to his father that he had been studying novels. Disdaining to answer, he had left his father's house in Bedfordshire for his aunt's in Middlesex, but, though "a tolerable proficienz [sic] in Geography," he had found himself in South Wales. When will the adorable Laura reward him for the sufferings his attachment to her has brought? " 'This instant, Dear and Amiable Edward.' (replied I.) We were immediately united by my Father, who tho' he had never taken orders had been bred to the Church."

The pair go to visit the aunt and there meet Edward's sister Augusta, a young woman of no sensibility. Laura overhears her asking Edward how he is to support a wife without conciliating his father, to whose satisfaction he has never willingly contributed since he was five. Love, says Edward, scorns such base things as "Victuals and Drink." Lady Dorothea appears at the house and shows herself, like Augusta, devoid of "refined Sensibility." Then Sir Edward arrives, to be greeted by his son's heroic defiance. While the others are presumably petrified with admiration, Edward takes Laura to his father's carriage and they are driven to the house of his friend Augustus. They are welcomed by his wife Sophia, a creature of infinite sensibility, then by Augustus, who had been out. The young men embraced each other in ecstasy, and Laura and Sophia "fainted Alternately on a Sofa" (suggested perhaps by the stage direction in Mr. Puff's play, "They faint alternately in each other's arms," in Sheridan's *The Critic*, III.i).

Aunt Philippa soon married "a young and illiterate Fortune-hunter," thereby depriving Edward and Laura of the expectations she had nourished; but they were readily prevailed on to live with Augustus and Sophia. That hospitable couple, however, had also married against parental wishes and had no money except the rapidly dwindling remains of what Augustus "had gracefully purloined from his Unworthy father's Escritoire." "But they, Exalted Creatures! scorned to reflect a moment on their pecuniary Distresses & would have blushed at the idea of paying their Debts." The reward for such disinterested behavior was the arrest of Augustus and notice of bailiffs' coming to take possession. "Ah! what could we do but what we did! We sighed and fainted on the sofa."

Edward went off to condole with Augustus in prison and did not return. The two wives took a carriage to London and asked every decent-looking passerby for news of Edward but did not stay for an answer. Laura's order to drive to Newgate was countermanded by Sophia, who could not endure the sight of Augustus there; so they went back to the country. They had no helpers to turn to: Laura had forgotten to mention the death of her parents and Isabel had married and gone to Ireland. But Sophia recalled a relative in Scotland who would receive them. As they were leaving their inn a coroneted coach arrived, and Laura's heart told her that its elderly occupant was her grandfather. He at once acknowledged her, and Sophia, as his grandchildren, and also two young men who now appeared. Lord St. Clair discharged his grandfatherly duty by giving each of the four a fifty-pound note and left. Laura and Sophia fainted, and on recovering found the young men gone with all the money.

They are rescued by the Scotch cousin, Macdonald, and taken

home to his young daughter Janetta. She, who has a soul, is to be
married to a man of her father's choice, one Graham, who has
none: he could never have read *The Sorrows of Werter* (the title
of the 1779 translation). But Laura and Sophia convince her of
the wrongness of submission and see her off to Gretna Green
with a man she likes. The father learns this only when he comes
upon Sophia removing a fifth banknote from his drawer: in revenge for such a violation of her privacy she tells him of Janetta's
elopement with a man whom he calls an unprincipled fortune-
hunter. Sent away on foot, the two wives rest for a while beside a
murmuring brook, sheltered on one side by a grove of full-grown
elms, on the other by a bed of full-grown nettles. Laura thinks of
Edward and Augustus, but Sophia cannot bear to be reminded of
her husband's fate, whether he is still in Newgate or hung; her
sensibility will not permit inquiry. Everything Laura says is a
painful reminder of Augustus: the elms recall his noble grandeur,
the white streaks in the sky his blue-satin waistcoat with white
stripes.

Sophia's thoughts were diverted by "a most fortunate Accident," the overturning of a phaeton on the road. They saw two
elegant gentlemen weltering in their blood—Edward and Augustus! "Sophia shreiked & fainted on the Ground—I screamed and
instantly ran mad." These frenzies continued for an hour and a
quarter, "Sophia fainting every moment & I running Mad as
often." But a groan from Edward was a sign of life. They im-
plored him not to die. " 'Laura (said He fixing his now languid
Eyes on me) I fear I have been overturned' "; and he expired.
Laura raved madly for two hours, without the least fatigue, but
was checked by Sophia's speaking of evening dampness. They
were given shelter in a cottage by a woman and her daughter; the
latter, though civil and obliging, had no delicate feelings and was
only an object of contempt. But Sophia's faintings on the ground
had given her a chill and in a few days galloping consumption
carried her off. Her last solemn words adjured Laura to take
warning from her unhappy end: "Run mad as often as you chuse;
but do not faint."

Sophia buried, Laura took a night coach to Edinburgh. The
morning light revealed that an "unprincipled Scoundrel" who
had snored was Sir Edward. The reader, though inured to sur-

prises, shares Laura's astonishment in finding that other fellow passengers are Augusta, Lady Dorothea, Isabel, and the two young men who had stolen her and Sophia's banknotes; further, the driver of the coach is Philippa's husband. This happy reunion enables Laura to tell them her story—which evokes from Isabel some pity but mainly censure of her faultless behavior—and to learn the experience of the others. Augusta, inspired by William Gilpin's account of the picturesque Highlands, had persuaded Sir Edward to take her and Lady Dorothea to Scotland. Philippa's husband, having spent her fortune, has turned their coach into a public conveyance and Philippa regularly accompanies him. The two young men, the natural sons of Lord St. Clair's daughters and uncertain tradesmen, had taken all their mothers' capital, spent it, become strolling actors, enjoyed a holiday on the money stolen from Laura and Sophia, and are about to resume acting in Edinburgh. The erstwhile scoundrel, Sir Edward, grants Laura, as his son's widow, four hundred pounds a year, on which she has since lived in melancholy solitude in a Highland village. Sir Edward has married Lady Dorothea and begotten an heir. The soulless Augusta is married to the soulless Graham whom Janetta had fled from. The two actors now perform at Covent Garden. Philippa has died but her husband still drives the coach from Edinburgh to Stirling. Poetic justice may seem to have worked somewhat unevenly.

The cult of sensibility or sentimentalism had been growing throughout the so-called age of reason, in England and, partly through English influence, on the Continent. Four major prophets, who spanned the century, were the philosophic Lord Shaftesbury, Richardson, Rousseau, and the young Goethe (whose gospel for young lovers is cited, as we saw, by the heroine of *Love and Friendship*). A very complex movement cannot be capsuled, but it may be said that various kinds of rationalism—in Puritanism, in Stoic, Cartesian, and Hobbesian philosophy and science, in neoclassical literary standards—provoked a reaction which urged the claims of benevolence, feeling, sympathy, and taste, of the soft loving heart against the hard analytical head. The cult spread rapidly and in much the same way as in our century the doctrines of Freud, simplified and misinterpreted, were reduced to a few formulas. The formulas of sentimentalism were abundantly exemplified and popularized in literature, especially the literature of romantic love. Comedy sought to evoke, not laughter, but tears. In fiction, such famous works as *Sir Charles Grandison* (1753–54) and Henry Mackenzie's *The Man of Feeling* (1771) swam in the tears of sensibility, of suffering innocence and benevolence. Sentimentalism was indeed so potent that, in addition to its direct fruits, it could affect even its satirists. Although the robust Fielding disliked what he saw as sentimentalism in Richardson, Tom Jones's lapses from morality are excused by his open generosity of heart, which is contrasted with the hypocritical meanness of Blifil and others. In Sheridan's *The School for Scandal* the loose-living but warm-hearted Charles Surface ranks far higher in the moral scale than his hypocritical brother; but both really belong to the sentimental line. Jane Austen remained immune.

Love and Friendship gives due prominence to that standard manifestation of sensibility, fainting: a notorious instance was the climax of *The Man of Feeling*. (This practice was still in full spate when Macaulay, reading bad novels to enjoy their badness, kept at the back a ledger of fainting fits; his arithmetic would have been baffled by Sophia's continuous faintings.) The tale also makes abundant use of what had been an element of much popular fiction ever since the Greek romances—continually surprising incidents: anyone may appear, anything may happen, at any time, regardless of narrative logic and coherence. And the young author does not forget that common ingredient of sensibility, an affected delight in picturesque scenery, which nourishes the soft and sublime emotions.

But, for the future novelist, satire of sentimental affectations is less important than moral satire. As a sound and realistic Johnsonian, Jane Austen always shared the moral attitude partly expressed in that chapter heading in *Rasselas*, "The Dangerous Prevalence [i.e. predominance] of Imagination." In the moral realm—though *The Man of Feeling* was decidedly against sin—excessive sensibility brings self-indulgent evasion of moral standards (along with stilted and incongruous moralizing), invulnerable egoism, self-righteousness, and hypocrisy that know nothing of genuine benevolence or love, that sustain contempt for ordinary decency, and that warrant injuring and robbing the "unworthy." We may be reminded of that modern hallmark of emancipation, undiscriminating contempt for "bourgeois values." Indeed, while the surface manifestations of eighteenth-century sentimentalism have long vanished, we are still in the broad deep trough of the movement, although in modern novels, plays, and films sentimentalism has commonly taken inverted forms and is disinfected by a flood of sexual "explicitness" and tough language. To come back to *Love and Friendship*, for a girl of fourteen and a half it is a precocious display of critical observation, comic and satirical invention, and moral criteria which do not lose their force in a farcical setting. And the fun depends largely, as the bits quoted make clear, on the young author's fastidious sense for words and style.

By the time she was sixteen or seventeen, extravagant burlesque shifted to a more ambitious plane, to serious presentation, within the frame of comedy, of ordinary life and individual character; and, for her, that meant more or less realistic social satire. We may notice two stages of growth in a short and a longish story, both of 1792. A thirteen-page epistolary tale, *The Three Sisters*, is concerned with a common problem of impecunious gentility, mercenary marriage. Some critics have thought it a promising start, or much more than that, in the difficult new genre; but the unbelievably crude manners of Mary Stanhope, the oldest sister, work against realistic verisimilitude. Her opening letter, telling a friend of a proposal, is that of a petulant child. Mr. Watts

is quite an old Man, about two & thirty, very plain, *so* plain that I cannot bear to look at him. He is extremely disagreable & I hate him more than any body else in the world. He has a large fortune & will make great Settlements on me; but then he is very healthy. In short I do not know what to do.

If the matter of age is a comic trifle that anticipates Marianne Dashwood's view of Colonel Brandon, other parts suggest Lydia Bennet: "I know the Duttons will envy me & I shall be able to chaprone Sophy & Georgiana to all the Winter Balls." Mr. Watts, strongly supported by Mrs. Stanhope, is resolved on one of the girls, any one; he is as flexible as Mr. Collins. Mary would refuse him at once if she were sure that neither of her juniors would accept him and that he would not propose to one of the Duttons;

but, since she cannot run such a risk, she thinks she will take him—provided he will have his new carriage blue with silver spots, not the "plain Chocolate" that he wants. The two younger sisters have gleams of higher ideals, and grace enough to be ashamed of Mary's public behavior: her crass vulgarity, however overdone, is contrasted with Georgiana's ironic sense and taste. The young author has stepped out in a significant direction, but she has not got far enough away from the exaggerations of burlesque.

A much wider and better path toward the novels is an unfinished narrative of forty-eight pages, *Catharine* [also called *Kitty*] *or the Bower*, dated August 1792, when Jane was sixteen. The orphaned heroine lives in the care of a well-to-do and loving but sternly decorous aunt, Mrs. Percival, who is on guard against all young men for fear of Kitty's falling imprudently in love. Kitty's two close friends, daughters of Mr. Wynne, the village clergyman, had been left without resources by the death of both parents: one had been sent to India to find a husband, which she did (Jane here makes unwonted use of family history, the experience of her cousin Eliza's mother, who had recently died); and the other had been taken by a relative, Lady Halifax, as a companion —and inferior—to her daughters. Kitty, in her loneliness, loves a bower that she and her two friends had made in her aunt's garden; there she reads, works, draws, and dreams. Her aunt has now at last consented to have distant relatives, the Stanleys, for a visit, especially as the son, being abroad, will be no hazard for Kitty. The Stanleys are "people of Large Fortune & high Fashion." The daughter, Camilla, is an elegant, frivolous, self-centered product of shallow education, and Kitty soon finds little attraction in her butterfly mind.

A ball is to be given by the Dudleys, the successors of the Wynnes in the village rectory, a family whose aristocratic pride suffers from their social and financial position. Kitty's eager anticipations of the ball are frustrated by tooth-ache, which her aunt attributes to the dampness of the bower, but Mrs. Stanley thinks Kitty's affection for her bower does credit to her sensibility. An hour after the others have left for the ball Kitty, feeling better, decides to dress and follow in her aunt's carriage. But a flustered maid announces the arrival of a handsome young stranger, who proves to be the Stanley son Edward, and Kitty is more charmed than puzzled by his airy self-confidence. They will go to the ball together, and he takes more than half an hour to powder his hair. The entrance of the couple fills Mrs. Percival with "anger & astonishment" over the multiple improprieties of her niece, who is severely lectured. Kitty escapes with Edward, who leads her to the top of the next dance, an honor which, because of Kitty's mercantile origins, offends Camilla and her mother. Kitty remains too happy to care about the indignation she has awakened on all sides, indignation to which Camilla gives full vent on the way home. Kitty's sincere apologies mollify Mrs. Stanley and Camilla, but not her aunt. Indeed, the next morning Mrs. Percival harangues Mr. Stanley on the necessity of his son's leaving the house and on Kitty's outrageous impudence. The father's expostulations only stimulate Edward's attentions to Kitty, and Mrs. Percival is "in tortures the whole Day."

Kitty's liking for Edward grows rapidly, but thunder again falls on her when Edward, kissing her hand passionately, darts out of the bower—he, though not Kitty, has seen Mrs. Percival bearing down. Her speech relates Kitty's profligacy to her own prime article of faith, the total degeneration of modern England. Kitty humbly replies that she has "done nothing this evening that can contribute to overthrow the establishment of the kingdom." And she adroitly changes the subject by hinting at evening dampness in the arbor, from which the alarmed Mrs. Percival anticipates a winter's rheumatism for herself. Kitty, though as yet not actually in love, is hurt by learning from Edward that his attentions to her had been prompted by his desire to vex her aunt. But his amiable vivacity, which he knows so well how to turn on, wins over Kitty as it had often placated others. By the end of the evening "she felt almost convinced again that he was really in love with her," and she went to bed in high spirits, determined to study his character the next day.

But the morning's news dashed her hopes: Edward, the evening before, had ordered the carriage for early departure. Kitty castigates herself for "insufferable vanity," for building castles in the air. Yet she listens with pleasure to Camilla's report of Edward's high esteem for her and his hope that she might not be married before he returns: he had gone abroad again only because of his father's insistence, though it interfered with all his other plans, and "other plans," according to Camilla, can only mean marrying Kitty. Such talk, from a flighty sister about a flighty brother, may be true, and Kitty even persuades herself that, in the anguish of love, Edward could not trust himself to see her before he left. The Stanleys depart, with warm invitations to Kitty to visit them in London, invitations promptly declined by Mrs. Percival because her niece is not to be trusted in such a hot-house of vice.[2]

This substantial fragment has moved far from the early burlesques. It is a serious comedy of manners and character, set in a country village in the social milieu of the novels, and spiced with satire, especially of snobbery and affectation. The author has entered the domain she was to make her own. Her theme was in the central tradition of the eighteenth-century novel. Fielding and Smollett had carried young men through their first experience of the world, and Richardson and Fanny Burney had done the same with young women (whose normally sheltered life permitted tragic or melodramatic misfortunes). If Fanny Burney's *Evelina* (1778) established the type for Jane Austen, the historical commonplace contains as much untruth as truth, since Miss Burney created plots, adventures, comic episodes which have a rather crude energy and variety but small significance for the heroine's inner self. Jane Austen largely abandoned that sort of thing; she had disposed of it in her burlesques. In *Catharine*, her first effort in her own line, she followed her sound instinct and placed the scene in the kind of quiet village she knew, not in Fanny Burney's kaleidoscopic London, and the characters and action are in keeping. About two fifths of the space are given to dialogue, dialogue which reveals character and in some degree forwards the story. The main "events" are a ball and the arrival of a young man; but the real events are the feelings and thoughts that go through Kitty's mind.

[2] The remaining four paragraphs Mr. Southam (18) thinks, on good grounds, were neither composed nor transcribed by Jane but were probably added by one of her literary nephews or nieces. These paragraphs say that Kitty lapsed back into her old way of life, now savorless except for the charms of the bower, which is associated with Edward. Camilla's letters cease to mention him. The story breaks off on the topic of a visit to an Exeter theatre and "the necessity of having some Gentleman to attend them."

Mrs. Percival, Camilla, and Edward, the chief persons apart from the heroine, have more or less actuality, which is more or less comic or satirical, although—as in Fanny Burney—their somewhat overdone "humors" can give them a touch of caricature. Kitty is at first something of the sentimental stereotype—an orphan, but not, like her orphaned friends, the Wynne girls, thrust into the harsh world. Yet she becomes a clearly recognizable Austen heroine. She is a good-hearted, right-minded, immature girl, with a love of reading as well as dancing, and, above all, preoccupied with ideas of love and marriage. Her romantic sensibility—partly represented by her bower—does not altogether outrun sense as she takes her first uncertain steps through delusive fancies toward knowledge of reality, though this last phase remains unrevealed. At any particular moment—after the opening —Kitty seems a real person, although the moments do not add up to entire consistency: for instance, the sometimes naive and credulous girl could hardly take the measure of Camilla or frame that reply to her aunt about the overthrow of the establishment. (Aunt Jane was later to warn a novel-writing niece to keep characters consistent.) Kitty makes us think especially of Catherine Morland, even if Edward is no Henry Tilney; and she sees through Camilla's pretensions as Catherine was to see through Isabella Thorpe—though the one experience has nothing of the significance of the other. *Catharine* shows how far, at sixteen, Jane Austen has progressed along her own path, and also how far she has still to go.

Lady Susan, written about 1793–94, might be said to carry on from *The Three Sisters* rather than from *Catharine*, since, while far more brilliant and sophisticated than the short tale, it has a relentless hardness which makes it unique in the Austen canon. The hardness is concentrated in the wholly unprincipled Lady Susan Vernon, a young widow left with small resources except her beauty and intelligence, who seeks to maintain and enhance her social position and her power over others. Indeed, she deliberately causes so much real and lasting pain and injury to a number of persons, including her daughter, that the story breaks the expected mold and tone of social comedy. One probable reason for Jane Austen's reverting, after *Catharine*, to the epistolary form might have been that Lady Susan's letters present, much more effectively than narrative could, the self-revelations of a versatile actress who sees wickedness only in opposition to her unscrupulous designs and actions. In writing to her loyal confidante, Mrs. Johnson, Lady Susan can mix some candor with her hypocrisy; otherwise she employs her skillful arts only in deceiving and manipulating whoever can be of use. Perhaps a while after finishing the letters the author added a three-page "Conclusion," which began by mocking the epistolary mode and went on to sardonic reporting of the fortunes of the several main characters.

As critics have observed, *Lady Susan* is a decidedly literary product; the roles of the "heroine" and her victims were all familiar in fiction and drama before Jane Austen undertook to deal with them. (Opinions differ as to whether she got suggestions for Lady Susan's style and character from the Comtesse de Feuillide and the Lloyd girls' grandmother, who treated her daughter cruelly; the negative case is well put by Mr. Southam.) For all the mordant cleverness of the writing, it is hard to make a real response to a story so closely focussed on a female monster who becomes increasingly artificial and unreal; she might be said to be nearer Barry Lyndon than Becky Sharp (who does one good deed). The unrelieved harshness of the satire is not the vein of the Jane Austen we know, and we feel that her developing skill is wasted on old-fashioned material which is drawn more from books and uninformed fancy than from experienced observation and intuition, and which evokes only a very limited portion of her instincts and powers.

Apart from *Lady Susan*, the few youthful pieces we have noticed are enough to indicate the directions in which those instincts and powers were growing. If we still feel a considerable gap between the juvenilia and the first novels, we must remember that we do not have these novels in their original form and that the author's growth was rapid.

4

Northanger Abbey

Although Jane Austen's six novels are probably less uneven than those of any other English author, they carry on the process of growth so clearly manifest in the juvenilia. Apart from the last of those, *Lady Susan* (*c.* 1793–94), an unexpected piece of unmitigated satire, the chief early writings had progressed logically from farcical burlesque to social comedy. But the first three of the mature novels to a considerable degree frustrate the tracing of the author's evolution because they cannot really be placed in chronological order, the reason being that we do not know the extent and the nature of the revision they all underwent. The order of publication gives no help: *Sense and Sensibility*, November 1811; *Pride and Prejudice*, January 1813; *Northanger Abbey*, December 1817 (dated 1818). About the dates of composition of these and later novels there are some precise facts recorded by Cassandra Austen in a memorandum.[1] *Sense and Sensibility* was first written, in epistolary form, as *Elinor and Marianne*, about 1795, a year or two after *Lady Susan*. *Pride and Prejudice*, originally called *First Impressions*, was begun in October 1796 and finished, in this first version, in August 1797. In

---

[1] Reproduced in facsimile in *Minor Works* (facing 242) and printed in Southam (53) and Hodge (209).

November 1797 Jane began rewriting *Elinor and Marianne* in narrative form.

Northanger Abbey was written during 1798–99. It was apparently somewhat revised a little later: in an "Advertisement, by the Authoress," written in 1816–17 and prefixed to the first edition, the novel was said to have been finished in 1803 and intended for immediate publication. It had been sold to the publisher Crosby in the spring of 1803 and advertised by him, although he had not printed it. (The original title, *Susan,* was later dropped, probably because another novel of that name had appeared; the familiar title was adopted by Henry Austen when the work was published.) In April 1809 a letter of inquiry, perhaps drafted by Henry, elicited from Crosby a curt reply, including an offer to sell the manuscript back for its original price, £10. This offer was not accepted until 1816. (It is satisfactory to know that Henry then informed the publisher that the book was by the author of the highly successful *Pride and Prejudice.*) In March 1817 (Letter 141) Jane told Fanny Knight: "Miss Catherine is put upon the Shelve for the present, and I do not know that she will ever come out." The revisions of 1803 and later years were presumably small. In the author's "Advertisement," already cited, readers were asked to forgive "those parts of the work which thirteen years have made comparatively obsolete," since "during that period, places, manners, books, and opinions have undergone considerable changes." But it was not too late for burlesque of Gothic and sentimental romance: Eaton S. Barrett's clever and funny but overdone *The Heroine* (1813) was deservedly popular in both England and the United States. Jane Austen enjoyed it highly (Letter 92: March 2, 1814). And, as we saw (c. 2, n. 9), Scott in 1814 listed Gothic and sentimental romances among four types of current fiction.

It is clear that Jane Austen's first three novels, more or less rewritten as they were, cannot be simply placed as first, second, and third; but *Northanger Abbey* was the earliest to be completed and, of the early novels, probably the nearest to its original form. Further, if we knew nothing of dates but wished to pick out the one that seems earliest in character, two central reasons would point to this work. It is the only one of all the novels that must have been conceived as a burlesque, in large part a very refined one, to be sure, and it thereby links itself with Jane's earliest writings. (She had indeed combined a mildly Gothic landscape and atmosphere with sentimental benevolence in a short burlesque, *Evelyn*, written in the spring of 1792 and included, with *Catharine*, in her *Volume the Third*.) In *Northanger Abbey* the ironic burlesque of both Gothic and sentimental romance begins at the beginning, and the later Gothic business at the Abbey is the only weak part of it. Secondly, this is the only one of the novels that is close to the eighteenth-century pattern—represented by Fanny Burney's *Evelina* and in some degree by *Catharine*—in launching a young girl upon the world, the social and amatory theme that occupies the largest and best part of the book.[2]

While *Northanger Abbey* has its eighteenth-century roots, Jane Austen is commonly and rightly credited with perfecting, if not inventing, the novel of ordinary life, the kind of novel in which the smallest and most commonplace incidents are made significant in the consciousness of the heroine. *Northanger Abbey* is (like *Persuasion*) shorter than the other novels, and—if we allow for the dual purpose of parody and realism—it has a linear simplicity of design. The young, simple-minded Catherine Morland, removed from her family into a new scene, has to make decisions for herself. Mrs. Allen, unlike the conventional duenna or guardian (such as Mrs. Percival in *Catharine*), is only an amiably inert body, and Catherine's mother, as counsellor, is only a vessel of simple proverbial wisdom. Catherine's instinctive right-mindedness is tested and confirmed in a succession of small happenings, which also, in time, sharpen her judgment of other people, in particular Isabella and John Thorpe, who have no principles; Isabella's combination of affected sensibility and moral obliquity recalls the sentimental heroines of *Love and Friendship*.

---

[2] It has been argued that this main part, the Bath sequence, was written about 1794 (despite Cassandra's dating of the book), and that the Gothic element was added about 1798 (C. S. Emden, *Review of English Studies* 19, 1968, pp. 279–87, elaborating an earlier note of his own). If there were such different elements composed at different times, surely the large Bath portion, for the most part done in the author's maturely felicitous vein, would have come after, not before, the relatively crude Gothic portion. Moreover, the Gothic section and the preparation for it, which begins early, seem to be an integral part of the plan, not an afterthought. In any case, Jane Austen was a pioneer in anti-Gothic satire.

Thus, like all Jane Austen's novels, this one is, with all its light-
ness and humor, firmly based on questions of moral right and
wrong. And, even more than the other novels, it has a pervasive
atmosphere of youthfulness, because all the elders except General
Tilney are background figures and especially because of the character of the two principals, Catherine and Henry Tilney. And
while these two, along with Mrs. Allen and Isabella and John
Thorpe, exist in their own right, they are also everyday counter-
parts of stock figures in romantic fiction—the ideal heroine and
hero, the duenna, the confidante, the repellent suitor.[3]

The book might have been entitled, in all seriousness, *Love and
Friendship*, since Catherine's formative experience is com-
pounded of both. She meets Henry Tilney one day before she
meets Isabella Thorpe, and, as Henry cannot remain steadily in
Bath, the girls' mutual devotion grows apace. "Friendship," says
the author, "is certainly the finest balm for the pangs of disappointed love" (iv). The theme and characters recall the fragment
Catharine of 1792 and show an immeasurable advance in every
way: characters are far more fully, consistently, and convincingly developed; dialogue is more economical and functional, better integrated in a forward-moving story and more revealing of
character. Camilla was presented only as a snobbish, affected, self-
centered, feather-brained creature of fashion; Isabella is all of
these, but mainly she is a vigilant man-hunter who conceals her
predatory instincts behind gushing affection for the younger
Catherine. Kitty was, like Catherine, naive and romantic (though
she had read more than novels), but, unlike Catherine, she had no
experiences that really illuminated or tested her character: she
discerned Camilla's shallowness too quickly to become a real
friend or be seriously disillusioned; and she would get over her
regard for Edward Stanley with little of the grief that Catherine
feels when she thinks that Henry may be, or is, cut off from her.
If ardent love is one of Catherine's maturing experiences, the
other is the break-up of friendship with Isabella and the reasons
for it.

Quite apart from the Abbey episode, the novel as a whole is a

[3] See especially Henrietta Ten Harmsel, *Jane Austen: A Study in Fictional Conventions* (The Hague, 1964), and Kenneth L. Moler, *Jane
Austen's Art of Allusion* (University of Nebraska Press, 1968).

comedy in which a genuine and charming love story is given a
frame and texture of quietly ironical burlesque:

No one who had ever seen Catherine Morland in her infancy,
would have supposed her born to be an heroine. Her situation in life,
the character of her father and mother, her own person and disposition, were all equally against her. Her father was a clergyman, without being neglected, or poor, and a very respectable man, though his
name was Richard—and he had never been handsome. He had a
considerable independence, besides two good livings—and he was not
in the least addicted to locking up his daughters.

No other of the Austen novels opens in this strain of playful
mockery of the heroine and her milieu, mockery that embraces
both the sentimental novel and the Gothic romance (which took
sentimental unreality still further). From the start the emphasis is
on Catherine's ordinariness; she is far from having the dazzling
beauty, glamor, and accomplishments of the romantic heroine. As
a child she was very plain and a good deal of a tomboy. At fifteen
she had become better-looking and more feminine in her tastes;
yet by seventeen she had not fallen in love with a lord, a baronet,
or a foundling, these romantic properties not being available in
the Wiltshire village of Fullerton. Apart from the seventeen-year-
old Marianne Dashwood, Catherine is Jane Austen's only immature heroine (Fanny Price is of the same age but older in mind
through harsh experience), and, having better luck, more sense,
and a less intense sensibility, she is to achieve maturity by a
considerably less painful ordeal than Marianne's. Fanny Burney's
Evelina is also seventeen, but her social experience in London
runs the whole gamut from amorous men about town and the
paragon Lord Orville, her eventual husband, to the boisterous
vulgarities of Madame Duval, Captain Mirvan, and the Branghton
family. These people—and many in Fanny Burney's *Camilla*, a
book mentioned in *Northanger Abbey* (v, vii) and *Sanditon* (*M.
W.*, 390) and recalled in the earlier letters—get the heroine into
situations that threaten to lower her, or do lower her, in her
lover's esteem; the Thorpes play a similar role in regard to Catherine and the Tilneys. Evelina's escapes can hardly be said to
advance her growth as a person; Camilla's more harrowing experiences affect her deeply. Catherine Morland's problems are

mostly very small, but they involve attitudes or decisions that are not insignificant for her or for Henry's view of her.

In the first three chapters, which take Catherine to Bath and launch her on her social career, the strain of antiromantic mockery is dominant, and throughout the book the author reminds us of her amused awareness of the aberrations of romantic fiction in contrast with her own picture of ordinary life; we see the heroine in a double perspective (as in the more complex and subtle *Emma*). Full enjoyment of *Northanger Abbey* is happily possible without the reading of earlier and long-dead novels that scholars have resurrected in illustration of Jane Austen's satirical points. She manifests a quite serious literary consciousness, though her tone partakes of levity, when, apropos of Catherine and Isabella shutting themselves up to read novels together, she puts forth the famous (and here uncharacteristically intrusive) defense of novels—not foolish ones—as delightful works of genius which hold their own with the most respected kinds of writing (v). The next chapter, returning to overt irony, gives the girls' talk about *The Mysteries of Udolpho* and other desirably "horrid" books "as a specimen of their very warm attachment, and of the delicacy, discretion, originality of thought, and literary taste which marked the reasonableness of that attachment."

From the beginning of her acquaintance with Henry Tilney, Catherine shows a natural degree of sensibility: his absence from Bath after their first meeting invests him with the "sort of mysteriousness, which is always so becoming in a hero." Her native good sense, however, is in control. In the assembly rooms she sees the much-desired Henry with a young woman on his arm, but she does not turn pale or fall in a fit because she immediately guesses his companion to be his sister and not his wife (viii). When, in company with the Tilneys, Catherine regrets her inability to judge the picturesque, the author remarks, with evident reference to the well-intentioned but "precipitant" and unfortunate Camilla and her mentor-lover, that "The advantages of natural folly in a beautiful girl have been already set forth by the capital pen of a sister author" (xiv). Catherine so well absorbs her mentor's lecture on the picturesque that she voluntarily rejects "the whole city of Bath, as unworthy to make part of a landscape." Henry indulges in some gentle raillery at women's understanding: "In my opinion, nature has given them so much, that they never find it necessary to use more than half." One of Catherine's weaknesses which Henry takes some pains to correct is her loose use of words, such as "nice" (though her girlish ignorance is innocent, as Isabella's insincere extravagance is not): rational thought and rational life require discriminating precision of language.

Toward the end, as "tell-tale compression" indicates that "we are all hastening together to perfect felicity," the author's literary consciousness shows some mock-concern with technical questions. When Henry has come to the Morlands' home to propose to Catherine and we are told the sorry tale of his father's motives and changes of mind, the author takes a humorous flick at romancers' sometimes labored rationalizations (xxx): "I leave it to my reader's sagacity to determine how much of all this it was possible for Henry to communicate at this time to Catherine, how much of it he could have learnt from his father. . . ." A little later, we have a bit of burlesque romantic contrivance: concerning the young peer whose marriage to Fleanor Tilney softens the General into permitting that of Henry and Catherine, the author —who does not bother to give him a name—says she is "aware that the rules of composition forbid the introduction of a character not connected with my fable." The remark might be taken as a prophetic reminder that, even in her more densely populated books, Jane Austen's minor characters do have functional connections with the story.

The last sentence of the novel starts on a note which seems to be more than comic, which might indeed be allowed to carry very serious ironic overtones: "To begin perfect happiness at the respective ages of twenty-six and eighteen, is to do pretty well." But the sentence continues in the author's normal vein: she is convinced that the General's interference served to improve Henry's and Catherine's knowledge of each other and strengthen their attachment, so that—here is an ironical touch of sentimental didacticism—"I leave it to be settled by whomsoever it may concern, whether the tendency of this work be altogether to recommend parental tyranny, or reward filial obedience." It is evidence of the creative and persuasive power of Jane Austen— and of such looser artists as Fielding, Sterne, Thackeray, and

Trollope—that, while her personal comments (granted of course her legitimate satirical vein) are less numerous and obtrusive than theirs, she, like them, can shatter illusion by reminding readers that they are only reading a novel and yet, most of the time, make them feel themselves direct witnesses of life.

Along with the author's irony, direct or implied, goes that of Henry Tilney, the only ironist and humorist among Jane Austen's sober heroes. He has at the same time the eighteenth-century role of mentor, a normally serious role (witness Edmund Bertram or the older George Knightley) but one that for him encourages a light touch. Henry is indeed a charming as well as sensitive and sensible young man. If we are at first surprised to find that he is a clergyman, as unromantic a hero as could be found, we may well conclude that—like Henry Austen—he could compose excellent sermons and cheer if not spiritualize his parishioners. One of the most attractive strains in this love story is the way in which the perceptive hero comes to see, respect, and love the goodness and warmth of heart and complete honesty that underlie the heroine's ignorance and naiveté. After one barren evening at the assembly rooms, a second brings felicity, the master of ceremonies' introduction of Henry to Catherine—a meeting still further from romantic fiction than that of Marianne Dashwood and Willoughby. While they have tea after dancing, he adopts a simpering air and takes her through a mock-catechism of the conventional questions for visitors to Bath, ending with "Now I must give one smirk, and then we may be rational again." He makes gentle fun of the journal she surely keeps and suggests how he should figure in it. He is even able to converse with Catherine and Mrs. Allen about muslin (a topic not lacking in Jane Austen's letters). When they part, Catherine at least is prepared, regardless of female propriety, to be in love.

From now on, Catherine's object in life is to see more of him. But when, after some days' absence, Henry appears again, with his sister, Catherine cannot dance with him because of being engaged to the casual and boorish John Thorpe, who fails to claim her. This is the first of the vicissitudes, due mainly to the Thorpes, that mar her happiness. Renewed conversation with Eleanor Tilney explains Henry's absence and Catherine unwittingly reveals to Eleanor her very special interest in him (x). Each day brings "its hopes and fears, mortifications and pleasures." In the drama that goes on in Catherine's eager heart nothing is trivial. She has become able to resist the pressures of the Thorpes and takes a most enjoyable walk with the Tilneys. Before their next meeting she hears from Isabella of her engagement to her brother James and, fond as she is of both, she cannot keep up with Isabella's ecstasies and encomiums. At the next dance Henry's brother, Captain Tilney, appears and wants an introduction to Isabella, who had assured Catherine that her heart was with the absent James and that she would not dance; but Catherine soon sees the couple on the floor. She thinks that Captain Tilney, observing Isabella as a wallflower, had good-naturedly rescued her. Her ascription of such a motive elicits from Henry the first tribute he has paid her, that she herself is "superior in good-nature . . . to all the rest of the world," and she is almost in a daze of joyful confusion (xvi). Much later, when they are talking of Isabella's and the Captain's unscrupulous tricks, Henry pays another tribute, ironical in phrasing but sincere in meaning, that her "mind is warped by an innate principle of general integrity, and therefore not accessible to the cool reasonings of family partiality, or a desire of revenge" (xxvii).

Near the end, just after the two have become engaged, the author says that, although Henry was now sincerely in love with Catherine, it must be confessed that his affection had originated in nothing better than grateful recognition of her partiality for him: "It is a new circumstance in romance, I acknowledge, and dreadfully derogatory of an heroine's dignity; but if it be as new in common life, the credit of a wild imagination will at least be all my own" (xxx). In spite of the reminder that we are reading a novel, and in spite of all the antiromantic satire, the author has steadily deepened our sense of the real worth and affection that unite the young pair.

The author might also have said that Catherine's affection had originated in gratitude: after that first dismal evening in the assembly rooms, dancing and talking with Henry had been her first experience, outside her family, of being treated as a person, here a person of interest to an intelligent and attractive man. What that meant we can imagine from the suggestive glimpse she gives him —not at all in the way of complaint—of her life at home in contrast with life in Bath (x):

". . . I walk about here, and so I do there;—but here I see a variety of people in every street, and there I can only go and call on Mrs. Allen."
Mr. Tilney was very much amused. "Only go and call on Mrs. Allen!" he repeated. "What a picture of intellectual poverty! However, when you sink into this abyss again, you will have more to say. You will be able to talk of Bath, and of all that you did here."

Much later we have such an intimation of Catherine's gratitude as this: dancing, she "enjoyed her usual happiness with Henry Tilney, listening with sparkling eyes to everything he said; and, in finding him irresistible, becoming so herself" (xvi). But Catherine's ardent and worshipful sensibility never asserts itself over her good sense and right-mindedness—except in regard to Henry's home and father.

The visit at Northanger Abbey and Catherine's dismissal occupy nine chapters (xx-xxviii), of which three (xxv-xxvii) deal with the problem of Isabella, James Morland, and Captain Tilney and with the inspection of Henry's parsonage at Woodston. The burlesque of Gothic romance seems to be the chief memory many people have of the novel, perhaps mainly because it stands out as untypical of the mature Jane Austen. While it cannot spoil the charm and authenticity of the earlier and much larger part, the elaborate episode may be thought, in spite of some good details, a conspicuous failure. It comprises two stages: first, Catherine's romantic fancies about the mysteries to be expected in a house of such antiquity, fancies that culminate in her suspicions of General Tilney's criminal behavior in the past; and, secondly, the hitherto effusively hospitable General's sudden, unexplained expulsion of his young guest. This second incident cannot afford to be taken as burlesque, though it looks like that. Certainly neither incident could be imagined at all in the other normally realistic novels.

It is not that the author has not carefully prepared for both climaxes but that no amount of preparation will make the incredible credible. Quite early Catherine—who has hitherto en-

joyed such novels as Jane Austen's favorite *Sir Charles Grandison*
—is introduced by the sophisticated Isabella to Mrs. Radcliffe and
she is enthralled by the exotic excitements of *The Mysteries of
Udolpho*; such qualms as she feels are banished when she learns
that even Henry Tilney had been unable to lay the book down.
Then on the drive to Northanger Abbey (xx) Henry playfully
builds up a graphic picture of the Radcliffian mysteries and horrors Catherine may encounter. When he drops his diverting *jeu
d'esprit* she assures him that she really has no such expectations;
and her first view of the stately home seems to promise only
luxurious modern comfort. But two mysterious objects in her
room arouse her curiosity. Attracted by a large chest, she uses all
her strength to open it—and discovers a folded counterpane.
Undressing for bed during a violent storm, she notices a cabinet,
manages to unlock it, and finds a roll of written papers. Snuffing a
candle to get a better light, in her agitation she puts it out, and,
trembling with horror, she jumps into bed to wait for morning—
when she finds that the writing is a laundry list (xxii). This
anticlimax, appropriately handled in a paragraph of *Love and
Friendship*, might have been funny; here it is—for Jane Austen—
labored and flat.

But there is more to come. While in general Jane Austen only
laughs at Gothic romance, it now threatens to warp moral
judgment—as sentimental romance so effectively does in *Love
and Friendship*. Catherine, her head full of Gothic horrors, misinterprets quite innocent actions and words of the General and
Eleanor and reaches the weird notion that Mrs. Tilney's sudden
death, years before, had been brought about by her husband.
Exploring unvisited rooms in quest of evidence, she accidentally
meets Henry, and the nature of her suspicions comes out (xxiv).
Henry, astonished and frank but not unkind, brings her back to
the world of common sense. "The visions of romance were
over." Catherine is stricken not only with shame for her folly but
with grief for having, as she thinks, forfeited Henry's respect and
affection and all her hopes. We are intended to see a naive girl,
who has been carried away by romantic fiction, cured of bringing such "horrid" fancies into real life. But, from our knowledge
of Catherine, it may be hard to conceive that her naiveté could,
by the reading of thrillers, be led to such a pitch of ill-bred

curiosity and absurdity. A young woman's advance through delusion to recognition of reality (Jane Austen's persistent theme) is
nowhere else achieved through acceptance of fantastic unreality
—even though here Henry Tilney is a catalyst. Yet, however
strained the incident itself, Catherine's youthful wisdom con-
quers guilt and humiliation: English people are not, like characters in exotic fiction, either angels or fiends but mixtures of good
and bad; even Henry and Eleanor might reveal some slight imperfections. "Her mind made up on these several points, and her
resolution formed, of always judging and acting in future with
the greatest good sense, she had nothing to do but to forgive
herself and be happier than ever"—a process much assisted by
Henry's generous reticence on the subject.

The General on his side has been nursing a not altogether
romantic delusion about Catherine. In Bath she had observed him
and John Thorpe talking, evidently about her; the substance of
the conversation is not given until the second-last chapter, but
Thorpe, who has his own axe to grind, tells Catherine at the time
that the General thinks her "the finest girl in Bath." (The reference to this talk is a small reminder of what critics have often
noted in regard to Jane Austen's tact and concern for verisimilitude, that she does not dramatize the conversation of men by
themselves; the presence of a woman or women determines the
matter and tone.) From this point on the General is assiduously
attentive to Catherine, who is finally invited to visit Northanger Abbey (xvii). From his multiplying hints it is clear to the
reader as to Henry and Eleanor, if not at first to Catherine, that
the General sees her as Henry's prospective wife. Later, Henry's
and Eleanor's conviction that their father would never allow his
older son and heir to marry a girl of "Isabella's want of consequence and fortune" awakens anxious thoughts about herself,
though she remembers the General's "most generous and disinterested sentiments on the subject of money."

Just as Eleanor and Catherine agree on the prolonging of her
visit, the General returns from London in evident agitation and
sends the greatly embarrassed Eleanor to tell Catherine that he
and his family are engaged for a fortnight's visit with friends and
that Catherine is to be sent home at once and without an escort
for the seventy-mile journey. Catherine of course has no notion

of how she has given offense but, with sensitive unselfishness, accepts the General's pretext and tries to comfort the unhappy Eleanor. When, a few days later, Henry appears at the Morlands' home, he explains, as best he can, that Catherine "was guilty only of being less rich" than his father, misled by John Thorpe, had supposed her to be; Thorpe, met again in London, had unsaid all he had said before about the Morlands' wealth—hence the abrupt banishment of an undesirable daughter-in-law.[4]

Although Catherine's fancies about General Tilney are part of the burlesque of Gothic fiction and show an impressionable young mind confusing it with actuality, his actual character and conduct, his choleric temper, his arrogant pride in his possessions and position, his excessive attentions to Catherine (and his equally ill-bred abuse of servants), the chilling effect of his presence on his grown-up children and on Catherine, all this, culminating in her rude dismissal, belongs to real life, but it seems hardly less unreal than her idea of him. In reality as well as in Catherine's mind he becomes almost a fairy-tale ogre, the only specimen of the kind in Jane Austen (unless Mrs. Ferrars in *Sense and Sensibility* is a subdued female counterpart). And we cannot help asking how a man of the world, a General who gives reading and thought to national affairs, could converse at all with the crude and irresponsible John Thorpe (whom even the naive Catherine had seen through), or, having conversed, could believe what he· heard and act on it in the choice of a daughter-in-law, and later believe and act on the same informant's contrary story. It is a commonplace of criticism that Jane Austen employs some relatively sensational incident or revelation to bring about the

---

[4] K. L. Moler (38) and others cite Montoni's removal of Emily St. Aubert from Udolpho (*The Mysteries of Udolpho*, Everyman ed., c. xxxi, 2, 58 f.). Catherine had earlier (xxiii) seen in the General "the air and attitude of a Montoni."

In *Camilla*—which, as we saw, was in Jane Austen's mind when she wrote *Northanger Abbey*—a mercenary Major Cerwood is similarly misled about Camilla's expectations by her brother (an Oxford student and irresponsible playboy) and, compelled to propose just after learning the truth, is saved only by being rejected (ed. 1802, 3, bk. vi, c. x). A partial analogue to Catherine's dismissal is in a novel Jane Austen may not have known, Robert Bage's *Hermsprong* (1796: 3, xvi; c. lxvi in reprint ed. V. Wilkins, 1951): the ogreish Lord Grondale orders the spirited Miss Fluart out of his house because she aids and abets the daughter he oppresses.

denouement, but nowhere else does she resort to a device which would strain the limits of farce and indeed belongs, like the laundry list, to the wild logic of *Love and Friendship*.

Lionel Trilling, in his important essay on *Mansfield Park*, speaks of *Northanger Abbey* in illustration of the author's directing irony not only upon some characters but upon the reader:

We are quick, too quick, to understand that *Northanger Abbey* invites us into a snug conspiracy to disabuse the little heroine of the errors of her corrupted fancy—Catherine Morland, having become addicted to novels of terror, has accepted their inadmissible premise, she believes that life is violent and unpredictable. And that is exactly what life is shown to be by the events of the story: it is we who must be disabused of our belief that life is sane and orderly. The shock of our surprise at the disappointment of our settled views is of course the more startling because we believe that we have settled our views in conformity with the author's own.[5]

Professor Trilling's insight carries high authority, a number of good critics have followed or expanded his view of *Northanger Abbey*, and it may be entirely right. But, if Jane Austen intended to demonstrate both that the terrors of Gothic fiction are utterly remote from real life and that real life can be a close parallel to Gothic fiction, one may think that the difficulty of the double proposition, especially its second part, led her into self-defeating extravagance. It is true that Catherine, back at home, after hearing Henry's account of his father's motives and behavior, can decide, with understandable exaggeration, that in her suspicions "she had scarcely sinned against his character, or magnified his cruelty." But that is a simple and natural reaction, it is not a revelation of a new view of life. One may discern no evidence that the Abbey episode shocked Catherine into the belief that life is violent and unpredictable. After Henry had exploded her Gothic suspicions, she had, as we observed, reached the sensible conclusion that real people are mixtures of good and bad qualities, not simply black or white, as in romance; and after her dismissal, although the General still looked pretty black, and although Catherine has learned that life and her own feelings have

[5] "Mansfield Park," *The Opposing Self* (New York: Viking Press, 1955), 207. The essay is reprinted in the anthologies of Heath and Watt.

more complexity than her mother's maxims allow for, she settles down with her husband at the parsonage to enjoy a sane and orderly life. In *Northanger Abbey*, as in the other novels, significant events are determined by character. To extract from one quite unconvincing incident a large and radical philosophical doctrine is surely to lift Jane Austen out of her age, her recognized principles, and her view of life and set her down in the twentieth century among the exponents of violence and "the Absurd."

As we have seen already, *Northanger Abbey* provides a contrast with the literary unreality and comparative artistic failure of the Abbey episode: Catherine's total disillusionment with the scheming Isabella Thorpe is an authentic experience in Jane Austen's real vein. This, like almost everything in her novels, is prepared for, and, as usual, such preparation contributes to the suspense that leads the reader on. From the beginning, of course, the reader is some steps ahead of Catherine in doubting Isabella's sincerity and honesty; but Isabella, who is four years older and far more worldly-wise, is the first friend she has ever had, and, for all Isabella's affectations and her and her brother's unscrupulous attempts to detach her from the Tilneys, juniority and youthful idealism dispose Catherine to enjoy her company and high spirits and think the best of her as long as she can. But Catherine grows more and more troubled as Isabella seems to forget her brother James, to whom she has just become engaged, in her efforts to capture the more rewarding Captain Tilney. One item is Isabella's ill-concealed disappointment—in spite of her rapturous professions about love in a cottage—over the provision James's father can make for him. In the end, Isabella's throwing over of James when she thinks she has landed a bigger fish (unlike Lucy Steele, she fails), and the false story she tells in trying to get Catherine to win James back when the flirtatious Captain evades her clutches—all this puts an end to friendship and enlarges the good-hearted Catherine's knowledge of life. It is this disillusionment, based on moral principles and human relations, not the briefly distressing experience at the Abbey, which, along with happy love, brings her to maturity, to knowledge not only of life but of herself. Here, as in the later novels, the heroine (sometimes the hero as well) has a capacity for growth which sets her or him apart from the other, mostly static characters.

Brief comment may be made on two matters of technique. One is "point of view," that perennial problem of Jane Austen's heir, Henry James. In this, the simplest of her stories, Catherine is present in all scenes as participant, observer, or hearer, and the reader follows events mainly through her eyes and ears and head and heart. But, since she is a simple soul, her reactions to experience and the reader's view of her are endorsed, modified, or interpreted by ironical or direct hints and comments from both the author and her surrogate, Henry Tilney. Further, after the opening chapters have set the stage, the story advances through a succession of dramatic scenes, one or two in each chapter, with narrative links; it is only at Northanger Abbey that narrative largely takes over, and a good part of that is a recital of Catherine's thoughts and feelings. Jane Austen did not invent the dramatic novel, since from antiquity onward fiction inevitably had more or less drama; but she did, among other things, order and refine the functional and economical use of dialogue. She came as near as any novelist to following the dramatic rule (not yet enunciated, I think, in her time) that every speech should in some way or degree alter the relations of the characters.

One may hazard the opinion that in *Northanger Abbey* dialogue has more consistently colloquial naturalness than the other early novels. *Sense and Sensibility* has rather frequent scraps of stilted utterance (quite apart from Marianne's rhetoric of sensibility) which can be momentarily jarring; and even *Pride and Prejudice* has some unnaturally elaborate syntax and diction in some highly emotional speeches. In *Northanger Abbey* there are extremes of vulgar colloquialism in the talk of John Thorpe (who has no parallel in any other of the novels) and in Isabella's gushing expression of her artificial sensibility, but Catherine and the rest—except General Tilney—speak in what may be called everyday style; Henry Tilney's moments of mock-formality are of course special bits of comedy. Along with the everyday quality of the characters and most of their doings, the normal naturalness of speech heightens the incongruous unreality of the Abbey episode. And the last three chapters, composed mainly of narrative summaries of feelings and events, do not altogether restore the dominant tone and easy flow of the earlier, much larger, and much better part of the novel.

5

The Watsons

I<small>N</small> 1804–05 J<small>ANE</small> A<small>USTEN</small> <small>WROTE</small> nearly 18,000 words of a novel which her nephew, when he printed the fragment in the *Memoir* in 1871, called *The Watsons* (*M. W.*, 314–62). A number of possible reasons may explain her giving up the work: that she was too much disturbed by recent personal sorrows and by the unsettled life she was then sharing with her mother and Cassandra; that she was dispirited by the non-appearance of *Susan* (i.e. *Northanger Abbey*); and that she was dissatisfied with the way the new story was going. That she worked on it carefully is clear from the many minute changes made in the manuscript, which was evidently a first draft. The fragment has been a good deal discussed on account of both its intrinsic interest and a theory that it contained the germ of *Emma*, a theory which may be thought wholly unconvincing.[1]

[1] The normally cautious Chapman (*Jane Austen*, 51) briefly and approvingly summarized points urged or accepted by some critics. (He did not mention the most elaborate argument, that of Mrs. Leavis, in *Scrutiny* 10, 1941–42, pp. 75–87: cf. their exchanges in the *Times Literary Supplement*, November 20, December 4 and 18, 1948.) Chapman wrote: ". . . *The Watsons* may with some plausibility be regarded as a sketch for *Emma*. The scene of both is Surrey. Mr. Watson is a faint adumbration of Mr. Woodhouse. Mrs. Robert Watson is strikingly suggestive of Mrs. Elton.

The initial and, so far as the fragment goes, the central situation is the sudden and complete eclipse of fortune for Emma Watson, a girl of nineteen who has been brought up in cultivated elegance by a rich and affectionate uncle and aunt: the widowed aunt has unexpectedly married an Irish captain and gone to Ireland and Emma has just come home to share the genteel poverty of her family. Cinderella has returned to her humble fireside, but after fourteen years in another world. The author has to accommodate to her own vein "the story of a distressed heroine, the staple character of sentimental and Gothic fiction" (Southam, 65). Emma is the first of the three isolated heroines, the others being Fanny Price and Anne Elliot: these three are almost immune from the author's irony. At the moment two of Emma's sisters, the older Penelope and the younger Margaret, are away visiting; the eldest, Elizabeth, whose spirit is not quite broken, has the responsibilities of the household and the care of their semi-invalid father, a retired clergyman and a widower. They live in a village several miles outside a town in Surrey.

Half of the fragment is taken up with the town's first winter ball, at which Emma is to make her first public appearance in the neighborhood. Elizabeth, driving her to town, unfolds much local and family history. Emma is warned against the well-to-do and flirtatious Tom Musgrave, who had once been attentive to Elizabeth and who Margaret thinks is now in love with her. Some years back, Elizabeth had been about to marry a friend of their brother Robert, but Penelope, an unscrupulous husband-hunter, had broken up that match without gaining the man herself. Elizabeth's story includes some grim facts and comments: ". . . you know we must marry . . . my Father cannot provide for us, & it is very bad to grow old & be poor & laughed at." "Poverty," says Emma, her style reflecting her different past and outlook, "is a

---

Emma Watson is very like Jane Fairfax in situation, and—so far as we get to know her—not unlike Emma Woodhouse in character." In view of Jane Austen's limited range of material, the first three particulars do not take us very far into *Emma*, and the two final statements are surely wrong: Emma Watson's situation is not like that of Jane Fairfax, who, during the time we know her, is engaged to the rich Frank Churchill and re-engaged after a short break; and Emma, who has ample knowledge of herself and clear perceptions of other people, is remote from Emma Woodhouse. One may think the theory was cogently disposed of by Mr. Southam.

great Evil, but to a woman of Education & feeling it ought not, it cannot be the greatest.—I would rather be Teacher at a school (and I can think of nothing worse) than marry a Man I did not like." Elizabeth would rather do anything than be a teacher; she thinks Emma's easy life has made her too refined for the taste of the sharp-tongued Penelope. Their brother Sam has his troubles too; he, a mere surgeon, aspires vainly to the hand of the rich Miss Edwards. The more pushing brother Robert, who had been an attorney's clerk, has got on by marrying his employer's well-dowered daughter.

The young Lord Osborne, the great man of the district, attends the ball ("to please the Borough") with a party which includes his mother and sister, Reverend Mr. Howard, formerly Lord Osborne's tutor and now clergyman of his parish, and Mr. Howard's widowed sister, Mrs. Blake, with her small son. Only one incident in the whole fragment gives Emma the aura of charm that belongs to an Austen heroine: when the Blake boy, who loves dancing, is bitterly disappointed by Miss Osborne's breaking her promise to him, Emma impulsively invites him to dance with her, and his woe turns instantly to joy. The partnership draws the attention of Tom Musgrave and even the cold Lord Osborne; it also leads to the introduction of Mr. Howard, who asks for two dances, thereby enabling Emma to refuse Tom Musgrave, to his surprise and discomfiture. Lord Osborne shows a growing interest in "that beautiful Emma Watson," but Emma likes Mr. Howard. The next morning, when the Edwardses, who have put up Emma for the night, are talking over the ball, Tom Musgrave appears with a message from Elizabeth about Emma's getting home. When he inquires what she thinks of Lord Osborne, Emma gives an opinion like Elizabeth Bennet's first impression of Darcy: "That he would be handsome even, tho' he were *not* a Lord—& perhaps—better bred; More desirous of pleasing, & shewing himself pleased in a right place."

Two days later, when the Watsons are about to have dinner, Lord Osborne and Tom Musgrave are ushered in. Emma is very conscious, as Elizabeth is not, of their humble style of living. Lord Osborne, in the course of his awkward efforts to converse, learns with regret that Emma doesn't ride: every woman should. "But every woman may not have the inclination, or the means. . . .

Female Economy will do a great deal my Lord, but it cannot turn a small income into a large one." Struck by such quiet candor, Lord Osborne feels for the first time what is due to a woman in Emma's situation, and he now talks to her "with a degree of considerate propriety." When the two men leave, with an invitation from Lord Osborne to attend next week's hunt, the sisters are astonished over the call, and Emma is flattered, but she wonders why Mr. Howard did not come too.

For a week or more Emma and Elizabeth enjoy each other's company, with increasing affection. But their quiet life is broken by the arrival from Croydon of their brother Robert and his "pert and conceited" wife, who come to bring Margaret home and to see Emma. Margaret's behavior alternates between "artificial Sensibility" and peevishness. Robert and his wife blame Emma's aunt and uncle for depriving her of the fortune she had been brought up to expect, but Emma defends them. Tom Musgrave appears again, at tea-time, and they play cards (the Vingt-un preferred at Osborne Castle). Margaret gets Elizabeth to invite him to dinner, and the next two days are spoiled by Margaret's preparatory commotion and her bad temper after he fails to come. Emma escapes to sit quietly with her father, "a Man of Sense and Education," and to read and think. Here the author abandons drama to summarize Emma's thoughts about her past, present, and future. However rhetorically composed, the summary is as bleak a page as any in Jane Austen; what we have seen already is a sufficient clue to the substance. It is plain that, unlike some other Austen heroines, Emma has no romantic illusions to grow out of, only a happy past to forget and a presumably dismal prospect to contemplate.

The story breaks off with Emma's declining an invitation to go home with Robert and his wife for a visit; she has had all she can take of them.

When printing the fragment in the *Memoir* the editor appended a note about Cassandra's knowledge of the author's intentions. Mr. Watson was soon to die and Emma was to become dependent for a home on her brother and sister-in-law. She was to refuse a proposal from Lord Osborne, and "much of the interest of the tale was to arise from Lady [*sc.* Miss] Osborne's love for Mr. Howard, and his counter affection for Emma, whom he was finally to marry." (Fanny Price was to make a partly parallel choice.)

These indications seem to point toward a quite typical story and atmosphere. But the fragment we have is quite untypical in being focused on a semi-genteel family that suffers from straitened income and its frequent accompaniments of drabness and meanness of life and outlook, with all the special problems confronting four young women who must achieve marriage, almost any kind of marriage, or face shabby, dependent spinsterhood. If this strain was going to be kept up by continued attention to Emma's sisters and her underbred brother and his wife, it would have resulted in harsher "comedy" than Jane Austen was wont to create. It is not that she did not elsewhere show an awareness of poverty, still more of the vulgarity of spirit that exists on all levels, but that in the other novels such evils are much less unrelieved and abrasive. Further, Jane Austen might have grown uneasy over the fact that, although the fragment runs to nearly fifty pages, the reader is kept more conscious of the social milieu and the oppressiveness of the Watson household than of the heroine as a person. If we think once or twice of Elizabeth Bennet, we think more often of Fanny Price in Portsmouth with her family (who, to be sure, are much below the Watsons in the social scale and in civility). But Fanny—not to mention her continuing security at Mansfield Park—is a developed and developing character, a substantial person, and Emma, though she makes assured and perceptive judgments of people and situations, has not become a commanding center of interest; the ordeal of adjustment to her new life has barely begun. Indeed, for all the space she gets, Emma may remain less alive in our minds than her also unhappy sister Elizabeth.

So much of the story is carried on through dialogue—a technical emphasis heightened by revisions—that it reads almost like a play with more or less copious stage directions; but although the acts and scenes have continuity they need a more ample frame and content. The dialogue, if it falls short of Jane Austen's mature subtlety, is still highly successful in revealing diverse characters and their diverse social positions and backgrounds. Thus, in the seven pages of talk between Elizabeth and Emma as they drive to the ball, the realistic colloquialism of the home-bred

Elizabeth (increased, Mr. Southam notes, in manuscript revisions) is distinguished from the more elegant style of Emma, who—to catch her at her worst—can say, sententiously: "If my opinions are wrong, I must correct them—if they are above my situation, I must endeavour to conceal them." Although we hear far less talk from the other characters, what there is reflects their individual dispositions and social levels, from the reserved and condescending Lord Osborne and his hanger-on, the casual and conceited Tom Musgrave, through the genially expansive Mr. Edwards down to Robert Watson and his wife, who differ in their kinds and degrees of vulgarity.

Altogether, this "work in progress" is of considerable interest to any student of Jane Austen's developing art and outlook, since it comes between *Northanger Abbey*, which had been virtually finished in 1803, and the final revisions, some years later, of *Sense and Sensibility* and perhaps *Pride and Prejudice*. However inadequate and uneven the treatment, in theme and atmosphere the story, or at least its substratum, might be called more "modern" than anything she had yet written or indeed was to write (unless *Sanditon* be excepted). Its drably realistic strain may make us think less of eighteenth-century types and motifs than of, say, the much grimmer lives of the sisters in George Gissing's *The Odd Women*.

6

Sense and Sensibility

We may briefly recall the chronological record. *Sense and Sensibility* was first written in epistolary form as *Elinor and Marianne*, about 1795.[1] In November 1797, after finishing the first version of *Pride and Prejudice* (1796–97), Jane Austen began to revise *Elinor and Marianne* in narrative form. During 1798–99 she wrote *Northanger Abbey*, which she said later was ready for publication in 1803. In 1804–05 came the fragment called *The Watsons*. In 1809–10, when happily settled at Chawton, Jane made the last—and inadequate—revision of what had become *Sense and Sensibility*. This was, we remember, the first novel to be published (November 1811).

The antithesis of the title was a frequent concern of eighteenth-century moralists and novelists and, with very little stretching, it would more or less fit all the Austen novels. Indeed *Love and Friendship* had in its farcical way contrasted the sensi-

---

[1] Critics have wondered how, unless the original plot was very different, this story could have been told in letters. In the revised version the sisters are always together, as the plot seems to demand they should be. Parts of the story could have been reported by others, but not the main part, the sisters' thoughts and feelings, since each is the other's only real confidante. Besides, Elinor, bound by her pledge to Lucy Steele, cannot for four months share her anxiety about Edward Ferrars with anyone.

[77]

bility of Laura and Sophia with the plain sense of Augusta and
Lady Dorothea. Among Jane Austen's six novels *Sense and Sensibility* is unique in having two heroines, and that in itself posed
problems of story-telling. Also, it is a much longer, more ambitious, and more thickly populated novel than the simple *Northanger Abbey*. And there was the large complication that the original epistolary version had to be radically changed in being recast
as a narrative.

It is not surprising, then, that such a transitional work is not a
complete success, that some central and incidental flaws go along
with some scenes, characters, and symbolic details that approach
or rival the author at her best. Such unevenness is nowhere dis-
played more strikingly than in the first two chapters. Whereas
the other novels open with arresting and more or less ironical
animation, this one begins with a rather flat account of the recently widowed Mrs. Dashwood and her daughters and the inadequate provision made for them by the will of her husband's
uncle; the affluent stepson John had promised to do everything to
make them comfortable. We are told that the nineteen-year-old
Elinor possesses right-minded judgment and stability, that Marianne is an impetuous embodiment of romantic sensibility, and
that Mrs. Dashwood is an older Marianne whose volatile imprudence Elinor has some trouble in curbing. The end of the
chapter is a brief report, not a dramatization, of their reactions to
the death of the father and husband: Elinor's quiet fortitude is
contrasted with the violent, self-indulgent emotionalism of Marianne and her mother. But in the second chapter, a brilliant one
(which could hardly have had a place in the epistolary *Elinor and
Marianne*), the author gets into her satiric stride. John Dashwood, who proposes giving Mrs. Dashwood and her daughters
£3000, is brought, in a face-saving dialogue perfectly suited for
the stage, to agree with his wife Fanny that he will amply fulfill
his father's wishes if he helps his relatives to find a house and
makes an occasional present of fish and game. In fact, he does
nothing at all. From now on, it might be remarked, money is to
be seen, in the foreground or background, as the chief asset or
chief aim of these and other characters.

The moral antithesis of the title is serious and central in Jane
Austen's view of life, but in this novel it is worked out through a

plot and contrasted sets of characters which hardly escape the appearance of artificial arrangement. The chief difficulty is that the contrast between Elinor and Marianne is too insistent: they seem quite often to be not so much persons as personifications of opposed qualities. Yet it is an essential part of the design that one sister should learn the value and necessity of the quality she has lacked and despised, and that she and we should recognize in the other the strong sensibility she has appeared to lack. The two suitors make a corresponding contrast. Edward Ferrars (Fanny Dashwood's brother) is said to have a good mind and disposition but is diffident, shy, and unambitious. Marianne thinks him quite stuffy; he has no feeling for poetry, drawing, or nature. Up to the second-last chapter he is shackled and largely silenced by his secret, youthful engagement to Lucy Steele, and his behavior might warrant an old dramatic critic's comment on an actor, that he displays every attribute of a poker except its occasional warmth (a phrase that applies also to the older Colonel Brandon). But Edward has his moments. While he acknowledges the sincerity of Marianne's love of the picturesque, his common sense shows up her very literary romanticism (and his own limitations): he prefers "tall, straight, and flourishing" trees to "crooked, twisted, blasted" ones and "a troop of tidy, happy villagers" to "the finest banditti in the world" (xviii). Although Marianne's first meeting with Willoughby is less romantic than it might have been in an earlier age—instead of saving her, like Sir Charles Grandison, from abduction by a vicious baronet, he only carries her home after she has sprained her ankle—she is instantly enraptured by an eager, ardent sensibility which seems completely in tune with her own.

Jane Austen follows a simple but fairly successful method in carrying on the parallel and contrasted stories of the two pairs of lovers: when a crisis threatens or overtakes one pair, she shifts to the other, without entirely neglecting the first. While the Dashwoods are still at Norland, two chapters (iii–iv) serve to kindle love between Elinor and Edward, without benefit of dialogue; after the move to Devon, Elinor longs for his company (xi). Chapters ix–xv take us from that first meeting of Marianne and Willoughby up to the point of a presumed engagement and his sudden, unexplained departure, which leaves Marianne and her family in misery. Chapters xvi–xxiv tell of Edward's continued silence and of Lucy Steele's confidential revelation to Elinor of her and Edward's secret engagement four years earlier. This heartbreak Elinor has to endure by herself; she feels sure that he loves her but is a prisoner in possessive hands. Now the scene changes to London (xxv f.), where Willoughby's cold rejection of Marianne's fervid appeals reduces her to uncomprehending anguish. Willoughby being disposed of (he is soon married to the heiress he has had in view), we return to Elinor's further trials and the results of Anne Steele's disclosure of Lucy's and Edward's engagement (xxxiii–xli): one result is that the angry Mrs. Ferrars disinherits Edward in favor of his younger brother Robert. Colonel Brandon unwittingly turns the knife in Elinor's heart by asking her to tell Edward he may have a living in the Colonel's gift. Chapters xlii–xliv contain two main events: Marianne's serious illness, brought on by her weeks of torment and an act of despairing, self-destructive imprudence; and Willoughby's rushing down from London on a report of her being near death. The impassioned story he pours out to Elinor is (to omit complications) that what he had begun as a flirtation had turned into real love, but that he could not conquer his dread of poverty; his candor and remorse somewhat soften Elinor's hitherto severe judgment, though later she—and Marianne—find him guilty of incurable self-indulgence.

We noticed the conspicuous disparity in craftsmanship between the first two chapters of the book, and, before we come to the dubious conclusion, we might juxtapose two passages which likewise illustrate the difference between the immature and the mature Jane Austen. After Willoughby breaks with Marianne, Colonel Brandon, her hovering, diffident admirer, feels free to unburden himself of what has troubled him for some time; readers may think he should have done so much earlier. He tells Elinor that Willoughby had seduced and abandoned his young ward (the daughter of his own first love by the first of her illicit lovers); the ensuing duel had left the villain unharmed—unlike the avenging duel at the end of *Clarissa Harlowe*. All this is a regrettable lapse into threadbare melodrama (xxxi). As a small antidote we might remember John Dashwood's saying to Elinor that Marianne's bloom is gone, that she cannot now expect a husband worth more than five or six hundred a year.

The second passage (xl) has to do with a matter referred to above, Colonel Brandon's bestowal of a living upon Edward Ferrars. Since the Colonel knows Edward, there seems to be no logical reason for his not making the offer directly instead of employing Elinor, but the awkward device, as critics have said, is perhaps justified by the result. Elinor has the cruelly ironic mission of giving Edward the news that will enable him and Lucy to marry, and the scene between the two anticipates the author's later subtleties. Edward thanks Elinor for a benefaction he owes to her. She is thinking of him and Lucy, he apparently thinks she is going to marry the Colonel, and neither can speak of the torment uppermost in their minds. Edward soon goes, in a perturbed state, to return thanks to the Colonel, and Elinor expects that the next time she sees him he will be Lucy's husband.

The denouement begins with a shock which the author, when more experienced, would not have used or would have prepared for. The Dashwoods' manservant, returning from Exeter, reports that Lucy Steele and Mr. Ferrars are married: he had seen them both in their carriage and brought the message from her. Elinor turns pale and Marianne has hysterics (we remember Mrs. John Dashwood's hysterics—not caused by sympathetic love—on a parallel occasion). But the appearance of Edward soon changes despair to ecstasy: he reports that Lucy has married his brother Robert, their mother's chosen heir. The rational, self-controlled Elinor "almost ran out of the room, and as soon as the door was closed, burst into tears of joy, which at first she thought would never cease." Edward having taken a walk to gain courage to do what he has come for, his proposal and her acceptance are despatched in two sentences, and he is one of the happiest of men, "not only in the rapturous profession of the lover, but in the reality of reason and truth"—a very Austenian phrase. At last able to talk freely, Edward tells his story, a total contrast to Willoughby's. His unhappy bond with Lucy had been broken by a letter from her after she had captured a much more prosperous husband. Her ambiguous message from Exeter to the Dashwoods had been a last bit of deliberate malice. (Since the manservant had been familiar with Edward, it may seem odd that he should have mistaken Robert for him; it may seem still more odd that Lucy, clever as she is, could have beguiled the very knowing Robert.) But of course Edward has to be set free.

Elinor's felicity is now complete except for the prompting of "sense" in regard to Edward's meager income; but Mrs. Ferrars is, reluctantly, won over to relax her purse-strings. Lucy, at first under a dark cloud, proves as successful with her mother-in-law as she had been with Robert, and is soon established as a favorite. Her felicity

may be held forth as a most encouraging instance of what an earnest, an unceasing attention to self-interest, however its progress may be apparently obstructed, will do in securing every advantage of fortune, with no other sacrifice than that of time and conscience.

This, and a further report on the relations of Lucy and Robert with each other and with the hostile John Dashwoods, are more akin to Fielding's broad irony than to that of the mature Jane Austen.

One piece of unfinished business requires a miracle, bringing Marianne to marry Colonel Brandon (who from the start might have seemed the foreordained husband of Elinor). The author, conscious of the difficulty, calls attention to Marianne's extra-ordinary fate: a girl who believed that a person could love only once, and only a young person love at all, found herself happily united, "with no sentiment superior to strong esteem and lively friendship," to a man who had loved once before, who seemed too old for marriage, and who still wears a flannel waistcoat in cool weather. As for Willoughby, however real his regret, he was not forever inconsolable: we must not imagine, says the antiro-mantic author, that "he fled from society, or contracted an ha-bitual gloom of temper, or died of a broken heart." Though Marianne remained his ideal, his wife was not always out of humor and he always had sports. Unlike the Willoughbys and the Robert Ferrars, the two worthy couples had of course the sub-stantial reward of close and unbroken harmony.

Even a bald outline of the main movement of the novel sug-gests the considerable skill with which the author keeps the stories of the two heroines going. Elements of suspense are partly of the external kind which does not outlive a first reading, but there is also something of the psychological suspense which, as in the later novels, gains rather than loses with rereading. Our interest in the four young lovers (and Colonel Brandon) varies from person to person; only Marianne, and at times Elinor and Willoughby, come alive. One reason—along with problems noticed at the beginning of this chapter—is that the author's total pattern in the end demands a more complete subordination of sensibility to sense than her own sympathies, however unequally mixed, can altogether support, and that this entails some unconvincing manipulation.

If for most readers the name of Jane Austen evokes the automatic thought of social comedy, it is plain that, while this novel has some (supplied chiefly by minor characters), the story of both Elinor and Marianne is serious and largely painful, that the book is nearer tragedy than comedy and has more sharp satire than humor. The characters can all be classified, strictly or loosely, by the criteria of sense and sensibility. Elinor and Colonel Brandon of course exemplify disciplined soundness of both head and heart, which includes acquiescence in social conventions as well as a notably unselfish concern for others. Edward Ferrars' goodness is likewise presented as rational and steadfast, though his holding to a loveless engagement seems more quixotically honorable than ideal or even sensible; and we, like Elinor, observe that his indulgence of affection for her left her in the lurch. On the other side, we go along with the author in seeing Marianne as a creature of excessive, self-centered, unconventional, and intolerant sensibility—though evidence is supplied for more than that. Mrs. Dashwood and Mrs. Jennings have an instinctive goodness of heart along with their shortcomings in sense or taste.

The other characters are more or less severely condemned or satirized in proportion to the nature and degree of their culpability—primarily Willoughby, the half-sincere actor, and Lucy Steele, the complete actress, but also John and Fanny Dashwood, Mrs. Ferrars and her son Robert. The root of ill-doing in all of these is callous or unscrupulous selfishness, which can masquerade as "sense." Much less grave but common faults are vacancy of mind and vulgarity of spirit, represented in various ways by the Steele sisters, Sir John and Lady Middleton, Mrs. Palmer and her rude husband (who scorns everyone around him, especially his wife), and, for all the sense and kindness she reveals, the boisterous Mrs. Jennings. If, by the way, we ask whether Jane Austen was interested in heredity, we may observe three trios: one of Mrs. Jennings' daughters, Mrs. Palmer, is like herself, while the other, Lady Middleton, is elegant, cold, and insipid; Marianne is like her mother, Elinor is not; Robert Ferrars and Mrs. John Dashwood are both like their mother, Edward is not. Such patterns are more mechanical than the later novels would have allowed.

We may ask where *Sense and Sensibility* stands in regard to the problem Jane Austen commonly assigns to her heroines, the journey through illusion to acceptance of reality. Elinor can hardly be charged with romantic illusions; the obstacle in the way of her fulfillment is an external one, the situation in which Edward is entangled. Marianne is the most extreme example of romantic sensibility in all Jane Austen. Her moral guide is her own instinctive feeling—the doctrine, as critics remark, of the philosophers of sentimentalism. But if Jane Austen's youthful impulse toward antisentimental satire went into the original conception of Marianne, it was considerably qualified in the creation of a vital human being. For all her adolescent extravagance, we recognize the frequent rightness of Marianne's feelings and we are compelled to believe in the passionate intensity of her love for Willoughby and of her prolonged misery after her disillusionment with him; in comparison with Marianne's high fever of mind and body, which is described with almost clinical detail, Catherine Morland's Gothic ailment is only a touch of literary indigestion. We may be less sure that through suffering Marianne achieves rational stability; at least we may (with Elinor) smile at the programmatic zeal of her reformation, since she is still a creature of extremes. Her acquisition of sense is, necessarily, given much less, and less dramatic, presentation than her joys and sorrows of sensibility. That her reformation could extend to her marrying the once despised Colonel Brandon requires the unwilling suspension of disbelief that accompanies a happy ending.

It is of course more than a happy ending. Marianne both prizes and possesses qualities which go beyond the stereotype of romantic sensibility. Her complete trust in the rightness of her own feelings and the wrongness of any different feelings, her impetuous sincerity and candor, her lack of decorous self-control at times make her, whether right or wrong, inconsiderate, intolerant, and rude: "it was impossible for her to say what she did not feel, however trivial the occasion; and upon Elinor therefore the whole task of telling lies when politeness required it, always fell" (xxi). Such qualities have led some critics to see Marianne as a solitary, valiant nonconformist smothered by the suppressions and hypocrisies of conventional society—a view very congenial to our age. Jane Austen might have made Marianne such a person, but she does not; she gives full value to what is right in the girl's instincts and behavior, but—with her always active awareness of social order—she also makes clear what she sees as faults that Marianne must learn to overcome. The conclusion alone is a sufficient refutation of the theory: if Marianne were a wholly admirable exponent of nonconformity, her marriage to Colonel Brandon would have been, would have had to be, presented as a final defeat, a proud spirit's capitulation to society. But the author never approaches that idea: however conscious of the difficulty of convincing us, she takes the marriage as proof of Marianne's attainment of "sense"; "and her whole heart became, in time, as much devoted to her husband, as it had once been to Willoughby."

Probably many readers find Elinor objectionable, and certainly her moral pronouncements can at times be stiff and forbidding. She is, at nineteen, the standard of both personal and traditional reason and rectitude by which all the other characters are judged; her opinions of them have the author's open or tacit endorsement and become, or should become, ours. Elinor is, like the more engaging Henry Tilney, in the eighteenth-century tradition of the mentor. But she is not merely an exponent of the author's moral principles and of general sobriety and poise, though she does not lose those qualities when she fences skilfully with the malicious Lucy Steele or when she, no less than Marianne, is kindled by love. And her sensibility is not effervescent, intolerant, and self-centered. Throughout the book, almost from the beginning, she is under heavy emotional strain, which she has to endure by herself. If Edward, in his difficult situation, seems no inflammatory object, that must not prevent our recognizing the intensity of Elinor's feeling, an intensity which her reason and sense of duty are bound to repress until fortune brings release. She has to struggle to achieve and maintain a right balance between feeling and reason. And, in the midst of trouble, she is capable of wry humor: when the well-meaning Mrs. Jennings brings for the sick Marianne a glass of the wine that had helped her husband's "cholicky gout," Elinor, since Marianne is asleep and in need of rest, drinks most of it, reflecting that "its healing power on a disappointed heart might be as reasonably tried on herself as on her sister" (xxx). So far as we fail to appreciate Elinor, the fault is partly in the presentation but perhaps more in our instinctive, "romantic" undervaluing of rational self-discipline.

Since Jane Austen was to become a superb mistress of dialogue, and is that in some scenes in this book, we may take brief account of artistry which here seems more uneven than it was in *Northanger Abbey*. One general premise is that in novels convention had established, for the well-bred, a more rounded formalism than prevailed in actual speech—a point which can be readily verified from Jane Austen's novels and letters. At the same time we might note the high praise given, in the *British Critic* of March 1818, to the extraordinarily lifelike naturalness of her dialogue,[2] a quality quite often manifest here.

In *Sense and Sensibility*, as in all the novels, style is a more or less subtle index or reflection of moral and cultural differences. Thus the style as well as the matter of Anne Steele's gabble proclaims her vulgarity; and, though the more self-conscious, clever, and ambitious Lucy uses better English than her sister, she is labeled "illiterate" by Elinor. Of Lucy's letter announcing her marriage to Robert Ferrars Edward says it is the only letter he ever received from her "of which the substance made . . . any amends for the defect of the style." The speech of Mrs. Palmer, Mrs. Jennings, and Robert Ferrars likewise reveals types of crude or fashionable vulgarity. With such persons the author's touch is sure, and the difference between sincerity and affectation is always clear.

2 Southam, *Critical Heritage*, 81.

With the style of Elinor and Marianne the author is less consistently successful; there may be some survivals from the epistolary version of the book. Both girls at times make much longer speeches than belong to real life. Even in ordinary dialogue, whether because of Elinor's special role as the exponent of sense or because of the author's relative inexperience in serious fiction, Elinor's habitual mode of utterance tends to be more formal than that of later heroines. When Marianne, Willoughby, and Elinor are chatting (x), the forceful colloquialism of the two individualists makes Elinor, the voice of reason and order, sound like an elderly schoolmistress. Willoughby says:

"Brandon is just the kind of man . . . whom every body speaks well of, and nobody cares about; whom all are delighted to see, and nobody remembers to talk to."

"That is exactly what I think of him," cried Marianne.

Elinor defends him thus:

". . . He has seen a great deal of the world; has been abroad; has read, and has a thinking mind. I have found him capable of giving me much information on various subjects, and he has always answered my inquiries with the readiness of good-breeding and good nature."

"That is to say," cried Marianne contemptuously, "he has told you that in the East Indies the climate is hot, and the mosquitoes are troublesome."

"He *would* have told me so, I doubt not, had I made any such inquiries; but they happened to be points on which I had been previously informed."

The last two clauses might be taken charitably as rather heavy irony.

There are some moments when Elinor's speech can be almost incredible, as when, in London, Marianne is trying desperately not to suspect evil of Willoughby (xxix):

Elinor would not contend, and only replied, "Whoever may have been so detestably your enemy, let them be cheated of their malignant triumph, my dear sister, by seeing how nobly the consciousness of your own innocence and good intentions supports your spirits. It is a reasonable and laudable pride which resists such malevolence."

When Elinor has to tell Marianne that she has for four months known of Edward's and Lucy's engagement, her speeches about duty and endurance have the structured syntax of a moral essay, and the decorum of self-control is superhuman (xxxvii).

Marianne's speeches, short or long, of course reveal her warm sensibility, whether in the rhetoric of her farewell apostrophe to her beloved Norland (v, end) or in her normally more colloquial vein. That apostrophe might have appeared in *Love and Friendship*; on the next page comes the author's ironical description of Barton cottage as lacking the prescribed romantic features. Like Elinor, though much less often, Marianne can speak with stilted formality even in moments of deep feeling, for instance, at the end of a very long but relatively realistic speech in which she reproaches herself for having been preoccupied with her own troubles and inconsiderate of others, especially Elinor (xlvi).

But we should not exaggerate the amount or, what is more important, the effect of varying degrees of rhetorical utterance. Such elements keep us aware of civilized manners, even if the idiom is remote from ours, and, no less than vulgarities, they help to define and distinguish character. For the most part what we consider excessive formalism merges readily enough into the general texture, into the atmosphere of the fictional world, so that it probably does not much disturb modern readers. In a different vein, a last quotation, which begins with Marianne's portentously youthful assumption of stable maturity, might suggest a modern parallel, a rather special one (xvii):

"Undoubtedly. At my time of life opinions are tolerably fixed. It is not likely that I should now see or hear anything to change them."

"Marianne is as stedfast as ever, you see," said Elinor, "she is not at all altered."

"She is only grown a little more grave than she was."

"Nay, Edward," said Marianne, "*you* need not reproach me. You are not very gay yourself."

"Why should you think so!" replied he, with a sigh. "But gaiety never was a part of *my* character."

Except for a word or two, we might take oath that this was an extract from Ivy Compton-Burnett.

7

Pride and Prejudice

*P*ride *and Prejudice*, ORIGINALLY CALLED *First Impressions*, was first written between October 1796 and August 1797, soon after the first (epistolary) version of *Sense and Sensibility*. In November 1797 Mr. Austen wrote to a publisher offering to submit the book and saying that it was "about the length of Miss Burney's *Evelina*"—a rather loose statement, unless the original version was much longer than the one we have. The offer was declined by return mail. Whether or not the novel was written first in epistolary form, as some critics have thought it was, it must have been considerably revised, perhaps during 1809–12.[1] It was published in January 1813. On January 29 (Letter 76)

[1] Chapman, in the appendix to his edition, argued that Jane Austen, with her instinct for minute accuracy, fitted the events of the story to the calendar for 1811–12. This view, which seems to have been generally accepted, has been disputed by Ralph Nash (*English Language Notes* 4, 1967, pp. 194–98), who questions "extensive revision in 1811–12," and by P. B. S. Andrews (*Notes and Queries* 15, 1968, pp. 338–42), who argues especially for a substantial revision in 1802. Both views present difficulties. It is not easy to see brilliant revision or re-creation of *Pride and Prejudice* as done some eight years before the final and uneven revision of the very inferior *Sense and Sensibility* (though the main revision of *Northanger Abbey* was done by 1803); nor, unless the author had extraordinary facility in changing gear, is it easy to think of such work going on during the composition of the sober *Mansfield Park* (begun about February 1811).

Jane wrote to Cassandra: "I have lop't and crop't so successfully
. . . that I imagine it must be rather shorter than S. & S. altogether"; it is in fact slightly longer. Whatever the dates and
degrees of revision, the novel combines mature or semi-mature
art with the ebullient spirit of youth and comedy.

The original title, *First Impressions*, had in sentimental fiction
carried the special connotation of immediate surrender to sensibility, love at first sight—the kind of experience enjoyed in *Love
and Friendship*. The opposed view, that sensibility needed rational restraint, was enunciated by the exemplary Miss Byron
early in one of the novels Jane Austen knew well, *Sir Charles
Grandison*: "O Sir Rowland, I thought you were too wise to be
swayed by first impressions: None but the *giddy*, you know, love
at first sight."[2] The first title was discarded probably because it
was used for a book published in 1800. Both it, in a general and
ironical sense, and the final title would apply to both heroine and
hero. Both were mistaken in their first impressions of each other,
as Elizabeth was also in regard to Wickham and Darcy in regard
to Jane Bennet. And Elizabeth, as she later admitted to herself,
was guilty of prejudice based on pride in her own discernment,
Darcy—as he also came to admit—of prejudice born of his chief
fault, personal and social pride. The phrase "pride and prejudice"
has been observed in a dozen or more books, mostly of the later
eighteenth century, where Jane Austen might have seen it. The
most likely and significant source would be Fanny Burney's *Cecilia* (1782), where the phrase is used three times, in capitals, in a
paragraph of the last chapter: Dr. Lyster is summarizing the
moral of the work, the havoc wrought in young lives by their
elders' fanatical pride in an aristocratic name and lineage.[3] Jane
Austen set up a partly similar conflict between Darcy and Elizabeth and related conflicts within each of them. It requires experience and self-examination on the part of the heroine and hero, the
"intricate" characters who are capable of such reflection, to

----

[2] Ed. 1932, 1, Letter 9, p. 51. Mr. Southam (59) cites a later bit of
Grandison and *The Mysteries of Udolpho* (Everyman ed., 1, 5; cf. 1, 81–82).
Other critics cite other examples, notably Fanny Burney's *Camilla* (1796).

[3] Mrs. Leavis has argued that "the original conception of *First Impressions* was undoubtedly to rewrite the story of Cecilia in realistic terms"
(*Scrutiny* 10, 1941–42, p. 71), a view which surely involves much exaggeration and distortion.

recognize their failings and correct their view of themselves and others.

During their more than a century and a half of life, almost every one of Jane Austen's novels has been the declared favorite of sundry readers, but there can be no doubt that *Pride and Prejudice* has always been the one most widely read and most often reread. It is also the one that has chiefly invited dramatization, for both stage and film, partly perhaps because of its abundance of bright dialogue and its highly dramatic symmetry of structure. On the other hand, critics who do not allow irresistible charm to sway their judgment might say that, while *Pride and Prejudice* is far richer and more mature than *Northanger Abbey* and *Sense and Sensibility*, and has many more speaking characters than either, it is still a simple, slender tale which has almost too ideal a pattern and seldom achieves the realistic complexity, density, and subtlety of *Mansfield Park* and *Emma*. But few could disagree with the author's avowal, made when she received the first copy of "my own darling child": "I must confess that I think her [Elizabeth Bennet] as delightful a creature as ever appeared in print, and how I shall be able to tolerate those who do not like *her* at least I do not know" (Letter 76: January 29, 1813). Elizabeth is not, like the heroines of conventional fiction, endowed in a transcendent and flawless degree with beauty and all the virtues of heart and head; she is a thoroughly human mixture, above the average in her perceptive interest in people (complicated people), in independence, candor, in gaily satirical wit, in a balance of sense and sensibility—in short, very much like her creator. And she is the mainspring of the plot: along with her own personal development, it is through her and her effect on Darcy that her sisters (and also Charlotte Lucas) achieve the appointed end of comedy, marriage.

It is obviously because of the spirited heroine that *Pride and Prejudice* is the most captivating of Jane Austen's variations on the Cinderella theme. Elizabeth, to be sure, is not a real Cinderella but (as she declared in her grand duel with Lady Catherine de Bourgh) the daughter of a gentleman, a gentleman, however, far below Darcy in station and income. Her chief handicap is her "low connections." Her foolish and ill-bred mother and youngest sisters and her uncle Philips (a Meryton attorney) and his wife must, as Darcy says of Jane and Elizabeth, "very materially lessen their chance of marrying men of any consideration in the world" (viii). And Darcy, in point of social standing, estate, wealth, and personal pride, is the most exalted of Jane Austen's heroes. The social gulf between him and Elizabeth is in accord with the facts of contemporary life, it is not merely a fictional convention; but social divisions had been a great resource for novelists from Richardson onward and were to be through much of the nineteenth century, notably for Trollope. Thus *Pride and Prejudice* puts formidable obstacles in the way of a happy culmination, and suspense is aggravated and prolonged by other obstacles that develop in the course of the story.

The theme and tone of the novel are set by the famous opening sentence: "It is a truth universally acknowledged, that a single man in possession of a good fortune, must be in want of a wife." In a way characteristic of a stylist of ironic nuances, the mock-philosophical solemnity of the first clause is immediately deflated by a notion of marriage appropriate to high comedy. Further, while that opening sentence applies directly to the subject of the first chapter, the arrival in the neighborhood of a very eligible bachelor, this novel, like all the others, starts from a more comprehensive and more valid truth, that every young woman, with or without a fortune, is in want of a husband. Thus the initial generality is completely reversed by the second sentence, which affirms that a new arrival is considered by alert mothers "as the rightful property of some one or other of their daughters." Then, through the talk of one ill-mated couple, the goal is set up for their progeny. At the same time we are made aware of the genteel, gossipy families which make up local society and the competitive marriage market. The short chapter ends with a short paragraph which crisply defines the characters and minds of Mr. and Mrs. Bennet; it underlines what dialogue had already revealed.

While in the other Austen novels the heroine (even Emma, though unaware of her feelings) is in love from the start, in *Pride and Prejudice* dramatic tension is much heightened because romance begins with cool disdain on both sides—disdain which soon, like that of Beatrice and Benedick, gives unwitting evidence of mutual fascination. At a ball we are reminded of Lord Os-

borne's aloofness in *The Watsons* by Darcy's supercilious refusal
to dance with anyone except Bingley's sisters; we are reminded
also of Evelina's first encounter with her future husband, Lord
Orville (*Evelina*, Letter xii), by Darcy's disparaging remark
about Elizabeth, a remark audible to her. If this seems a doubt-
fully credible lapse in manners, even on the part of a proud, shy
man who is out of his element, it is an early preparation for what
is to offend Elizabeth in his proposal. Now, she has "no very
cordial feelings towards him," though she tells the story for fun
among her friends. But when Jane's illness takes her sister to
Netherfield as nurse for a few days, her fine eyes and her vivacity
and candor kindle an interest which Darcy comes to recognize as
dangerous bewitchment, and he deliberately sheers off.

Elizabeth, being more indifferent than positively hostile to
Darcy, has been in his company her unawed sparkling self. But
the next episode, acquaintance with Wickham, provides fuel for
strong aversion. Much attracted by Wickham's elegant looks and
manners, and curious about his relations with Darcy, she fails—as
the reader should not fail—to see the impropriety of a new acquaintance's volunteering a self-pitying autobiography. She swal-
lows without question his story of Darcy's thwarting his career
in callous disregard of his father's intentions (Wickham's father
had been the steward of Darcy's father's estate). Wickham
speaks also of Darcy's unbending pride, a quality shared by his
sister, and of his being expected to marry his cousin, Lady Catherine's daughter. Elizabeth's complete trust in Wickham is perhaps understandable in the circumstances, but it is the one case in
which her discernment is blinded by prejudice; even the mild
Jane Bennet, while not disposed to question Wickham's veracity,
is much less sure than Elizabeth that they have the whole truth.

Since Bingley and Jane have manifestly fallen in love, Elizabeth's feeling against Darcy is strongly intensified by what she
suspects to be his responsibility for the Bingleys' sudden migra-
tion to London and the blighting of her sister's happiness. Her
next meetings with Darcy (after the Netherfield dance) take
place at Hunsford, when she is visiting Mr. and Mrs. Collins and
Darcy and a Colonel Fitzwilliam are visiting their aunt, Lady
Catherine. In Lady Catherine's house—where Darcy has as much
reason to be ashamed of her ill-breeding as Elizabeth had of her

mother's—he, in smiling mood, converses amiably with Elizabeth, who, as usual, holds her own in liveliness. Darcy makes frequent calls at the parsonage and apparently seeks to meet her when she walks in the park, although he has little to say; she only laughs at Charlotte's notion that he is falling in love. Her hostility is greatly strengthened by Colonel Fitzwilliam's unwitting corroboration of her suspicion about Darcy's having separated Bingley and Jane. When alone, she is overcome by thoughts of such heartless conduct; declining to go with the others to have tea at Lady Catherine's, she sits down to reread Jane's letters from London, "as if intending to exasperate herself as much as possible against Mr. Darcy" (xxxiv).

At this moment, so artfully and naturally contrived, Darcy comes in, asks about her health, sits still, walks about the room, and after more silence approaches her "in an agitated manner" and says:

"In vain have I struggled. It will not do. My feelings will not be repressed. You must allow me to tell you how ardently I admire and love you."[4]

Elizabeth is too completely astonished to speak. Then gratification over "the compliment of such a man's affection" gives place to anger as his eloquent tenderness gives place to equally warm recognition of her family's defects—all this with no apparent doubt of his being accepted. He in turn is astonished and angry when she cites his offensive acknowledgment that he has forced himself to stoop, his ruining her sister's happiness, his cruel treatment of Wickham.

"You are mistaken, Mr. Darcy, if you suppose that the mode of your declaration affected me in any other way, than as it spared me the concern which I might have felt in refusing you, had you behaved in a more gentleman-like manner."

She saw him start at this, but he said nothing, and she continued,

"You could not have made me the offer of your hand in any possible way that would have tempted me to accept it."

Again his astonishment was obvious; and he looked at her with an

[4] Darcy's first words had been anticipated by Richardson's Mr. B.: "In vain, my *Pamela*, do I find it to struggle against my affection for you" (*Pamela*, Oxford, 1930, 2, 10; Everyman ed., 1, 227). The latter text lacks "find it to."

expression of mingled incredulity and mortification. She went on.

"From the very beginning, from the first moment I may almost say, of my acquaintance with you, your manners impressing me with the fullest belief of your arrogance, your conceit, and your selfish disdain of the feelings of others, were such as to form that ground-work of disapprobation, on which succeeding events have built so immoveable a dislike; and I had not known you a month before I felt that you were the last man in the world whom I could ever be prevailed on to marry."

"You have said quite enough, madam. I perfectly comprehend your feelings, and have now only to be ashamed of what my own have been. Forgive me for having taken up so much of your time, and accept my best wishes for your health and happiness."

And with these words he hastily left the room. . . .

Jane Austen's readers discover in time that almost the only proposals she stages in full are those that are rejected; these— including Mr. Collins' comic effort in an earlier chapter (xix)— have more dramatic possibilities than happy acceptances, which, summarily handled, run no risk of banality. Darcy's proposal gives us a pleasant shock of surprise in realizing Elizabeth's power over such a formidable man, though we knew he was bound to speak, since the growth of his interest has been steadily recorded. We are also given new evidence of Elizabeth's courage, family loyalty, and vigorous, unladylike candor—not to mention what she never thinks of, the allurements of wealth and position. We are left, almost exactly in the middle of the book, wondering if and how the chasm just created can be bridged; of course we know, but the story never grows stale.

The dramatic energy of the encounter undoubtedly achieves impressive success, as the test of memory proves, but it may provoke some marginal queries. Are Darcy's last words to be taken as an agitated and embarrassed lapse into lower-middle-class manners? We may even think of Dickens' Mr. Toots. When Elizabeth angrily declares that she has disliked him from the first moment of their acquaintance, are we intended to remember what she does not, the numerous occasions on which she enjoyed being "impertinent" in conversation with him, the occasions which had kindled his admiration and love (vi, viii–xi, xviii, xxxi–ii)? At any rate she remembers them near the end of the book (lx). A quite different question is whether Jane Austen, in working up this set piece, consciously or unconsciously adopted the high style fiction had consecrated to such bravura scenes: the passage quoted displays, in spite of Elizabeth's explosive emotions, an extraordinary control of complicated syntax which equals or outdoes Elinor Dashwood.

When Darcy the next day puts into her hand his long letter of self-defense, her first reaction, that it is "all pride and insolence," gives way, as she reads and rereads it, to exoneration on the two main charges. It is true that Jane's habitual composure might have convinced the most acute observer that she was not seriously in love, as—since the author prepares for everything—Elizabeth and Charlotte had once agreed (vi). As for Wickham, Darcy had shown much more generosity than he deserved: his life of dissipation, importunity, and reproaches had included an attempt to elope with Darcy's rich young sister. (This off-stage item, a fictional cliché, stops well short of the Willoughby affair in *Sense and Sensibility*, it links Darcy with Elizabeth in a parallel humiliation, and it gives him a second motive for intervening on Lydia's behalf.) As for Darcy's strictures on her family, and the family's share in wrecking Jane's prospects, Elizabeth feels "depressed beyond any thing she had ever known before."

Some critics have doubted the possibility of a proud, reserved man's volunteering "so much, and such, information . . . —unless under pressure from his author, anxious to get on with the story," since Elizabeth's whole impression must be revised before the visit to Pemberley.[5] But we may remember that the letter was written "in a dreadful bitterness of spirit" (lviii), when Darcy was greatly upset. It would be far less plausible and effective if he gave the necessary information *viva voce* and Elizabeth had no time to reflect on it. And surely high comedy is not traditionally bound by the strictest realism in every particular. Finally, the letter may be said to establish its credibility because at earlier stages in the novel most of its points had been lodged in our minds by casual evidence or strong hints.

In Elizabeth's mind Darcy, with good reason, is pretty well

---

[5] Mary Lascelles, 162. M. Mudrick (118) takes such a letter from such a man as the author's desperate effort "to weight the scales in favor of her predetermined hero." Most heroes are predetermined.

cleared of blame. She feels "absolutely ashamed of herself." She, who had been so proud of her discernment, "had been blind, partial, prejudiced, absurd." But this correcting of a mistaken judgment is given a larger dimension which belongs to the essence of Jane Austen. Elizabeth, since she cannot look to either parent or get much light from the gentle and uncritical Jane, must throughout the novel depend on her own experience, instincts, and judgment; and for the most part these had hitherto been or seemed reliable guides. But now a somewhat rhetorical outburst of self-condemnation ends with the plain statement: "Till this moment, I never knew myself." If that claim is not yet fully warranted, at any rate the attainment of self-knowledge is the first step in the process of replacing illusion with a grasp of reality.

In regard to Darcy, Elizabeth has at this point moved from strong hostility to benevolent neutrality: she is grateful for his attachment and respects his general character, "but she could not approve him; nor could she for a moment repent her refusal, or feel the slightest inclination ever to see him again" (xxxvii). We can imagine Jane Austen planning the best conditions for the next meeting between the two: it should be involuntary, the result of circumstances; Elizabeth should first see Pemberley, as a fresh image or reflection of its owner, and should hear testimony on his character from a trustworthy witness; she should encounter Darcy there, on his own ground, and find him quite altered in manner; and he should see her in the company of thoroughly presentable relations. All these conditions are fulfilled, within a legitimate range of contrivance, by the visit the Gardiners and Elizabeth pay to Pemberley.

First we see the grounds through Elizabeth's eyes, the eyes of a civilized but "natural" person who delights in nature that is "neither formal, nor falsely adorned," and she receives a visual impression of the owner's taste. She has the further feeling "that to be mistress of Pemberley might be something!" The interior of the house reflects the same fine taste and renews the exciting fancy, a fancy immediately saved "from something like regret" by the recollection that she would not have been allowed to invite her uncle and aunt there. She has, of course, no reason to think that a proud suitor, angrily rejected, would be disposed to try again; nor have we reason to think that, at this stage, she would be ready to accept him. The tour of the rooms with the housekeeper has much quiet ironic drama, since the Gardiners believe Elizabeth has some attachment to Wickham and complete antipathy for Darcy. But the housekeeper, after mentioning Wickham's generous upbringing and later wildness, pays warm tributes to the exemplary goodness and kindness Darcy has always shown as son, brother, landlord, and employer; she has known him since he was four and has never had a cross word. As Elizabeth looked at his portrait, "she thought of his regard with a deeper sentiment of gratitude than it had ever raised before." (Gratitude, we may remember, was in fiction—and no doubt has been in life—a not uncommon beginning of love: Miss Byron had both a special and a general reason for adoring Sir Charles Grandison, a rescuer, lover, and universal uncle on a plane of patrician loftiness and beneficence well beyond Darcy's.)

The housekeeper's testimony is a prelude to more direct and compelling evidence. As they leave the house they encounter Darcy himself. Elizabeth is horribly embarrassed at being found there, and Darcy, though quite civil, even gentle, in his inquiries about her family, is himself too confused to linger. "She longed to know" what he was thinking, "and whether, in defiance of every thing, she was still dear to him." Encouragement soon comes. Darcy, having collected his wits, puts himself in their way again while they are admiring the grounds. He asks to be introduced to Elizabeth's friends (whom he would be taking for "people of fashion"), and she rejoices in "every sentence of her uncle, which marked his intelligence, his taste, or his good manners." Darcy, to Mr. Gardiner's surprise, cordially invites him to fish whenever he likes, and Elizabeth, recognizing the compliment to herself, wonders too. She explains that the housekeeper had said he would not return until the next day. He had changed his plans and the next day the Bingleys will be arriving with his sister, whom he wishes to introduce to her. When they leave, the Gardiners are impressed but still suspicious, and on one point, Darcy's supposed ill treatment of Wickham, Elizabeth enlightens them.

All three are further enlightened when, the very next day, Darcy brings his sister and Bingley to call on them. It is pretty

clear to Elizabeth that Bingley is not in love with Miss Darcy but
is still in love with Jane. Darcy himself wears "an expression of
general complaisance," with no trace of hauteur; he seems anxious only to please. During the evening and part of the night
Elizabeth, recalling her angry and unjust response to his proposal,
can account for the miraculous change only on the conviction
that he is still ardently in love, and her gratitude swells. And—
since Jane Austen's stronger heroines are not passive—"she only
wanted to know . . . how far it would be for the happiness of
both that she should employ the power, which her fancy told her
she still possessed, of bringing on the renewal of his addresses."
But a happy ending must not come too easily, there must be
suspense and a closer, surer bond established, and the next seven
chapters (xlvi–lii) raise a new and presumably fatal obstacle. A
letter from Jane reports that Lydia has eloped from Brighton
with Wickham, that no one knows where they are, and that they
are probably not married. This is that relatively violent incident
that Jane Austen commonly uses to start the wheels rolling toward the denouement.

After much negotiation, Wickham and Lydia are married, and
Darcy, who has just called, is shocked and deeply concerned.
Sophisticated readers may laugh at Elizabeth's declaration that,
since Lydia has nothing to tempt Wickham to marriage, "she is
lost for ever"; but perhaps there is still enough support for the
institution to make her bourgeois feelings comprehensible. With
Darcy at hand, walking up and down, "his brow contracted, his
air gloomy," Elizabeth cannot help thinking that this crowning
family disgrace must extinguish his love. And the thought brings
understanding—less than full understanding—of her actual state
of mind: "never had she so honestly felt that she could have
loved him, as now, when all love must be vain." The author here
puts in a brief defense of Elizabeth's present feeling for Darcy as
founded on "gratitude and esteem" (a topic lightly touched in
the second-last chapter of *Northanger Abbey*), although such an
idea may offend believers in the common romantic doctrine of
first impressions, love at first sight—which she had given "somewhat of a trial . . . in her partiality for Wickham." She is not
unemotional, but she is unsentimental, or antisentimental, and
always honest.

After much negotiation, Wickham and Lydia are married, and

Elizabeth is enabled to extract from Mrs. Gardiner the information that Darcy had managed the whole business. She is cheered by the knowledge of his undergoing so much trouble, mortification, and expense (the expense of bribing Wickham); he had surely done it for her, yet can even he link himself with such a family and such a brother-in-law?

Elizabeth's change of heart has been convincingly brought about, but it must be made known to Darcy and he must be given an occasion to renew his proposal. First, however, Jane and Bingley are reunited, with Darcy's approval. Then Lady Catherine, having heard rumors, journeys to Longbourn to browbeat Elizabeth into a promise of refusing a possible offer from her nephew. The confrontation, in which Elizabeth stands up to the dragoness with such forceful dignity, is one of Jane Austen's stirring scenes—and very different from the overwrought rhetoric of Fanny Burney's Mrs. Delvile and the meek Cecilia (*Cecilia*, 4, bk. vii, c. 8). A few days later, having Darcy alone, Elizabeth says that she must thank him for what her family does not know of, the "unexampled kindness" and "generous compassion" he had shown in regard to Lydia; this of course leads at once to a proposal, Elizabeth's somewhat embarrassed acceptance, and Darcy's "heart-felt delight." We are not told whether Elizabeth had now been thinking how far "she should employ the power, which her fancy told her she still possessed, of bringing on the renewal of his addresses" (xliv); but later (lx), when the lovers are talking over the past, she says: "I wonder when you *would* have spoken if I had not asked you! My resolution of thanking you for your kindness to Lydia had certainly great effect." If Darcy can mold Bingley, Elizabeth can mold Darcy.

R. A. Brower, after skilfully analyzing the ironic ambiguities of dialogue between Elizabeth and Darcy, regrets the virtual disappearance of that double or multiple vision in the last third of the novel (after Lydia's elopement), in which the "events seem to belong to a simpler world where outright judgments of good and bad or of happy and unhappy are in place."[6] In Mr. Mud-

[6] "Light and Bright and Sparkling: Irony and Fiction in 'Pride and Prejudice,'" *The Fields of Light* (New York: Oxford University Press, 1951), 180. This valuable essay is reprinted in the critical anthologies of Heath and Watt and in *Twentieth Century Interpretations of PRIDE*

rick's more explosive terms, that last third sinks into Burneyan simplification of motive and will and "a fogbank of bourgeois morality," and the characters, especially Darcy, "fall automatically into the grooves prepared for them by hundreds of novels of sentiment and sensibility." But surely this romantic-realistic story had reached a point where—as when Beatrice says to Benedick, "Kill Claudio"—the hero and heroine must be seen, under stress, as their essential selves, above the ironic ambiguities of comedy, firmly joined in their judgment of good and bad; however unequal in worldly terms, they have the same moral values—however bourgeois these may be.

For the simple-minded reader the denouement offers much enjoyment. Darcy had been encouraged by his aunt's angry report of Elizabeth's refusal to give the promise demanded; Lady Catherine had also worked on him, less effectually than he had worked on Bingley. The happy talk of the engaged pair (lviii) is surely enough—along with all that has gone before—to blunt the traditional complaint about Darcy's incredible change of character. Some of his original "pride" had been the creation of Elizabeth's prejudice. For the rest of it, he had, like Elizabeth, arrived at self-knowledge; her vehement rejection had given him a new view of himself. He had been a selfish being all his life, "in practice though not in principle"; his right principles he had been left, "almost taught," to follow "in pride and conceit," and, when shocked and humbled by Elizabeth, he had broken out of the social shell in which he had grown up and resolved to show that he could become a different man, a sensitive individual. Although the total characterization of Darcy has been censured as both a wooden and an inconsistent stereotype, we may think that, in such a novel, such a reformation does not overtax our belief in a character of his strength, sincerity, and devotion. It might be called a large-scale development of Lord Osborne's conscious change of attitude when, in talking with Emma Watson, he realizes that she is a person who has her own dignity.

Elizabeth of course dominates the conclusion as she had dominated throughout. She is tempted to speak of Darcy's swaying

AND PREJUDICE, ed. E. Rubinstein (Englewood Cliffs, N.J., 1969). For Mr. Mudrick, quoted just afterward, see his *Jane Austen*, 119–20. Mr. Babb's chapter has, with other things, an able defense of the presentation of Darcy.

Bingley this way and that, but the common sense that can co-exist with love warns her that "he had yet to learn to be laught at, and it was rather too early to begin" (lviii). This item is one reminder of the tact with which Jane Austen compels our belief in genuine love (witness Elizabeth's talk with her father) while rounding out a conclusion in the vein of comedy. When trying to convince the incredulous Jane that she has fallen in love, Elizabeth jocosely dates it from her first sight of Pemberley—an idea which, on the plane of material possessions, Sir Walter Scott, that great admirer of Jane Austen, and some other hasty readers have taken seriously. One peak of comedy is reached in the dithyrambic ecstasies of Mrs. Bennet—who, in the awesome presence of her prospective son-in-law, is fortunately cowed into self-restraint. But Elizabeth evidently recognized a limit to taking risks, and at the beginning of the last chapter the author quietly draws a distinction: "With what delighted pride she [Mrs. Bennet] afterwards visited Mrs. Bingley and talked of Mrs. Darcy may be guessed."

We have seen something of the almost unfailing naturalness and ease—ease that comes from careful work as well as inspiration—with which Jane Austen builds characters and situations that forward the growth of love while creating both social comedy and suspense. And economy contributes much to the graceful, coherent symmetry of *Pride and Prejudice*. The author's own famous comment on the book is evidence enough of her deliberate avoidance of anything irrelevant to her story (Letter 77, to Cassandra: February 4, 1813):

The work is rather too light, and bright, and sparkling; it wants shade;—it wants to be stretched out here and there with a long chapter of sense, if it could be had; if not, of solemn specious nonsense, about something unconnected with the story; an essay on writing, a critique on Walter Scott, or the history of Buonaparté, or anything that would form a contrast, and bring the reader with increased delight to the playfulness and epigrammatism of the general style. I doubt your quite agreeing with me here. I know your starched notions.

Some references in the letters suggest how real to the author her characters were. One item of general significance is that, while she enjoyed the Liverpool Museum and the British Gallery, her avowed "preference for Men & Women" inclined her, as always, "to attend more to the company than the sight" (Letter 69: April 18, 1811). So Elizabeth Bennet, thinking of one man if not of people, was indifferent to all portraits but one in the Pemberley gallery. Two years later (Letter 80: May 24, 1813), when Jane and Henry visited an exhibition, she was particularly happy to see "a small portrait of Mrs. Bingley," which she described in detail as an exact likeness. But there and at another exhibition she was disappointed in finding nothing like Mrs. Darcy: she could "only imagine that Mr. D. prizes any Picture of her too much to like it should be exposed to the public eye," that "he w^d have that sort of feeling—that mixture of Love, Pride & Delicacy."

In *Pride and Prejudice*, as in the other novels, various pairs represent various attitudes toward love and marriage. Although, as we have seen, some readers think Darcy implausibly manipulated, the workings of pride and prejudice are not, like the workings of sense and sensibility, obtrusively molded in opposed patterns. We may note further that this novel, unlike most of the others, has no mentor whose rational wisdom establishes a point of view and scale of values. But to say that is to realize that the role is tacitly given to the spirited and highly intelligent heroine, who, though she can err grievously, is nevertheless the person through whose eyes and usually reliable mind we assess the other characters and the action. In every respect, in characters, plot, structure, dialogue, tone, *Pride and Prejudice* is very much lighter, brighter, more sparkling, and more maturely competent than its predecessor. Indeed, as its long popularity proclaims, this, more than any of the novels except *Emma*, maintains social comedy among fully realized characters with dramatic verve, frequent subtlety, and a fine blend of wit and serious feeling.

Sense and Sensibility has some good minor characters, notably Mrs. Jennings, but those of *Pride and Prejudice* are richer in themselves and even the most comic ones are put to more functional use. Whereas Willoughby came to be enveloped in melodrama, the new "villain," Wickham, is kept almost clear of that— though his lesser villainy goes along with less vitality; and there are no other really bad characters. Lydia Bennet is a robustly

successful creation, a girl who, while not vicious, is only a plea-
sure-loving animal devoid of mind and principle; she is her
mother's own daughter.[7] Satire, having less serious human faults
to work on, is less sharp and more humorous than it is in *Sense
and Sensibility*, but it does not spare the jealous and self-defeating
cunning of Miss Bingley, the crude and self-defeating arrogance
of Lady Catherine, the several kinds and degrees of imbecility
embodied in Mrs. Bennet, Mr. Collins, and Sir William Lucas, or
Mr. Bennet's irresponsible, often cynical, and sometimes callous
levity. Mr. Bennet, though, wins at least our retroactive sympathy when, in warning Elizabeth against marrying a man she
could not respect, he touches on the disparity—due of course to
his own bad choice—which had caused his retreat into cynicism
(lix). The spirit of Jane Austen's early burlesques survives in
such mature distillations as Mrs. Bennet, Mr. Collins (a comic
successor of serious clerics in the Richardson–Burney line), and
Lady Catherine (whose embryonic ancestress was Lady Greville
in the third of *A Collection of Letters*, *M. W.*, 156–60). Although we cannot imagine such broad caricatures in any of the
later novels, they scarcely jar with the less rigorous realism of
such a half-romantic comedy as *Pride and Prejudice*. Some
readers may wish that the author's diligent lopping and cropping
had included Mary Bennet, whose scraps of threadbare morality,
as satire on moralizing in the Richardsonian tradition, fall pretty
flat, though she can be said to represent a bookishness as remote
from life as her intelligent father's. Such characters resemble
some in *Sense and Sensibility* in being "humors," which were
Fanny Burney's very inferior stock in trade: everything, or almost everything, they say reveals one dominant trait, with a consistency which goes beyond the measure of predictability common enough in people of limited intelligence. This relatively
elementary kind of characterization, which can of course be very
funny, may be seen as a survival of Jane Austen's youthful relish

[7] Apropos of Lydia's interrupting Mr. Collins' reading aloud from
Fordyce's sermons, E. E. Phare observed that Lydia Languish, in Sheridan's
The Rivals (one of the plays acted by the young Austens), used pages from
Fordyce for curl-papers (*Notes and Queries* 11, 1964, pp. 182–83; cf. F.W.
Bradbrook, *ibid.*, 421–23).

for high coloring. Even Mrs. Norris and Lady Bertram and Mr. Woodhouse and Miss Bates have more than one facet.

Some of Jane Austen's fictional principles are enunciated by Elizabeth in early conversations at Netherfield. One concerns the village world of the novels (ix):

"I did not know before," continued Bingley immediately, "that you were a studier of character. It must be an amusing study."

"Yes; but intricate characters are the *most* amusing. They have at least that advantage."

"The country," said Darcy, "can in general supply but few subjects for such a study. In a country neighbourhood you move in a very confined and unvarying society."

"But people themselves alter so much, that there is something new to be observed in them for ever."

Some later remarks from Elizabeth (xi) touch the lighter side of Jane Austen's satirical creed. She agrees with Darcy that the wisest and best of men "may be rendered ridiculous by a person whose first object in life is a joke," but, she says: "I hope I never ridicule what is wise or good. Follies and nonsense, whims and inconsistencies *do* divert me, I own, and I laugh at them whenever I can." We may note that, as usual, Elizabeth's feminine instinct is drawn to the natural and individual, Darcy's masculine mind to the rational and general.

Throughout the book the main vehicle of characterization, comedy, and satire is dialogue; narration and description are given largely to placing conversation in its setting and summarizing characters' thoughts and feelings. The talk of Elizabeth and Darcy especially, as Mr. Brower and others have shown, carries frequent ambiguities of meaning and tone which, whether in or outside the speaker's consciousness, are left to the perceptive reader to interpret, with or without a hint from the author. And many things are said which, in addition to being appropriate at the moment, recall or anticipate things said or done earlier or later. One brief and straightforward example (xi) shows the unregenerate Darcy revealing, with unconscious irony, the armor of self-assurance which Elizabeth is destined to pierce with more than a hidden smile. He says that

". . . it has been the study of my life to avoid those weaknesses which often expose a strong understanding to ridicule."

"Such as vanity and pride."

"Yes, vanity is a weakness indeed. But pride—where there is a real superiority of mind, pride will be always under good regulation."

Elizabeth turned away to hide a smile.[8]

We noticed, in Elizabeth's heated replies to Darcy's first proposal, some unexpected examples of complicated syntax, and once in a while we come upon a speech which sounds like a remnant from the first version of the book. One example, too long to quote, is Elizabeth's exhortation to her father to put some restraint upon Lydia (xli). Apropos of Lady Lucas' offering condolence and aid in regard to Lydia's elopement, Elizabeth's comment to Jane begins with entire naturalness and shifts into the formal rhetoric of Fanny Burney and Dr. Johnson (xlvii):

"She had better have stayed at home," cried Elizabeth; "perhaps she *meant* well, but, under such a misfortune as this, one cannot see too little of one's neighbours. Assistance is impossible; condolence, insufferable. Let them triumph over us at a distance, and be satisfied."

But, in comparison with *Sense and Sensibility*, such speeches are rare. For the most part the texture of both dialogue and narrative is—allowance being made for a standard of elegance—informal, spontaneous, and easy. It warrants the author's comment on "the playfulness and epigrammatism of the general style." The first chapter above quoted the exquisite picture of Lady Catherine sallying forth to scold the cottagers into harmony and plenty, and there are many such satirical felicities of idea and phrase. The social gifts of Bingley's sisters are summed up in a manner which suggests their brittle smartness: "Their powers of conversation were considerable. They could describe an entertainment with accuracy, relate an anecdote with humour, and laugh at their acquaintance with spirit." Mrs. Bennet of course is constantly quotable. The clever Mr. Bennet enjoys his own fastidious

[8] Harriet Byron, already in love with the paragon Sir Charles Grandison, discerns in him one fault, pride, which he acknowledges and does not seek to correct (*Sir Charles Grandison*, 2, Letter 19, pp. 145–46). Later he says to her: "I have vanity, madam; I have pride, and some consequential failings, which I cannot always get above" (5, Letter 32, p. 219).

ironies, chiefly at the expense of his wife and daughters, but Mr. Collins, the pompous toady, is a prime butt for parody: "You judge very properly, . . . and it is happy for you that you possess the talent of flattering with delicacy. May I ask whether these pleasing attentions proceed from the impulse of the moment, or are the result of previous study?" (xiv). Even the amiable but hardly brilliant Bingley is given one gem: "I declare I do not know a more aweful object than Darcy, on particular occasions, and in particular places; at his own house especially, and of a Sunday evening when he has nothing to do" (x).[9]

While Jane Austen's stories of young love all of necessity present obstacles in the way of fulfillment, the temporary disappointments of Jane and Elizabeth, though painful, are not treated like the passions and ordeals of Marianne and Elinor Dashwood; the marriage of Charlotte Lucas and Mr. Collins is distressing to contemplate, but she chooses it as the lesser of two evils and makes the best of it. Whatever the dark spots, from this to the affair of Wickham and Lydia, our main impression is of gayety, humor (broad or subtle), grace, warmth, and happy love. Criticism cannot really analyze the secret of the novel's unfading charm. It is, in quality as in point of time, the last of Jane Austen's youthful works, and nowadays critics generally seem to rank it below the three that were still to come; but—if we are not too superior—we just keep going back to it to enjoy the story and the company of its characters and their creator.

[9] A little earlier in this conversation Darcy had charged Bingley with an indirect boast in avowing a needless precipitance in all his actions: in the morning he had declared "Whatever I do is done in a hurry" (ix). It may be noted that Charles Bingley had a fictional namesake, a baronet, who was accused (wrongly, he said) of being "the most changeable fellow in the world." See Regina M. Roche's popular and long-lived romance, *The Children of the Abbey* (1798: ed. Philadelphia, 1827, 2, c. ii, p. 25). The tale was a favorite of Harriet Smith in *Emma* (iv).

8

Mansfield Park

Mansfield Park WAS BEGUN about February 1811, finished in the summer of 1813, and published in May 1814. Thus it was the first of the novels written (and was perhaps conceived) at Chawton, when Jane Austen was 35–37, whereas the two previously published and the unpublished *Northanger Abbey* were revisions of early work. Even without knowledge of dates, readers of *Mansfield Park* could hardly fail to recognize a strain of moral seriousness not new in kind but new in its predominance. No one would say of it what the author said of *Pride and Prejudice*, that it "is rather too light, and bright, and sparkling; it wants shade. . . ."; she feared it would be "not half so entertaining" (Letters 77 and 81: February 4, July 3, 1813). The novel may, as Lionel Trilling says in his canonical essay, appear to be a total contradiction of its predecessor. It has bits of sparkle, to be sure, but these come mostly from the author and, in a different vein, from Henry and Mary Crawford, whose light-minded worldliness and want of principle the author condemns. Apparently some readers have found in *Mansfield Park* a heavy excess of "shade," an uncharacteristic, obtrusive, antipathetic moralism, and—most strangely —a lack of irony. But insensitive and violent criticism has helped in recent years to stimulate much fresh insight into both the moral quality and the art of the novel.

Mansfield Park is indeed a test case for critics and readers. The hostile minority have damned both the moral and social principles the author upholds and the fable in which she embodies them; for some, such principles are wrong *per se* and Jane Austen's exposition of them shows a lamentable failure of intelligence and honesty. But those who condemn the book are refusing to accept the author in her full dimensions, refusing to recognize her most serious self; with dogmatic prejudice they set up for exclusive admiration the detached, ironic, sparkling, and incomplete mistress of high comedy who wrote *Pride and Prejudice* and *Emma* (although these novels, so far as they go, are in thorough accord with the ethical standards of the more sober work). *Mansfield Park*, far from being crudely simplistic in its morality, is a more deeply analytical novel than Jane Austen had yet written or was to write. Its theme, carried in a positive way by the heroine and the more vulnerable hero, and in a negative way by many other characters, is the problem of maintaining the moral values, individual and social, which traditional wisdom and the enlightened individual conscience validate, against the pressure of the looser values of the world at large. The kind of ethical antithesis openly declared in such titles as *Sense and Sensibility* and *Pride and Prejudice* is still central in *Mansfield Park*, but opposed ways of feeling, thought, and action are treated with much more depth and complexity. Charles Austen complained that the novel "wanted Incident"; but, even more than in Jane Austen generally, incidents are psychological and ethical. And, in spite of the author's own strong commitment, she does not deal in black-and-white contrasts but gives the "good" some unattractive deficiencies and the "bad" some attractive virtues and talents. Although she comments and judges more than usual, she also leaves more than usual to the attentive reader; countless tiny details have implications that enrich an intricate but coherent pattern. In recent years *Mansfield Park* has been increasingly considered Jane Austen's most profound work. It has also been called, for example by Mrs. Leavis, the first modern novel, an anticipation of George Eliot and Henry James.

Sir Thomas Bertram and his family represent the landed gentry on a level between the squirearchy and the aristocracy. Fanny Price, one of the many children of Lady Bertram's sister (who had made an ill-starred marriage with a lieutenant of Marines), is removed from her down-at-heel family in Portsmouth to be brought up among the young Bertrams in luxurious elegance— though not on a plane of equality with them and their expectations. Fanny is a Cinderella with a difference; the old theme of a young woman launched upon the world is given some new twists. Like most of the Austen heroines, Fanny is uprooted from her familiar surroundings and has to work out her own salvation in another world; but, unlike the others, she is only ten, she is set down among grand relatives who are total strangers, and her transplantation is not only radical but permanent. And "the world" is here the microcosmic world of Mansfield Park, which with its connections provides a sufficient spectrum of genteel society. *Mansfield Park* is significant as the only title Jane Austen chose that is the name of a place (*Northanger Abbey* was a title bestowed by Henry Austen on a novel its author had referred to as *Catherine*, and *Sanditon* was not her choice). It is signal evidence of her discriminating sense of values that she makes the house and estate a symbol of a traditional, desirable stability even while she lays bare the excesses and defects of the persons who live there.

The opening sentences of *Mansfield Park*, quoted in the first chapter above, expose with deadpan irony the commercial view of marriage so generally accepted in the world of Jane Austen's fiction, and we might assume that the curtain is rising on another satirical comedy like *Pride and Prejudice* or *Emma*, in which no clouds are very dark or lasting. But as we get into the story, especially after the introduction of Henry and Mary Crawford, we begin to expect deeper conflicts of personality and outlook than the lighter comedies explore. The first three chapters make us acquainted with all the inhabitants of Mansfield Park, and most closely with that virtual inhabitant, the aggressive, self-centered, self-righteous busybody, Mrs. Norris,[1] who is quite different

---

[1] Mrs. Norris is so vivid a character that some critics—on a dubious principle—have thought she must be drawn from life. I have not seen mentioned the possibility that some suggestions came from Miss Margland in *Camilla*, a novel Jane Austen knew well. She also is a penny-pinching busybody, who tries to get Indiana married to Edgar and continually attacks Camilla, whose lover-mentor he is. Other characters in *Mansfield Park* also recall those of eighteenth-century fiction, but they are so far re-created that the prototypes are of remote interest.

from her sister, the passively self-centered and bovine Lady Bertram. These characters are presented in part through the author's commentary, in part through discussions among Mrs. Norris and Sir Thomas and Lady Bertram about the problem of bringing up Fanny. The only other conversation of account is between the forlorn little Fanny, soon after her arrival, and her sixteen-year-old cousin Edmund; his active kindness, then and later, has a natural result, that "she loved him better than any body in the world except William," her brother.

The third chapter, which brings Fanny to the age of sixteen, sends Sir Thomas to Antigua, supposedly for a year, to look after his ailing interests; he takes with him, for safekeeping, his extravagant heir, Tom. Edmund, a prospective clergyman, becomes the temporary head of the house. Sir Thomas has been a well-meaning, upright father and uncle but he has also been incapable of warm concern and intimacy, and with his departure his daughters Maria and Julia feel only welcome relief from restraint. They, "now fully established among the belles of the neighbourhood," are on the marriage market; Fanny stays at home, humbly but not unhappily, as Lady Bertram's companion. (The author, by the way, never loses an opportunity to make the odious—and stingy—Mrs. Norris more odious, and sometimes comic: she is so haunted by fear of an evil fate for Sir Thomas that she is "obliged to take daily refuge in the dining room of the park.")

The beautiful Maria attracts the young, rich, and stupid Mr. Rushworth and, being now twenty, begins "to think matrimony a duty"; "by the same rule of moral obligation," it was her evident duty to marry him if she could and thereby secure the enjoyment of a larger income than her father's and a house in town, "which was now a prime object." This idea is zealously forwarded by Mrs. Norris; and Sir Thomas, having been given wholly favorable reports, is "truly happy in the prospect of an alliance so unquestionably advantageous." ("Advantage," for most Austen characters—including Mary Crawford—means chiefly estate and income.) Edmund, who has assessed the suitor's mentality, is the only dissenter in the family.

Now, when Fanny has reached seventeen, agents of trouble appear as guests of Dr. and Mrs. Grant at the parsonage. Henry and Mary Crawford, the half-brother and half-sister of Mrs. Grant, had grown up in the dubious care of their ill-mated uncle and aunt, Admiral Crawford and his wife; after Mrs. Crawford's death the widower, an evident exception among Jane Austen's naval officers, had installed his mistress in his house and thereby occasioned Mary Crawford's coming to Mansfield. She had come reluctantly, fearing the boredoms of rusticity, but she is pleasantly surprised by the families of both the parsonage and the Park. Within three hours of her arrival Mrs. Grant unfolds her plan that her sister should marry Tom Bertram, since a baronet's heir is "not too good for a girl of twenty thousand pounds." Even the restless Henry is glad to stay a while, and Mrs. Grant has also provided for him: he shall marry Julia Bertram. This Mary declares an impossible idea because Henry is "the most horrible flirt"; "the admiral's lessons have quite spoiled him"—a playful charge which is to lose its ironical quality. Henry himself, quoting *Paradise Lost* (5.19) with ironical emphasis, considers a wife "Heaven's *last* best gift." His sister thinks otherwise. "Matrimony was her object, provided she could marry well," and she is ready to like Tom Bertram. But she is no idealist. She so vehemently assails marriage as a universal cheat that Mrs. Grant says the Admiral's house has been a bad school; but Mansfield shall cure them both. These early exchanges forecast much of the future.

Henry proved "the most agreeable young man" the Bertram sisters had ever known, "and they were equally delighted with him" (v). The author, with characteristically satirical wording, remarks that Maria's engagement made Henry "in equity the property of Julia, of which Julia was fully aware. . . ." For his part, Henry had "no object but of making them like him"; despite his good sense and temper, he "allowed himself great latitude on such points." Mary finds Edmund's company increasingly pleasant and his growing admiration for her increasingly troubles Fanny. Fanny's own secret devotion to Edmund is the one constant attachment from the beginning to the end of the novel, and since, though Edmund rarely fails in attentive kindness, it appears more and more likely to be disappointed, her jealous anxiety for both his happiness and her own is constant too; or rather, it becomes more and more strongly grounded.

Young people of fortune, with or without engaging manners, are common enough in the Austen world, but the two Crawfords are novel and special figures. Mary is very pretty and Henry, if not handsome, is captivating. Both are highly intelligent and are lively and clever talkers; both are good-natured (if good impulses do not conflict with other inclinations); they have real affection for each other, much more than the young Bertrams have; and—what is most important—both are emancipated individuals whose sophistication goes well beyond the social attitudes represented by the rural Bertram family. Their emancipation, however, is limited; they are in general as fully and shallowly conformist as the Bertrams in reflecting the *mores* of their own social world, that of Regency London. Since Mansfield Park is by no means Eden, we cannot call them Satanic; but, by simply being themselves, they become an unsettling, even corrosive, element in a supposedly stable little society. We may think of the broad comic effects Trollope achieved by bringing the emancipated Stanhopes back from Italy to stir the quiet waters of Barchester Close; but Jane Austen is far more serious in developing contrasts and consequences.[2]

The general structure of *Mansfield Park* differs from that of the preceding novels. In *Sense and Sensibility* blocks of narrative were given alternately to the sister heroines; in *Northanger Abbey* and *Pride and Prejudice* the relatively simple story was focused throughout on the heroine and hero. But in *Mansfield Park* there are six young people, Fanny Price, Edmund and his sisters, and the Crawfords, whose characters and relationships are the chief material, and the author accomplishes the more difficult feat of advancing simultaneously, without apparent strain, on all fronts. In keeping with that movement, at intervals she brings people together in a prolonged dramatic episode (a method begun on a small scale in *Sense and Sensibility*), in which rela-

[2] Some critics have seen an original for Mary Crawford in Jane Austen's cousin, the brilliant Comtesse de Feuillide, who had married Henry Austen in 1797 and who may have had a share in overcoming, for what was to be a long time, his thoughts of taking orders. Mrs. Leavis (*Scrutiny* 10, 1941–42, pp. 114–42) argued that the courtship gave the basis for *Lady Susan* and that *Mansfield Park* was developed out of *Lady Susan*. This is a very strained theory (Southam, 136–45).

tionships are further defined and tensions develop on or below the surface.

The first such episode is the visit made to Sotherton to give Mr. Rushworth's intended "improvement" of his estate the benefit of Henry Crawford's taste (viii–x).[3] (It would not be beyond Jane Austen's irony to imply that Mr. Rushworth and others are not concerned with improving themselves.) Discord begins as they start, when, at Mrs. Grant's suggestion, Julia gets "the envied seat, the post of honour," on the box of the barouche with Henry (we remember Mrs. Grant's plan for him). Maria—Mr. Rushworth's fiancée, we also remember—remains sunk "in gloom and mortification," while Julia and Henry chatter merrily; however, when they get into the Sotherton domain, Maria's "Rushworth-feelings" assert themselves over her "Crawford-feelings." Fanny and Mary sit side by side, unlike "in every thing but a value for Edmund." Some of Jane Austen's own instincts are divided, not quite fairly, between the two: Mary's preoccupation with men and women (such as her creator felt at the art gallery: Letter 69, quoted in chapter 7 above) is noted as a defect. In contrast with Fanny's pleasure in the scenes along the way, even "the difference of soil," Mary "had none of Fanny's delicacy of taste, of mind, of feeling; she saw nature, inanimate nature, with little observation; her attention was all for men and women, her talents for the light and lively."

Viewing of the interior of the house brings quietly dramatic approaches to the novel's central theme: the house and Mrs. Rushworth and Fanny and Edmund in their several ways represent tradition, the Crawfords rootless alien modernity. Whereas Mary "had seen scores of great houses, and cared for none of them," Fanny's romantic and religious feelings are stirred by Mrs. Rushworth's tales of the past, including the chaplain's prayers in the chapel, a custom the previous Mr. Rushworth had left off. " 'Every generation has its improvements,' said Miss

[3] The visit had grown out of a discussion (vi) which touched on a great controversy of the period. Edmund and Fanny are on the conservative side, against Henry, as they are later (xxv) when he proposes radical changes at Edmund's parsonage. The historical and fictional topic is fully treated by A. M. Duckworth, *The Improvement of the Estate: A Study of Jane Austen's Novels* (Baltimore and London, 1971), 38–55.

Crawford, with a smile, to Edmund," and Fanny's protest evokes Mary's mockery of a custom especially empty in an age when, she fancies, "parsons were very inferior even to what they are now." Fanny feels "too angry for speech," but Edmund, after hesitation, says that Mary's "lively mind can hardly be serious even on serious subjects," and makes some corrective remarks. Just then Julia, seeing Mr. Rushworth and Maria standing side by side, observes to Henry that they look as if they were about to be married. Henry, smiling acquiescence, steps forward and whispers to Maria, "I do not like to see Miss Bertram so near the altar"—the first hint of a preference replacing that which he had formerly, in a teasing mood, professed for Julia (v). Julia, carrying on her joke, exclaims that if Edmund were but in orders he could perform the ceremony directly. At this revelation Mary is so upset that even Fanny pities her, and she apologizes for her disparagement of the cloth. When, prompted by "one wish for air and liberty," the party move outdoors, Mary expresses her surprise over Edmund's choice of a profession: "A clergyman is nothing." He says that she is thinking of London, he of the nation at large, and in that broad sphere the clergyman is the guardian of religion and conduct. Mary's judgment of the profession, which goes along with her general worldliness and a strain of cynicism, is henceforth to be a cause of recurrent and aggravated doubts on both sides.

After some walking Fanny sits down to rest and Edmund and Mary go on, to "be back in a few minutes." Fanny now becomes an involuntary witness of a very remarkable bit of drama (x). When she is found by Maria, Henry, and Mr. Rushworth, it is decided—to get rid of the unwanted fiancé—that they must survey the house from a knoll in the park and the owner goes to get a key for an obstructing gate. But for Maria there is no "liberty" outside; the grounds and the gate and the owner symbolize confinement (into which, of course, she had sold herself). Henry renews his hint of regret for her approaching marriage. She, after a moment's embarrassed fencing, speaks of his recent enjoyment of Julia's company on the box. Appeased by his ingenious excuse, she adapts her present physical situation to her marital one: the scene is smiling, "But unluckily that iron gate, that ha-ha, give me a feeling of restraint and hardship"; and, she says—alluding to Sterne's *Sentimental Journey* ("The Passport")—"I cannot get out, as the starling said." Henry carries on her *double-entendre*:

And for the world you would not get out without the key and without Mr. Rushworth's authority and protection, or I think you might with little difficulty pass round the edge of the gate, here, with my assistance; I think it might be done, if you really wished to be more at large, and could allow yourself to think it not prohibited.

Fanny has apprehended at least enough to give Maria a warning of danger, but Maria proceeds, successfully, and her reply has further overtones: "Thank you, my dear Fanny, but I and my gown are alive and well, and so good bye." Such veiled exchanges go beyond ambiguities in the earlier novels. Returning with the key, Mr. Rushworth feels a natural resentment against Maria and especially Henry for deserting him: "In my opinion, these Crawfords are no addition at all. We did quite well without them"—an opinion Fanny endorses with a sigh. The promised "few minutes" of Edmund's and Mary's walk have turned into an hour; they have evidently had a good time.

When the party are reassembled in the house, Henry and Maria are gay, Fanny and Julia and Mr. Rushworth are gloomy— though Julia revives when the prudent Henry invites her to share the box again. Apart from Mrs. Norris' exulting in the loot she has collected from the housekeeper and gardener, those inside the barouche drive home in silence. "It was a beautiful evening, mild and still." The Wordsworthian sentiment is an ironic prelude to a question which "might occupy the meditations of almost all"— that is, "whether the day had afforded most pleasure or pain." These chapters, recording a series of outwardly trivial incidents, are surely the most extended and subtle drama Jane Austen had yet written.

The next episode that brings the *dramatis personae* together is the prolonged business of preparing to act a play (xiii–xx). But before that, two chapters, mainly of dialogue, develop several kinds of unhappiness. Maria thinks of "the black month" of November, the month of her father's return and her marriage to a man she despises; she can only cling to a vague hope that "Much might happen in thirteen weeks." Sir Thomas' return will also bring Edmund's ordination, which sticks in Mary's crop because she has transferred her interest from the indifferent Tom to his brother. Henry's absence for a fortnight has afflicted the Bertram sisters, but he came gladly back to Mansfield to trifle further with both. "Each sister believed herself the favourite."

The project for a dramatic performance itself creates an elaborate drama which, like the Sotherton expedition, aggravates old and stirs new tensions and thereby yields a further revelation and moral assessment of all the characters. This time clashes are numerous and open. The impresario is the irresponsible Tom Bertram (who had returned from Antigua in advance of his father). The initial agent of this general threat to the stable order of Mansfield Park is Tom's feather-brained acquaintance, the Honorable John Yates; as a nobleman's son, who brings the idea from another nobleman's house-party, Mr. Yates brings also—at least for Sir Thomas, later—a whiff of aristocratic and alien folly or depravity. Edmund raises vigorous but vain objections to the enterprise: want of feeling when their father is absent and in danger (from the climate, the sea, and the French); his certain disapproval of acting for his daughters, especially the engaged Maria, as a breach of decorum; the wrongness of taking liberties, expensive liberties, with his house; and, later, the choice, for well-bred young women, of such a play as Lovers' Vows (Mrs. Inchbald's popular version of Kotzebue), an orgy of sensational-sentimental emotionalism. This was a happy choice by Jane Austen for causing an immediate imbroglio and for foreshadowing the Mansfield actors' later behavior. There is ethical significance even in such small items as Fanny's declaring that she "cannot act" and thinking (with others) that Henry Crawford is "considerably the best actor of all." Fanny, sharing Edmund's objections, declines, like him, to participate;[4] and she observes, with some amusement,

[4] A. W. Litz quotes correspondence between Philadelphia Walter and her (and Jane Austen's) cousin, the Comtesse de Feuillide, about acting in private theatricals, which illustrates some of Fanny's objections (Jane Austen: A Study of Her Artistic Development, New York: Oxford University Press; London: Chatto and Windus, 1965, pp. 118–21). Fanny does, reluctantly, consent to read an innocent part when Mrs. Grant cannot come to the big rehearsal, and in being obliging she makes some compromise with her principles—but the arrival of the deus ex machina spares her the ordeal.

Lovers' Vows is conveniently reprinted in Chapman's edition of Mansfield Park.

the jealous friction over the casting and one another's acting. Julia withdraws in resentment because of Henry's preference for Maria in the part involving scenes with him (which they incessantly and needlessly rehearse, by way of amatory titillation): the also observant Mary "would not give much for Mr. Rushworth's chance, if Henry stept in before the articles were signed." Edmund makes Fanny miserable by going back on his early decision: he takes the clergyman-lover's part in order to spare Mary the embarrassment (which she feels) of playing her amorous role with the stranger Tom wants to bring in; we can imagine a further reason which Edmund might not admit to himself. The Sotherton visit had ended with no one entirely happy except Mrs. Norris, and the present affair has much the same result. But this time one of Jane Austen's boldest uses of coincidence provides a dramatic climax (at the end of the original volume one): just as the company is beginning its first regular rehearsal, Julia reports that her father has returned and is in the house. Amid the general consternation Henry continues to press Maria's hand to his heart—a sight which inflames Julia.

Postponing our welcome to Sir Thomas, we may take account of opposed views of the author's view of these theatricals. Some critics, expressing what they assume many readers feel, have seen no moral issue at stake and concluded that Edmund, Fanny, Sir Thomas, and Jane Austen are all incomprehensibly stuffy, that the ironical satirist of shams is here guilty of a lamentable lapse into genteel, finicky propriety. Our general respect for Jane Austen's intelligence and moral integrity forbids hasty acceptance of such a brash judgment—and recent critical opinion seems to be mainly on her side.

This episode is clearly a signal example of the moral urgency that distinguishes *Mansfield Park* as a whole. We think of the novels as in all essentials timeless because they deal with the unchanging essentials of human nature, and hostile critics of this novel can say that the treatment of the theatricals represents only the narrow moral outlook of a particular person (or the Evangelical party) in a particular age. But, even if that were true, it would also be true that, to repeat, our major premise must be well-grounded respect for Jane Austen's standards of conduct, for what Virginia Woolf (in *The Common Reader*) called her "impeccable sense of human values."

First, we may note two facts of different kinds. The characters who eagerly join in or approve of the theatricals are three of the young Bertrams, the Crawfords, Mrs. Grant, Mrs. Norris, Lady Bertram, Mr. Rushworth, and Mr. Yates: of these ten, at least nine do not constitute a jury one would appeal to on a question involving moral sensitivity—although the dismay occasioned by Sir Thomas' return includes, in most of the players, a sense of guilt. A second fact is that in the earliest opinions of the novel (partly cited below) the author's relatives and friends, who were quite candid about their dislikes, gave no hint of any disapproval of her handling of this affair; so far as we can tell, they endorsed the recorded objections. It might of course be said that the latter group were old-fashioned and the fictional group sophisticated, but sophistication is not an automatic proof of wisdom. Two other items, often adduced, may be set aside because they are not relevant to the moral situation: one is Edmund's distinction between professional acting, which all can enjoy, and amateur incompetence; the other is the common citing of the performances in the Austen household in Jane's youth, which obviously have nothing to do with Edmund's objections.

The central issue is the meaning and validity of decorum, which, while it includes Edmund's objections, is far larger: it concerns Jane Austen's moral attitude in all her novels and above all in this one. Decorum, in the tradition in which she wholeheartedly writes, operates on different levels of value. One kind is good manners, the lubrication of civilized intercourse, but good manners may adorn the bad as well as the good: witness such polished "villains" as Willoughby, Wickham, Walter Elliot, and —though he is decidedly above them—Henry Crawford, all of whom are, in a general sense, more or less insincere, self-centered "actors." In good people, however, at least in the best, good manners are only the surface expression of fundamental virtues, self-knowledge, self-discipline, unselfish regard for others, a conscious, sincere effort to judge, feel, and act rightly in accordance with the traditional standards set by religion and by the experience and wisdom of humanity. On this large subject there is no

better witness than Henry Crawford (at a later time), even
"though he was too little accustomed to serious reflection to
know" good principles "by their proper name." (These phrases
remind us of Jane Austen's discriminating concern with the language of moral value, a concern she gives to such thoughtful
characters as Fanny and Edmund and others in other books.)[5]
Having discovered his love for Fanny,

> when he talked of her having such a steadiness and regularity of
> conduct, such a high notion of honour, and such an observance of
> decorum as might warrant any man in the fullest dependence on her
> faith and integrity, he expressed what was inspired by the knowledge
> of her being well principled and religious. (xxx)

That decorum, in its fundamental sense, is not working among
the actors at Mansfield Park is made pragmatically clear by the
selfish desires and discords which develop from the start, which
are a microcosmic example of moral and social disintegration, and
which compel us to see the theatricals as a bad thing. Behind
Edmund's objections we feel, on one side, the symbolic significance of the Park (whatever the moral deficiencies of most of its
inhabitants), and, on the other, the moral vacuum of Regency
London in the Crawfords. In the course of the rehearsals, as
Edwin Muir said, "a sense of pervading evil gradually fills the
scene, and the corruption of the Crawfords, only latent until
then, diffuses itself over the whole company."[6] So discerning a
critic as A. W. Litz speaks of "The antagonism between art and
morality which weakens so much of *Mansfield Park*—an antago-

---

[5] See, e.g., Howard Babb's chapter; David Lodge, "The Vocabulary of
'Mansfield Park,'" *Language of Fiction: Essays in Criticism and Verbal
Analysis of the English Novel* (London and New York, 1966); Robert A.
Donovan, "*Mansfield Park* and Jane Austen's Moral Universe," *The Shaping
Vision: Imagination in the English Novel from Defoe to Dickens* (Ithaca,
1966).

[6] "Jane Austen and the Sense of Evil," *New York Times Book Review*,
August 28, 1949. The rewritten piece in Muir's *Essays on Literature and
Society* (London: Hogarth Press; Cambridge, Mass.: Harvard University
Press, 1965) omits the words quoted but has these broader remarks (200):
"Compared with *Pride and Prejudice*, *Mansfield Park* is like a full-scale
study of corruption. The Crawfords . . . are at the heart of it; the corruption spreads from them." Lionel Trilling, following up his essay on *Mansfield Park*, pursues the theme of "the negation of self through role-playing"
in *Sincerity and Authenticity* (Cambridge, Mass., and London, 1972).

nism reminiscent of eighteenth-century attacks on the irresponsibility of fiction"; but in Jane Austen's treatment of the theatricals one may be unable to see evidence of that large antagonism. The issue is between a strong sense of duty and right on one side and undutiful, irresponsible self-gratification on the other.

To come back to Sir Thomas' return home, he greets Fanny with more kindness than he had ever shown before. He is at first the happy life of the not altogether happy party. He is much less happy when he hears of the play and sees the changes wrought in some rooms (an outward sign of changes in the atmosphere of the Park); and, without feeling the need of giving reasons, he quietly makes it clear that the project is ended. Edmund, explaining it all in the morning, praises Fanny as "the only one who has judged rightly throughout, who has been consistent." Mrs. Norris is "a little confounded" by Sir Thomas' hints of her lack of judgment, but she manages to take home the green baize curtain. The aftermath of the play leaves Maria much the unhappiest person: she had counted on Henry's declaring himself, but he departs at once to meet his uncle in Bath, and "the agony of her mind" is "severe." Julia can both enjoy and pity her fate. Otherwise, after the unwonted stir of recent weeks and without the Crawfords' company, life at Mansfield Park under Sir Thomas' sway seems rather flat, "all sameness and gloom," even to Edmund—though not to Fanny.

But Sir Thomas' resumption of authority does not quiet the simmering or seething emotions of the young people. He is soon disturbed by perceiving both Mr. Rushworth's stupidity and Maria's carelessly cold treatment of him, and he asks her, with "solemn kindness," if she would like to be released. After a moment's struggle, she assures him of her wholehearted attachment, and her father is ready enough to suppress his misgivings and persuade himself that all will be well. Maria resolves not to let her behavior awaken further doubts. "Henry Crawford had destroyed her happiness, but he should not know that he had done it; he should not destroy her credit, her appearance, her prosperity too" (xxi). She must achieve independence and escape from the oppressive atmosphere of her father and Mansfield Park. The "very proper wedding," as described by the author, is a ceremonial display of artificial feelings.

Julia having gone away with the bride and groom, Fanny becomes a more important person at both the Park and the parsonage. From now on the story is focussed on the relations of Fanny,
Edmund, Mary, and Henry, who are bound to interact or clash
because of individual desires either allied with or divorced from
the integrity of principle; and for some there is inward conflict as
well. Fanny suffers from what appears to be a growing understanding between Mary and Edmund. Mary, however, is angered
by the assured approach of her admirer's ordination: she had
been thinking seriously of him and had believed she had more
influence; but if he can so command his affections, so can she. She
had more than once made clear her desire for wealth (though she
had plenty herself) and position: "A large income is the best
recipé for happiness I ever heard of."

But the main theme of chapters xxiii–xlv, a long stretch, comes
as a surprise, though one that is quite logical—the unoccupied
Henry's choice of a new diversion, "to make Fanny Price in love
with me": she has grown attractive in appearance and her reserve
is a challenge. Mary insists that he must not hurt her, "for she is
as good a little creature as ever lived, and has a great deal of
feeling." The author doubts whether even Fanny "could have
escaped heart-whole" from such a siege "had not her affection
been engaged elsewhere"; though "she thought as ill of him as
ever," she "felt his powers." And his opinion of "the capabilities
of her heart" rose when he saw her joy in reunion with her sailor
brother William, who had come to the Park on his long-awaited
visit. Fanny's new status in the family and her increasing prominence as heroine are established by the ball Sir Thomas gives in
honor of her and her brother (xxvi–xxviii). One small object
starts what might be called a chain reaction. Almost the only
ornament Fanny has is an amber cross William had brought her
from Sicily; he could not afford a chain.[7] She is doubly embarrassed by Mary's forcing upon her a necklace (which proves to
be a present from Henry) and by Edmund's buying her a chain.
Her pleasure in the latter gift is spoiled by Edmund's saying that

[7] This is one of the rare instances in which we can see Jane Austen using
a concrete personal experience: in 1801 her brother Charles had bought
"gold chains & Topaze crosses" for his sisters out of his naval prize money
(Letter 38: May 28, 1801).

she must wear both: "I would not have the shadow of a coolness arise . . . between the two dearest objects I have on earth." Symbolic suggestion does not stop there. And Fanny is not made happy—as Sir Thomas is—by Henry's attentions at the ball.

A new propulsion for this long segment of the story comes from Henry, who returns from a visit to London to astonish his sister with another announcement: he is "quite determined to marry Fanny Price" (xxx). He had begun with "idle designs" (as Willoughby had with Marianne Dashwood), but he had been completely won by the virtues which, as we saw, he had come to recognize: "I could so wholly and absolutely confide in her, . . . and *that* is what I want." Henry has enough grace to be attracted by his moral opposite (as Mary is, much less warmly, by hers). Mary's initial surprise gives place to real satisfaction in the prospect for both: "To have seen you grow like the Admiral . . . would have broken my heart." This is about the only time Mary questions the way of her world (later, when Henry does behave like the Admiral, her heart seems to remain intact). But Henry defends his uncle, who had let him have his own way—a revealing reason. It never occurs to either Henry or Mary that Fanny might not accept a husband so far above what the world would call her claims.

Fanny is overjoyed by Henry's report that he has, through the Admiral's influence, gained promotion for William; but, when he says he has done it all for love of her, she is repelled by what she regards as gallantry and by his taking advantage of having just conferred an obligation. From now on Henry, not of course aware that he is laying siege to "a pre-engaged heart," strives in every way, even after her refusal of his suit, to convince Fanny of his sincere love and steadiness. One way is through his expressive reading of Shakespeare, which compels her attention; it is significant that he could become every character in turn. It is even more significant that in his discussion of liturgical reading and preaching he treats these functions only as an actor's performances. The ball had been Sir Thomas' crowning recognition of Fanny's altered position in the family; but now, for rejecting Henry, she has to undergo her uncle's grave reproaches, worst of all for her ingratitude to himself—reproaches she might have blunted if she had stooped to tell of Henry and Maria. (Sir

Thomas, in spite of his strong displeasure, is magnanimous: finding that Fanny's sanctum is kept unheated by Mrs. Norris' direction, he gives orders for a daily fire.) Fanny suffers still more from gentle but insistent pressure from Edmund, who is at the moment on good terms with Mary and all the more eager for Fanny's acceptance of a really changed Henry. Even Lady Bertram is roused to give "almost the only rule of conduct, the only piece of advice, which Fanny had ever received from her aunt in the course of eight years and a half": "that it is every young woman's duty to accept such a very unexceptionable offer as this"—namely, "a man of such good estate." But Fanny has the courage to hold out against them all.

Her chief depression comes from the conviction that Edmund and Mary are nearer marriage than ever, that she has not lost her serious faults and that he no longer sees them; Fanny thinks her sorrowful judgment is made "independently of self." Meanwhile William has come for a visit and Sir Thomas, "in one of his dignified musings," has conceived the idea that Fanny shall go back with him to Portsmouth to visit her family. Sir Thomas does not communicate his motive—to make Fanny so sick of life in such a home that she will see Henry's proposal in a better light.

After the first pleasure of a return to her family—pleasure much overshadowed by the family's excitement about William's new ship—the visit becomes a wearing disappointment. Fanny cannot help feeling the smallness of the house, which intensifies the children's incessant noise and confusion, and the relative indifference to her presence on the part of her tired and incompetent mother and her coarse and alcoholic father. She is unfilial and unsaintly enough to put added value on the peace and order of Mansfield Park. This realistic episode is Jane Austen's one substantial account of low life—much lower in quality, though perhaps not in income, than that of the family to which Emma Watson returned. Only the older girl, Susan, who tries to improve her family's messy ways, becomes by degrees the kind of sister Fanny can love, respect, and help, as Edmund had helped her. To Fanny's surprise, Henry seeks her out to carry on his unwelcome purpose; she is ashamed, and ashamed of being ashamed, to receive him there (we may think of Emma Watson

when Lord Osborne called). Fanny can only hope that his present unselfish gentleness means that he will not long persist in his
distressing suit.

For further—and rapid—developments she, and we, are dependent on the economical medium of letters, chiefly from Mary and
Edmund. Henry is expecting to see the Rushworths, about whom
Mary and he are curious. Edmund has not proposed to Mary:
seeing her in London, he had found in her the reflection of her
mercenary, ambitious, cold-hearted friends, yet he cannot give
up the only woman in the world whom he could ever think of as
a wife. Henry's devotion to Fanny shows no sign of wavering; he
had appeared surprised by the coolness of Maria's greeting. Tom
Bertram has been brought home from Newmarket with a serious
fever. Fanny is not to believe a scandalous rumor about Henry
and Maria. This last cryptic message is soon explained by a newspaper report of the elopement of "Mrs. R." and "Mr. C." Fanny,
deeply shocked herself, imagines the shock felt at Mansfield Park,
especially by Sir Thomas and Edmund. This, like the elopement
of Lydia Bennet and Wickham, is the violent event that Jane
Austen relies upon to start the denouement. Here it upsets existing relationships and brings about a climactic reassessment of
Henry and Mary. News comes from Edmund of what now seems
only a minor blow, Julia's elopement with Mr. Yates, an act
induced by Maria's example and by Julia's fear of her father's
severity. Edmund will go to Portsmouth to bring Fanny home,
and Sir Thomas, kind even in his trouble, invites Susan to come
to Mansfield for a few months. Edmund is much shaken by these
events, by Henry's desertion of Fanny, and above all by his own
plight in regard to Mary.

Back at home (xlvii), Fanny thinks it would be poor consolation to Sir Thomas that her distrust of Henry had been well-
founded; and she does not doubt that "Edmund must be for ever
divided from Miss Crawford." Edmund, when he can bring himself to talk, tells Fanny of his calling on Mary, by invitation. He
had been utterly disillusioned by her attitude: "She saw it only as
folly, and that folly stamped only by exposure." He had felt
stunned. She said, to her credit, that Henry "has thrown away . . .
such a woman as he will never see again"; but she had gone on
to blame his behavior on Fanny's refusal of him. Mary, says

Edmund, feels and speaks like the people she has lived among: "Her's are faults of principle, . . . of blunted delicacy and a corrupted, vitiated mind." He would—as he had told Mary—endure all the increased pain of losing her rather than have to think of her as he does. Mary had been greatly astonished and angered, perhaps half-ashamed, and had, with affected indifference, uttered some gibes about his preaching. He had left the room, but she followed, to call him back, with a smile, "a smile ill-suited to the conversation that had passed, a saucy playful smile, seeming to invite, in order to subdue me. . . . I resisted." This scene of parting, as described by a disenchanted lover, leaves us to speculate about the feelings behind Mary's enigmatic last act and smile.

As they talk of how bad influences had corrupted her delightful nature, Fanny—not unnaturally but with something less than ideal charity—speaks of Mary's revealing that Tom's serious illness and the possibility of Edmund's becoming the heir had probably had a part in her desire for reconciliation. Edmund agrees, though he believes that Mary "had certainly been *more* attached to him than could have been expected. . . ." He could never meet with any woman who could take her place: "Fanny's friendship was all that he had to cling to." Whatever the manner of his breaking off, it is hard to see what else Edmund could do in the face of Mary's hard-boiled attitude (even when we allow for sisterly loyalty to Henry), an attitude amply prepared for in earlier pages and reinforced by her recent return to the London world of fashion. Her frequent "good feelings" are not the same as principles.

The last chapter begins with those much-quoted words: "Let other pens dwell on guilt and misery. I quit such odious subjects as soon as I can, impatient to restore every body, not greatly in fault themselves, to tolerable comfort, and to have done with all the rest." Such a half-serious, half-jocular statement has evoked varied responses. For one thing, the preceding 460 pages were not much given to "tolerable comfort"; the last word, a recurring one, means, as Norman Page says, emotional security and tranquillity. At any rate this chapter is composed mainly of judicial and depressing curtain calls. Fanny has reasons, not crowned until the very last pages, for being happy. Edmund has not, though by degrees he becomes fairly cheerful. Sir Thomas "was the longest to suffer," because of his realizing his failure as a father to inculcate in his daughters the practice of duty and self-discipline; he does not, as he might, blame Lady Bertram. Tom's grave illness has made him sober and responsible. Julia and her mindless husband are now humbly desirous of forgiveness. Maria's hopes of marrying Henry proved vain, and, after a separation and a divorce, Mrs. Norris, who was not allowed to give Maria a home at Mansfield, moved far away in order to do so; if this was her one good deed, her departure was a great felicity for Sir Thomas. His refusal to let Maria become "an insult to the neighbourhood" was doubtless in accord with his strict character. Some critics recall—as perhaps Jane Austen does not—Mr. Collins' letters to Mr. Bennet on the proper Christian treatment of Lydia (xlviii, lvii); but the offenses in question are hardly parallel. Maria has throughout been seen as a selfish, mercenary, rebellious daughter and a selfish, mercenary, contemptuous wife; possibly, however, the untold experience behind her final revolt, and her lasting exile with Mrs. Norris, may invite more compassion than the author feels.

As for Henry, the author, while stressing his own fatal propensities, makes him in some degree a victim of Maria. He had felt himself challenged by her coldness (the egoistic motive which had kindled his interest in Fanny), and resolved to win back his old power over her; but he had put himself in the power of her feelings, which proved stronger than he had supposed they were:

He was entangled by his own vanity, with as little excuse of love as possible, and without the smallest inconstancy of mind towards her cousin. . . . When he returned from Richmond, he would have been glad to see Mrs. Rushworth no more.—All that followed was the result of her imprudence; and he went off with her at last, because he could not help it, regretting Fanny, even at the moment, but regretting her infinitely more, when all the bustle of the intrigue was over. . . .

Jane Austen doubtless shrank, for various reasons, from dramatizing what would have been a lengthy prelude to the elopement, but a brief report and explanation are somewhat less than satisfying. In spite of the volatile Henry's free and easy ways and his early dalliance with Maria, he had felt himself really in love with Fanny; the author can even startle us by saying, near the end, that if he had persevered uprightly, and if Edmund and Mary had married, "Fanny must have been his reward—and a reward very voluntarily bestowed." Readers may have strong doubts concerning both parties, and may think, on the author's evidence, that Henry's ways were incurable and that such a flighty actor would soon have been lured from Fanny's side by the novelty of another role.

Our last news of Mary is that the Grants, moving to London, could give her a home, and that her beauty and fortune were long in attracting a suitor to "satisfy the better taste she had acquired at Mansfield, . . . or put Edmund Bertram sufficiently out of her head." Views of the author's judgments on the Crawfords range from full endorsement to angry—and myopic—denial of any moral guilt except in Jane Austen. But, however attractive some of their qualities are, "Lilies that fester smell far worse than weeds," and their good impulses have been subject to irresponsible vanity and meretricious ambition. In Jane Austen's view, there is too much at stake for easy tolerance.

The story of Fanny and Edmund is wound up with despatch. The author declines, with a playfulness appropriate to comedy but not here, to fix the precise time at which Edmund discovered that he had ceased to "care about Miss Crawford, and became as anxious to marry Fanny, as Fanny herself could desire." He had indeed always loved her as a younger sister, one much closer to him than his actual sisters, and his affection was greatly augmented when he found that she had always loved him. Fanny does not at all resent having been a second-best for so long. Their union joyfully fulfilled what had become Sir Thomas' wish: it had been one of his fears when the idea of bringing Fanny to Mansfield Park had first come up. And, "to complete the picture of good," on Dr. Grant's death Edmund acquired the Mansfield living. Even Lady Bertram and Susan are provided for: Susan succeeds Fanny as her aunt's companion—one concrete suggestion that life at the Park is renewing its steady course, a course presumably improved by shock and enlightenment. Providential

arrangements for a happy ending include a reminder of the main
theme: Sir Thomas could "rejoice in what he had done for them
all [the young Prices], and acknowledge the advantages of early
hardship and discipline, and the consciousness of being born to
struggle and endure." And the well-being of the hero and heroine
does not preclude a religious overtone in a commonplace phrase:
"the happiness of the married cousins must appear as secure as
earthly happiness can be." The phrase may also carry a touch of
sympathetic irony, since, for a virtuous hero and heroine, their
reward, by worldly standards, has been modest.

Criticism of *Mansfield Park* began, as some references have
indicated, with the very diverse reactions of the author's relatives
and friends, which she collected (*M. W.*, 431–35; Southam, *Critical Heritage*). Since some points have figured in sophisticated
modern criticism, a few opinions from those earliest readers may
be recorded. It would appear that none of them grasped or at any
rate attempted to define the moral and social theme. Of those
who compared the novel with its predecessor, *Pride and Prejudice*, six thought it better, twelve inferior. The Portsmouth episode was often singled out for praise, and, among characters, Mrs.
Norris. Fanny Price drew completely opposed judgments. Jane
Austen's brothers Francis and Edward (Knight), Edward's son
Edward and his daughter Fanny, and Martha Lloyd were delighted or pleased with her. Edward's son George "disliked" her,
and James Austen's daughter Anna (who was beginning to write
herself) "could not bear" her. The author's forthright mother
pronounced Fanny "insipid," and a Mr. Plumptre put a similar
view more mildly. The young Edward Knight objected to Edmund as cold and formal. Fanny Knight thought the ending
needed more love between Edmund and Fanny, and she could
not think it natural that Edmund should be so much attached to
an unprincipled woman like Mary Crawford or should promote
Fanny's marrying Henry. Two nephews thought Henry's eloping with Maria "unnatural"; the wife of Rev. James Austen
thought it "very natural." Nephew George was "interested by
nobody but Mary Crawford."

We must look further at the four principals, Edmund, Mary,
Henry, and Fanny, and at the author's much debated view of

them. Edmund is—next to the slighter and dimmer Edward Ferrars—the least obviously attractive of Jane Austen's heroes. According to her reliable friend, Mrs. Barrett, she said once, in answer to a question, that of all her characters she liked best "Edmund Bertram and Mr. Knightley; but they are very far from being what I know English gentlemen often are." Edmund is the only one of Jane Austen's young clergymen who is given, or could be given, occasion to expound and defend—as his father also does—the active professional guardianship of religion and morals; and he is honest enough to acknowledge that his commitment might have been fortified, though it was not induced, by the fact of a Mansfield living in prospect. Edmund is sober and often stiff, confessedly incapable of wit and gayety, but he has intelligence and insight (up to a point), strong principles (also up to a point), and genuine goodness of heart; the reservations are due to the effects of Mary's power over him. He is the only hero caught and held by a questionable passion which, because he is a clergyman, makes him doubly unhappy. He is the only hero who, in love, betrays some weaknesses of a kind which should help to offset the common critical label of "prig" and keep him really human and sympathetic.

While there are stumbling blocks on both sides, Edmund's love for Mary is much deeper and more disinterested than her feeling for him. He is more and more charmed by her beauty, grace, vivacity, and accomplishments, her insight into character, and the genuine good nature she often manifests. She appears at her best when Fanny, unwilling to act in the play, is crudely reminded by Mrs. Norris of "who and what she is" and Mary goes to sit by Fanny and cheer her up—an instance, in the author's words, of "the really good feelings by which she was almost purely governed." In proportion to his love Edmund is increasingly troubled by what appears to be the result of the kind of society she has grown up in, her habitual levity and her wrong scale of values. Mary, on her side, after having to abandon the idea of Tom Bertram, the baronet's heir, comes to like Edmund's sincerity, steadiness, distinctive good-breeding, his freedom from all idle gallantries; but, though she lessens her sniping at his vocation, she cannot lower her ambitions to the level of a country parsonage. We have reason to doubt whether Mary could ever really love anyone except her brother.

Mary and Henry are only the most conspicuous proofs that, on the practical level, the central and comprehensive theme of *Mansfield Park* is bad education, in the broad sense of religious, moral, and social environment. That is the root of the many problems that arise. Sir Thomas Bertram, with all his virtues, is aloof and unimaginative, and Lady Bertram is a sheep in the sun, so that Maria and Julia—as the author says (ii) and as their father laments, too late (xlviii)—have had no proper upbringing; their preparation for life's duties has been left to Mrs. Norris. Tom is the usual shallow, spendthrift heir, though more decent than most of his kind. Mr. Rushworth is a country fool, Mr. Yates a town fool. Henry Crawford, like Mary, has engaging animation, intelligence, and good nature, but, like her, he has grown up in a bad atmosphere, at home and outside. None of the erring persons in the novel violate principles, because, apart from Sir Thomas, they have none—except impulse and self-indulgence. These points are repeatedly enforced throughout Jane Austen's most didactic work, in revealing speech and action and in comments by the author and by Edmund and Fanny. Mary Crawford's bright vivacity is altogether charming to those readers who fail to see how much of it is brittle flippancy. As Virginia Woolf said, Jane Austen lets Mary

rattle on against the clergy, or in favour of a baronetcy and ten thousand a year with all the ease and spirit possible; but now and again she strikes one note of her own, very quietly but in perfect tune, and at once all Mary Crawford's chatter, though it continues to amuse, rings flat. Hence the depth, the beauty, the complexity of her scenes.

Fanny Price has some earmarks of the heroine of sensibility, though she has grown far beyond her predecessors in moral consciousness. She has a romantic regard for the past, for old avenues of trees, old houses, old traditions. Unlike most people of Mansfield, she reads and thinks: three books mentioned are in line with her creator's tastes, Crabbe's *Tales*, Dr. Johnson's *Idler*, and Lord Macartney's book on China (xvi)—not that these works belong to the world of sensibility. ("Fanny Price," by the way, is the name of a heroine in "Marriages," in Crabbe's *Parish Register*, who prefers a humble husband to "an amorous knight.") Fanny's rhapsodies on nature (for example, in xi and xxii) recall Marianne Dashwood, the heroine of *Udolpho*, and eighteenth-century ideas of the sublime: nature is sententiously moralized with the naive sincerity and self-consciousness of a youthful thinker. (The author's own scenic descriptions, such as the view from the Portsmouth ramparts in chapter xlii, are more direct accounts of Fanny's sensations.)

But this "unpromising heroine" has few romantic illusions to grow out of. We have seen in the earlier novels—and shall see in *Emma* and *Persuasion*—how much Jane Austen stresses the attainment of rational and emotional self-knowledge and self-control, responsible maturity, and nowhere is that idea or ideal so much emphasized as in *Mansfield Park*. The lack of self-knowledge is explicitly noted, usually by the author, with varying degrees of seriousness, in Mrs. Norris, the Bertram sisters, the Crawfords, Dr. Grant, and Mr. Rushworth. And the lack of self-knowledge, while related to all defects, is most closely linked with selfishness, an insistent theme throughout Jane Austen, not least in this novel. Fanny alone—since Edmund falls well short of her—gains the full self-knowledge and integrity born of almost unfailing self-discipline. And hers, like Anne Elliot's, is acquired through years of trying experience and much lonely reflection; it is not a rapid change of heart about a prospective husband, like Elizabeth Bennet's. It would not be altogether fanciful to think of Fanny, Edmund, and Mary Crawford as descendants of a trio perhaps unknown to Jane Austen—Spenser's Una, Red Cross Knight, and Duessa. (It might be added, without prejudice, that Fanny, when grown up, is in or near tears about as often as Una; but Fanny almost laughs several times.) If Edmund's and Fanny's initial instincts are due less to genes than to acts of God, he has been her mentor and the nourisher of sound principles, and in two crises she proves stronger than he. To quote a remarkable essay of 1870, by Richard Simpson, "Miss Austen seems to be saturated with the Platonic idea that the giving and receiving of knowledge, the active formation of another's character, or the more passive growth under another's guidance, is the truest and strongest foundation of love"[8]—an idea that operates also in *Northanger Abbey* and *Emma*.

Generations of readers and critics have considered Fanny Jane Austen's least attractive heroine—unless Elinor Dashwood claims that distinction. Doubtless many have shared A. C. Bradley's feeling: "I pity, approve, respect, and admire her, but I neither desire her company nor am greatly concerned about her destiny, and she makes me impatient at moments when I doubt if she was meant to." It is obvious that Fanny has nothing of Elizabeth Bennet's lively charm and that her goodness and seriousness lack most of the winning power those virtues have in the older Anne Elliot. Yet Fanny is not one of those "pictures of perfection" for whom Jane Austen was to express her abhorrence. "My Fanny" —at the beginning of the last chapter—is the only heroine so referred to in the novels, and "My" surely carries the author's special concern on her behalf. But it is not a protective concern which seeks to conceal Fanny's natural human imperfections: we have noticed some of the occasions on which love, jealousy, and antipathy can color her judgments. However, such frailties, which some critics refuse to see, are not dark enough to save her from disrepute. In general, of course, Fanny is presented as disinterested and right in her moral attitudes, and such a role piles up heavy odds against her in many modern minds (as it did for some of the author's relatives). Those who see her as an odious embodiment of odious virtue, and see the Crawfords as the rightful hero and heroine, are akin to the bygone sentimentalists who took Satan as the hero of *Paradise Lost*. Fanny is, as Lionel Trilling emphasizes, "a Christian heroine."

As observer and judge of character and conduct, Fanny comes nearest—nearer than Edmund—to being a surrogate for the author. Her point of view usually is or should be dominant in the reader's mind, even though, for more than half of the story, she is in the background; and she cannot at any time talk freely to anyone except Edmund and not at all to him about her chief concern. Moreover, since there are numerous characters, divided between the Park and the parsonage, the feelings and relations of individuals cannot all be brought, or brought fully, within the

[8] Southam, *Critical Heritage*, 244.

range of Fanny's awareness. Hence the author often steps in to summarize or comment upon the state of mind of Fanny especially, but also of Edmund and indeed everyone. She seeks to strengthen our respect for Fanny by stressing the circumstances which set her apart from all the other heroines. Her status, for a long time, is that of a poor relation. She cannot participate enough in family life to be established as a fully rounded personality; she inevitably appears to a large degree as a passive sufferer and sober moralist, in talk with Edmund or in her private thoughts. There is good reason for her self-effacing timidity, a timidity which, along with her lack of physical vitality, should heighten our sense of her moral strength in contrast with the strong, morally shallow Mary Crawford. During her chief trial, resisting pressure to accept Henry Crawford, Fanny even thinks of "right reason" (xxxii), that conception which—however little Jane Austen knew about it—had for twenty centuries been a bulwark of ethical and social order. Unlike those around her, Fanny does not try to impose her will on others, and she will not have Henry make her judgment his "rule of right": "We have all a better guide in ourselves, if we would attend to it, than any other person can be" (xlii). Fanny is the only character in the novel who has no clear social standing or identity, but—while Sir Thomas is too rigid and Edmund too yielding—this timid outsider is the only one who has a wise and consistent moral identity, who has "all the heroism of principle" (xxvii). She—at the cost of denying the wishes of its revered master and of his son, the man she loves—maintains the true or ideal character of Mansfield Park. And this is the novel that is said to have a fatal lack of irony!

Whatever discounts may be lodged by unsympathetic readers against Fanny and Edmund as heroine and hero and as the bearers of the ethical and social message, *Mansfield Park* is certainly the book in which Jane Austen conducted her deepest explorations of the human heart and head. It may be that, on the threshold of middle age and for reasons unknown to us, she felt a special need of getting some things said about her world. We cannot tell whether or not her always strong principles were here quickened, as many critics have suggested, by Evangelicalism (her sympathetic sentiments of 1814 were quoted above near the end of chapter 2). At any rate, in its corrective conservatism *Mans-field Park* remains true to the traditional ethos of comedy, but it also shows the maintenance of inward order against worldly pressures, and the tragic flaws and waste that attend the lack of such order, on a level well above the comic.

9

Emma

I F THERE WAS ANY SPECIAL cloud on Jane Austen's outer or inner horizon that helped to cause the predominant seriousness of *Mansfield Park*, it assuredly did not hang over *Emma*. It is remarkable that the novel commonly regarded as her masterpiece was written in less time (January 21, 1814–March 29, 1815) than any of the others except the shorter *Persuasion*. It appeared in December 1815 (dated 1816). We do not, to be sure, know whether the story had been growing in her mind before actual composition began; it is easy to imagine that it had been enriched by prolonged gestation. The author was, she wrote to the Prince Regent's egregious librarian, "very strongly haunted with the idea that to those readers who have preferred 'Pride and Prejudice' it will appear inferior in wit, and to those who have preferred 'Mansfield Park' very inferior in good sense" (Letter 120: December 11, 1815). Among the comparative (and mostly unsophisticated) verdicts she recorded from relatives, friends, and others (*M. W.*, 436–39), some twenty ranked *Emma* below *Pride and Prejudice*, some sixteen below *Mansfield Park*. Captain Francis Austen, while giving a judgment almost identical with the prophecy just quoted from Jane, still preferred *Emma*, "on account of it's peculiar air of Nature throughout"; a Mrs. Guiton "thought it too natural to be interesting"; Captain Charles Austen put it even above his favorite *Pride and Prejudice*. The great Francis Jeffrey, editor of the *Edinburgh Review*, "was kept up by it three nights."

Emma is a masterpiece in both positive and negative ways: in texture it is hardly less "light, and bright, and sparkling" than *Pride and Prejudice*; its exquisite craftsmanship is partly manifest, partly well below the surface; and it has no such faults as have been found in the other novels. Mainly because Jane Austen had taken "a heroine whom no one but myself will much like" (*Memoir*, c. x, p. 157), *Emma* is a much more complex and subtle work of art than *Pride and Prejudice*. Elizabeth Bennet's judgment of persons and situations is, apart from her one signal lapse, virtually identical with the author's and it guides our reactions; but *Emma* is in large part the story of the heroine's continual errors of judgment, errors which do more or less harm or injustice to other people. Thus while Elizabeth often used irony herself but was not much subjected to it, the very essence of *Emma* is the author's, and our, ironical view of the heroine, who must at the same time be kept from losing our favor and respect. The same thing might of course be said of *Northanger Abbey*, but, though *Emma* touches some romantic-sentimental formulas, it is far more serious and realistic, and literary irony or parody, of the kind exploited in *Northanger Abbey*, is almost invisible.

The first chapter—like so many chapters—is a small masterpiece in itself: it felicitously blends the three chief ingredients of fiction, narrative, a character's reflections, and dramatic dialogue. Five short paragraphs of descriptive narration present the twenty-year-old Emma Woodhouse as an ideal but still very human heroine, "handsome, clever, and rich, with a comfortable home and happy disposition," who "seemed to unite some of the best blessings of existence" and whose life had brought "very little to distress or vex her"—the implications are clear. Her older sister having married, Emma, from an early age, has been mistress of Hartfield, her widowed father's house. Her mother's place had for sixteen years been filled by Miss Taylor, first as governess, then as companion and close friend. Her judgment Emma had esteemed highly, while "doing just what she liked." "The real evils indeed of Emma's situation were the power of having rather too much her own way, and a disposition to think a little too well of herself," but so far these evils had not appeared as dangerous.

Emma has just encountered her first distress, which will be lasting: Miss Taylor has married the genial and well-to-do Mr. Weston, the wedding party has left, Mr. Woodhouse is as usual asleep after dinner, and Emma is alone with her thoughts of past, present, and future. Thus, at the moment of a great change in her way of life, we are taken, naturally and almost imperceptibly, inside her mind. Although "she had always wished and promoted the match," and although the Westons are to live only half a mile away, Emma thinks of long days and evenings stretching out before her, with no intimate friend to talk to. She dearly loves her father, but that valetudinarian, incapable of any "activity of mind or body," "could not meet her in conversation, rational or playful." The large village of Highbury contains many acquaintances but no possible friends.

Mr. Woodhouse, waking up, has to be cheered, since "his habits of gentle selfishness" make him averse to changes of any kind and matrimony in particular. After Emma has managed to induce a less doleful view of Miss Taylor's marriage, they have a welcome caller, Emma's brother-in-law and old friend, George Knightley, a gentleman-farmer of thirty-seven or so, who has just returned from a visit to London and brings news of his brother John and his family. The ensuing talk of the wedding launches the story on its course and shows that Mr. Knightley "was one of the few people who could see faults in Emma Woodhouse, and the only one who ever told her of them." For Emma claims to have made the match herself, at which Mr. Knightley shakes his head and Mr. Woodhouse wishes she would not make matches and foretell things, "for whatever you say always comes to pass. Pray do not make any more matches." Mr. Woodhouse is much too mindless to be a conscious ironist. Mr. Knightley insists that Mr. and Mrs. Weston made the match, that Emma only made a lucky guess. The chapter ends with Emma's declaring that she will make only one more match, that she must find a wife for the Highbury vicar, Mr. Elton. Mr. Knightley warns her: "Depend upon it, a man of six or seven-and-twenty can take care of himself."

Before we begin to follow Emma's execution of her enterprise two chapters fill in our knowledge of the present and prepare for the future. The first is one of the rare chapters in the novel in which Emma does not participate and one of the few which are wholly narrative: an account of Mr. Weston's earlier life and first marriage and the now grown-up son who had been adopted by his rich uncle and aunt and taken their name of Churchill and who is to be very prominent in the last two thirds of the book. The next chapter (iii), also narrative, introduces the girl who is to be a figure in Emma's machinations as Emma herself is to be in Frank Churchill's. We hear of the old friends whom Mr. Wood-house likes to have in for the evening, Mrs. Goddard, who runs a school, and Mrs. Bates, the widow of a former vicar who has come down in the world, and her daughter Miss Bates, a very good-hearted woman who cheerfully endures poverty, likes everyone, and, though a compulsive talker, is respected by all— all perhaps except Emma, who sees a silly, satisfied, smiling, un-fastidious chatterer. The momentous thing about this particular evening is that Mrs. Goddard, by permission, brings Harriet Smith, "the natural daughter of somebody," who has lately been elevated to the status of a "parlour boarder" at the school.

These two narrative chapters slip easily into and out of reports of people's thoughts, especially Emma's. She perceives that Har-riet, while not "remarkably clever" (the reader soon finds her remarkably stupid), is beautiful, good-natured, naive, and hum-bly worshipful toward the great Miss Woodhouse, who resolves to mold her mind and natural graces into true elegance. From now on, Emma keeps Harriet under her wing. The first chapter had given hints of Emma's ways, and her patronage of Harriet fully displays the complacent self-esteem and lack of wisdom which circumstances and temperament have combined to pro-duce in the first lady of Highbury, a young woman whose mind is active on the social and matrimonial level (not otherwise), who has lost her old friend and has nothing to do. At this first meeting she thinks she has found a wife for Mr. Elton. The future will show, as critics have observed, that Emma is a sort of artist *manqué*, creating romantic fiction out of the materials Highbury life affords.

The first necessity is to detach Harriet from friendship with the Martins, a farming family with whom she has just had a long visit; they are said to live creditably but "must be coarse and unpolished." Emma soon discovers Harriet's warm liking for Robert Martin, an excellent young man (a tenant of Mr. Knightley), and his strong attraction to her, and she proceeds, with snobbish hardness and without a trace of self-distrust, to extinguish that danger: Harriet is certainly a gentleman's daughter and must conduct herself accordingly. When Emma says that Mr. Martin will probably marry "some mere farmer's daughter, without education," Harriet doesn't think he "would ever marry any body but what had had some education." The bad English, especially in this context, deflates both Harriet's superior claims and Emma's estimate of them. Emma's snobbery and capacity for self-deception are repeatedly exposed. For instance, she assumes that Mr. Martin does not read, although Emma herself, as Mr. Knightley says, has been meaning to read more ever since she was twelve, and, with Harriet, she finds it "much easier to chat than to study." As Emma runs down Mr. Martin, she plays up Mr. Elton. The idea of the match seems so natural, so completely predictable, that she can have small merit in promoting it.[1] On this point Emma is her father's daughter: he was "never able to suppose that other people could feel differently from himself."

Apart from the few opening paragraphs, the first four chapters have revealed Emma almost entirely through her own thoughts, speeches, and actions, and, though their import was clear, the author felt the need for our seeing her in perspective through the judgment of friends, the need also for planting more seeds of future developments. We have now the novel's one chapter of dialogue in which Emma takes part only as the subject (v): we listen to the candidly critical Mr. Knightley and the indulgently defensive Mrs. Weston. This chapter carries on what began in the first, the establishment of Mr. Knightley as Emma's—and our—mentor, whom we come to see as Jane Austen's most reliable specimen of his kind. We observed his complaint that Emma

[1] Jane Austen could readily understand Emma's operations, even while condemning them. Writing to Cassandra, she said: "I have got a Husband for each of the Miss Maitlands;—Col[n] Powlett & his Brother have taken Argyle's inner House, & the consequence is so natural that I have no ingenuity in planning it. If the Brother sh[d] luckily be a little sillier than the Colonel, what a treasure for Eliza" (Letter 55: October 1, 1808). Cf. Letter 60: November 20, 1808.

has always been planning to read more: "She will never submit to any thing requiring industry and patience, and a subjection of the fancy to the understanding"—which touches Jane Austen's perennial theme, progress through illusion to reality. His main charge is related to that: "this great intimacy" between Emma and Harriet is bad for both; Harriet's ignorance continually flatters Emma's complacency, and Emma's flattery will only make Harriet uncomfortable with people of her own station. Other bits of talk have no less bearing on the whole course of the story. Mr. Knightley cordially endorses Mrs. Weston's picture of Emma's vivid, healthy beauty: "I love to look at her," he says, and he does not "think her personally vain . . . her vanity lies another way." We are already enough enlightened to see that he can reveal more than he is consciously aware of, but, being the sterling character he is, he does not suffer from coming within the range of the author's benevolent irony. While pouring scorn on Emma's many reading lists, he casually recalls that one she drew up at fourteen "did her judgment so much credit, that I preserved it some time." He wonders what will become of her: "I should like to see Emma in love, and in some doubt of a return; it would do her good. But there is nobody hereabouts to attach her; and she goes so seldom from home." We guess that he himself is to fulfill his wish, though we can hardly forecast that both he and she will be in doubt of a return. Mrs. Weston also wonders what will become of Emma; and, since the conversation has included reference to Frank Churchill, we understand the author's closing hint of the hopes cherished by her and her husband.

The Elton episode (iv–xvii) is so handled as to initiate readers into the ironic method. Although they could hardly fail, on their own, to have increasingly clear suspicions of Mr. Elton's object, the author makes doubly sure by having Emma somewhat puzzled by his behavior. He is a gushing attendant while she does a portrait of Harriet and, when he has volunteered to take the "precious deposit" to London for framing, Emma, though single-minded in her assurance, is just perceptive enough to think that she herself comes in for a pretty good share of his studied compliments, "But it is his gratitude on Harriet's account."

In the matter of Robert Martin's proposal, which Harriet would like to accept, Emma is at her worst. The girl is confounded by Emma's assumption that the only question is the wording of a refusal. While declining to give advice on the main question, Emma does a thorough job of brain-washing: the decisive point is that acceptance would end their friendship, since Miss Woodhouse could not visit Mrs. Robert Martin. Emma virtually dictates the letter of refusal. And she ends the colloquy with a bracing reference to Mr. Elton's ardor. The reader wholeheartedly welcomes Mr. Knightley's explosive wrath when he hears what has been done and by whom: Emma's opinion of inequality is absurd; the inequality is all on Harriet's side. (One playful remark of Emma's anticipates the most serious crisis of her life: "Were you, yourself, ever to marry, she is the very woman for you.") Elton, says Mr. Knightley, is far too worldly-wise to throw himself away; he "may talk sentimentally, but he will act rationally." Emma is left quite uncomfortable, but confidence in her feminine judgment soon returns.

Mr. Elton pursues his campaign and Emma pursues hers through the business of the charade or riddle (ix), which Emma of course misinterprets. When she has carried her further operations to what seems the brink of success, she has to leave the rest to Mr. Elton because she is occupied with visitors, the John Knightleys and their children. In *Emma* as in *Mansfield Park* Jane Austen at intervals collects her people in a dramatic scene which heightens tensions or widens complications. The first such occasion is the Westons' dinner for the Hartfield party and Mr. Knightley, Mr. Elton, and Harriet. Harriet is kept at home by a bad cold and Mr. Elton seems much more perturbed by fear of Emma's becoming ill than by Harriet's being so; and he is far from depressed in going to the dinner without her. Some hours before the event Emma is astonished by the shrewd John Knightley's suggestion that she is of special interest to Mr. Elton. She dismisses the idea and walks on, "amusing herself in the consideration of the blunders which often arise from a partial knowledge of circumstances, of the mistakes which people of high pretensions to judgment are for ever falling into. . . ." But during the evening Mr. Elton's behavior brings the idea back to her mind.

When they set off for home a mix-up over carriages lands Mr. Elton and Emma together in one. He seizes her hand and pours forth the most ardent professions of love. She thinks he has had "too much of Mr. Weston's good wine" and tries to shut him off with references to Harriet, which he brushes aside. He is angered by the notion that he would stoop to Harriet, and Emma by his aspiring to herself. Alone in her room, Emma miserably reviews the whole affair: her own misjudgment, the Knightley brothers' penetration, the blow now to fall on Harriet, the upstart Mr. Elton's presumption (perhaps encouraged by the special graciousness she had shown him on Harriet's behalf). The first and worst error was her own, in trying to bring two people together: "she went to bed at last with nothing settled but the conviction of her having blundered most dreadfully." But, in spite of her resolve to do no more matchmaking, Emma is not cured. She should have been satisfied with preventing Harriet from accepting Robert Martin: "There I was quite right." Harriet took her disappointment very well, with no grudge against her mentor. She shed many tears, but her artless grief had its own dignity; for the time Emma felt her young friend superior to herself. Although "It was rather too late in the day to set about being simple-minded and ignorant," Emma was confirmed in "every previous resolution . . . of being humble and discreet, and repressing imagination all the rest of her life." Emma's resolutions for herself, until her great awakening, tend to be as delusive as her plans for others.

This whole episode, rich in comic detail but not comic for the persons concerned, has been developed, as the story continues to be, with a double perspective, Emma's and the author's. Emma's occasional qualms about Mr. Elton's behavior she could explain away because of her obsessive aim and a view of her lofty position too assured to permit any suspicion of his object, which even the visitor John Knightley and Miss Bates and others could perceive. We, exasperated by her motives and her treatment of Harriet and the Martins, may feel that the scales have been weighted against the heroine to a degree that cannot be reversed. As for the ironic method, the reader's initiation may be said to be now completed: henceforth the author supplies fewer hints and relies more upon the reader's interpreting objective drama—as far as limited knowledge allows. A year before beginning *Emma* Jane

Austen had said to Cassandra, revamping a couplet from *Marmion* (6.38.1147–48: Letter 76, January 29, 1813):

> I do not write for such dull elves
> As have not a great deal of ingenuity themselves.

Mr. Elton's campaign did not—until he proposed—affect Emma's immediate personal concerns. But now, with Jane Austen's usual perfect timing, two actors appear on the Highbury stage who are in different ways to impinge on her life and prospects and inspire further delusions. These agents of complex and prolonged comedy, mystery, and suspense are the active Frank Churchill and the passive Jane Fairfax. Earlier references have prepared us for the ripples they cause among their relations and friends. (We are reminded, remotely, of the Crawfords' impact upon Mansfield Park.) We continue to see persons and events through Emma's eyes and mind, but we are by degrees enabled to make more intelligent guesses about Frank and Jane than Emma or other interested parties can. Frank has never in all these years come to Highbury, but the village, always curious about this glamorous figure, decided over the tea-tables that his father's second marriage should bring him for a visit; and he did send his stepmother "a very handsome letter." Even Emma has been enough attracted by hearsay to think that "if she *were* to marry, he was the very person to suit her in age, character and condition" (xiv); and she believes, with good reason, that the Westons have that hope. But Frank, being dependent on the selfish whims of his hypochondriac aunt, again fails to appear. Mr. Knightley condemns his weakness: he could always do his plain duty if he wanted to. Emma, who had said similar if milder things to Mrs. Weston, now defends Frank (xviii). She imagines him as a model of general information, conversational ease, and good manners. Mr. Knightley heatedly rejects the picture of a man of twenty-three setting up as "the king of his company"; he would be an insufferable puppy. Emma wonders why Mr. Knightley should be so angry; we see that he is not only showing his usual good sense but already unconsciously revealing jealousy.

Jane Fairfax, however, does come for a long visit with her aunt, Miss Bates. An orphan, brought up by a Colonel and Mrs. Campbell, she had been a close friend of their daughter; but the daughter had married a Mr. Dixon and gone to Ireland, where the Campbells are now joining her, and Jane is to stay in Highbury before looking for a post as governess. During her previous visits Emma had, somewhat guiltily, neglected her; she was, she had said in a petulant outburst to Harriet, tired of always hearing Miss Bates's talk of Jane and her letters. Now, seeing her again, she acknowledges her elegant beauty and distinction, pities her fate, and resolves to treat her better; but she finds her cold and reserved and continues to dislike and ignore her. The main reason, the candid Mr. Knightley had once told her, is that she sees in Jane the kind of really accomplished young woman she wants to be thought herself (xx). Thus Mr. Knightley's unconscious jealousy of Frank Churchill is given a parallel in Emma's unconscious jealousy of Miss Fairfax. But her interest is quickened by her overactive fancy: from Miss Bates's flow of talk she snatches enough to imagine that Jane has a secret love for Mr. Dixon (who at Weymouth had saved her from possible drowning). At Weymouth, too, Jane had become acquainted with Frank Churchill, "but not a syllable of real information could Emma procure as to what he truly was. . . . Emma could not forgive her" (xx).

Frank Churchill does eventually come and is quickly brought to Hartfield. Emma does "not think too much had been said in his praise." He is handsome, well-bred, readily talkative, and clearly intends to be friendly with her. Emma wonders if his compliments indicate his being conscious of "what might be expected from their knowing each other, which had taken strong possession of her mind" and evidently of Mr. Weston's. Frank speaks of Miss Fairfax in a way that suggests no great degree of acquaintance or even of admiration. In a second meeting Emma's questions about Jane elicit what appear to be candid answers: she has "A most deplorable want of complexion"; her musical talent, in the expert opinion of Mr. Dixon, was far above that of his fiancée, Miss Campbell; on her extreme reserve he agrees with Emma. These first encounters inaugurate the kind of dramatic finesse which is to govern many scenes where Frank appears: we must be on the alert for both positive and negative nuances and must constantly ask when and how far Emma, hitherto the would-be manipulator, is being manipulated. Her highly favorable opinion is somewhat shaken when, the next day, Frank dashes to London to have his hair cut—which confirms Mr. Knightley's opinion of his silliness.

The presence of Frank, Jane, and later Mr. Elton's bride stimulates several of those gatherings which serve such important dramatic purposes. The first of the series is a dinner given by the Coles, people "of low origin, in trade," who have risen in affluence and social ambition. Emma at first resolves to teach them their place by declining, although her less fastidious friends will be there, but she changes her mind. She enjoys guessing how Frank will behave toward her, how soon she might need to be cool toward him, and how people will react in seeing such a predestined couple together.

A small incident is used to illustrate Emma's mixed scale of values in regard to gentility. Meeting Mr. Knightley at the Coles' door, she congratulates him on coming "like a gentleman" in the carriage he rarely uses; when she learns later that he had got it out in order to transport Miss Bates and her niece, she warmly praises his characteristically thoughtful kindness. At the dinner the first lady of Highbury is "given all the consequence she could wish for," and "That very dear part of Emma, her fancy, received an amusing supply." A piano has been delivered for Miss Fairfax and she and her aunt have agreed that it must be a gift from Colonel Campbell. This news leads to some fencing with Frank. Emma, having pursued the question, shares with him her suspicion that the giver is Mr. Dixon, who, after proposing to Miss Campbell, had fallen in love with her friend. This communication to a new acquaintance savors more of a village gossip than of the elegant Miss Woodhouse. Frank accepts her successive arguments in a way that seems sincere to Emma and quite insincere to us. We link the piano with Frank's otherwise hare-brained expedition to London and are fully convinced of his talent for duplicity. The same clue suggests that there is more between Frank and Jane than a brief and casual acquaintance; it does not explain his increasing attentions to Emma or his relative neglect and even disparagement of Jane.

At this party, for the only time in the book, Miss Bates is present in body without being allowed a word (apart from the quoting of her grateful report of Mr. Knightley's beneficence).

The author is intent here upon stirring dim surmises in regard to Jane, Frank, and Emma. Jane is presented partly as a musician much superior to Emma, as Emma knows; partly as an object of Mr. Knightley's solicitude when, in spite of her cold, she is urged to continue singing; but mainly for a stronger reason. Emma receives a shock from Mrs. Weston's notion of a match between Mr. Knightley and Jane: he is always concerned about her, admires her gifts, and probably sent her the piano—an unwonted flight of fancy for the sedate Mrs. Weston. No, says Emma, "Mr. Knightley must not marry"; he must not cut off his small nephew Henry from inheriting his estate. We are amused and not deceived by Emma's clutching at this argument. Her real instincts, which she has never defined to herself, are more apparent when she declares that "every feeling revolts" at the idea of Jane Fairfax as mistress of Donwell Abbey; Mr. Knightley has no reason or desire to marry, he is perfectly happy as he is. Some things can jolt Emma out of her fantasies into the real world, if not, as yet, into self-knowledge. Frank Churchill's conspicuous attentions culminate, when dancing begins, in his leading Emma to the top of the dance. Looking about for Mr. Knightley, she sees that he is talking with Mrs. Cole and that Jane is asked by someone else, and, having "no longer an alarm for Henry," she thoroughly enjoys the dancing.

The next day, in retrospect, Emma is glad to have delighted the Coles by her condescension and to have gained "in the splendour of popularity." She has misgivings over having told Frank her suspicions of Jane and Mr. Dixon, yet his agreement "was a compliment to her penetration." Her other uneasiness, about her musical inferiority, was banished by an hour and a half of practising. Mrs. Weston and Frank appear, on their way to hear Jane's piano. Perhaps, says Frank, it is a poor one, and he is "the wretchedest being in the world at a civil falsehood." Emma's disbelief—"I am persuaded that you can be as insincere as your neighbours"—is not, now or later, a safeguard against the duplicity he enjoys.

The relations between Frank and Emma and the more mysterious relations between Frank and Jane are developed in tantalizing fashion through many chapters, and Emma's fancy continues active. For a time she is sure that Frank is in love with her and even thinks, mistakenly, that he is about to propose (xxx); his actual and abortive intention is not revealed until his long letter near the end of the book. She thinks also, for a shorter time, that she is in love with him, but finally decides that, although she likes him, she would refuse an offer. With her instinctive shrinking from serious involvement in life, she "did not mean to have her own affections entangled again" (xxxvii). Perhaps Frank might fall in love with Harriet. There is no charm, she reflects, equal to tenderness of heart, a quality which her father and sister and Harriet have and which she herself has not, though she prizes it. Harriet is worth a hundred cold Jane Fairfaxes: "happy the man who changes Emma for Harriet!"

At this point we are diverted from problems by a chapter of lively dramatic satire (xxxii), the introduction of a new and commanding figure on the Highbury stage, the well-dowered bride Mr. Elton had speedily won after his humiliation at the hands of the much richer Emma. Her maiden name, Augusta Hawkins, was a suggestive blend of pretension and commonness, and she gives a full display of both in a formal call. In Highbury society, she stands out, even more than her husband, as an alien from another world, that of town-bred people with money but without roots or good-breeding. Having, in her way, something of Emma's proprietary instinct, Mrs. Elton quickly takes Jane Fairfax under her wing and is officiously zealous in trying to find her a post as governess. All along Jane has maintained impenetrable reserve and has been manifestly unhappy, and Frank, when present, has seemed to enjoy tormenting her. Emma, in addition to her cherished idea about Mr. Dixon, is continually and naturally puzzled by Jane's conduct and manner. The value of the accumulating elements of mystery is not lost after our first reading of *Emma*; we only gain a finer appreciation of the author's ironic design and her skillful invention and placing of minute details.

The Westons' ball at the Crown Inn (xxxviii) is one of the increasingly significant gatherings in the last third of the novel. The ball is led by Mr. Weston and the bride, Mrs. Elton, with Frank and Emma second, and Emma is conscious of two things, that Frank behaves only as an old friend and that Mr. Knightley seems to be watching her—that is, her and Frank, who are hap-

pily guiltless of flirtation. There are two important incidents.
Harriet, left without a partner, is rudely snubbed by Mr. Elton,
and Mr. Knightley, who has always avoided dancing, leads the
delighted girl into the set. This act of chivalry is to have crucial
consequences for both Harriet and Emma, and we may not at the
moment relish the irony of Emma's observing the rescuer and
rescued with high satisfaction.

When, after supper, Emma acknowledges that she had been
completely mistaken in Mr. Elton, Mr. Knightley acknowledges
in return that Harriet would have been a better wife than the one
he has. The chapter ends with one of the simplest and most
pregnant bits of dialogue in all Jane Austen. The bustling Mr.
Weston calls on Emma and others to resume dancing and she
declares herself ready whenever she is wanted:

"Whom are you going to dance with?" asked Mr. Knightley.
She hesitated a moment, and then replied, "With you, if you will
ask me."
"Will you?" said he, offering his hand.
"Indeed I will. You have shown that you can dance, and you know
we are not really so much brother and sister as to make it at all
improper."
"Brother and sister! no, indeed."

These few words tell us that Emma is quite unconscious of her
real feeling about her old friend and mentor, and that he has some
consciousness, whether fully defined or not, of his real feeling for
her. In spite of all our previous complaints against Emma, we
recognize her invincible charm, and for the first time we see the
pair together in a situation—a reminder of the traditional symbolic link between dancing and matrimony—which establishes
them as worthy of each other and destined somehow to understand themselves fully. And the scene follows immediately upon
that incident of which the result, at the climax of the story, will
threaten to divide them.

The next morning Emma, thinking over the ball, is happily
confident that the Eltons' behavior will cure Harriet's infatuation
—a quite rational inference, though developments will give it an
ironical twist. On top of that comes a "romantic" incident
which will nourish one of Emma's last and largest delusions.

Frank Churchill appears, supporting the frightened Harriet, whom he had just rescued from a menacing gang of gypsies on the road. Such a rescue, thinks Emma, would convince the most hard-headed rationalist that Frank and Harriet could not fail to be drawn together—"How much more must an imaginist, like herself, be on fire with speculation and foresight!—especially with such a ground-work of anticipation as her mind had already made" (xxxix; cf. xxxi). She herself would not need to do a thing. She forgets, as the reader does not, or should not, that this is not the only time in the last twenty-four hours that Harriet has been rescued from an unpleasant situation.

The sequel appears to Emma to confirm her idea (xl). The first part of it is a bit of solemn farce, quite in keeping with Harriet's mentality: she comes to burn, in Emma's presence, her "Most precious treasures," the relics of Mr. Elton's attendance at Hartfield during the portrait painting, a piece of court-plaster and a leadless stump of a pencil. The second part becomes a strong link in the chain of Emma's delusions. Harriet avows that she will never marry because she loves a man too far above her to be an object of hope, though she cannot help worshiping him: "The very recollection of it, and all that I felt at the time—when I saw him coming—his noble look—and my wretchedness before. Such a change! In one moment such a change! From perfect misery to perfect happiness." The reader, not possessed by Emma's wishful idea, sees that Harriet's words fit Mr. Knightley's action at the ball far better than Frank's protecting her from the gypsies. If this conversation at cross-purposes somewhat strains credibility, it is made more plausible by Emma's plea for caution this time: "Let no name ever pass our lips." But she can, on her own premise, tell Harriet that her dream is not wholly impossible and that it shows her good taste. Thus Emma the "imaginist" has encased herself, though now passively, in another cloud of fancy.

An accidental meeting of some friends at Hartfield (xli) is a good illustration of the reliance Jane Austen is disposed to put on her readers' acuteness. The sight of Mr. Perry the physician on horseback leads to Frank Churchill's question about the report that he was setting up a carriage, and that leads, via Miss Bates, to our inference that Frank and Jane are corresponding—which, in the world of the novels, means a virtual or actual engagement.

Frank resorts to the game of anagrams in order to communicate with Jane about his blunder; he characteristically adds the word "Dixon," which indicates that he has told Jane of Emma's suspicion. Mr. Knightley, who has suspected Frank of double-dealing with Jane and Emma and who is our guide through this scene, waits after the rest have gone to ask Emma, "with earnest kindness," whether she knows the actual relations between Frank and Jane. Emma's confusion seems to him to declare her own affection engaged to Frank; she insists that there is nothing between him and Jane. "That is, I *presume* it to be so on her side, and I can *answer* for its being so on his. . . ." Her confidence and satisfaction send Mr. Knightley home much depressed.

The mysteries and tensions centered in Jane, Frank, and Emma are deepened and quickened in the drama that develops, on or below the surface, during picnics on successive days at Donwell Abbey and Box Hill (xlii–xliii). Emma is an observer at the first, a participant in the second. Not having been at Mr. Knightley's place for a long time, she feels increasing respect for the spacious, unpretentious home of "a family of such true gentility." The relating of the external scene to states of mind, though different, recalls the splintered Sotherton party in *Mansfield Park*. The supposed unity of jolly picnickers does not exist. In the heat they walked "over the gardens in a scattered, dispersed way, scarcely any three together," and "insensibly followed one another" along a tree-shaded avenue which "led to nothing." But it does give a view of the Martins' Abbey Hill Farm, "a sweet view—sweet to the eye and the mind," a completely English image of idyllic order and security. Emma sees Mr. Knightley and Harriet together, facing the Farm, but Emma no longer fears its effect on Harriet. Frank Churchill, who had promised to come, does not. Emma meets Jane slipping away to walk home; she refuses Emma's offer of her father's carriage. Her fatigue is not physical; "from an overcharged heart" she exclaims on "the comfort of being sometimes alone!" Frank soon arrives, in a bad humor, and supposes the party will be breaking up: "I met *one* as I came— Madness in such weather!—absolute madness!" Emma is glad to be no longer in love with a man so discomposed by a hot morning; but Harriet will not mind that. After food and drink he is somewhat better, though he is "sick of England" and of being thwarted; he will stay over for the Box Hill party "if *you* wish me to. . . ."

At Box Hill (xliii) disunity and discord become more open and Emma is now in the center of it. Initial pleasure gives way to "a languor, a want of spirits, a want of union, which could not be got over." Prospects improve when they all sit down. Frank Churchill grows talkative and gay, making Emma "his first object," and she, glad to be enlivened, not sorry to be flattered, is gay and easy too, and gives him as much encouragement as in the days when she thought they were in love. She indulges or forces this mood mainly because she feels less happy than she had expected to be. Mr. Knightley gives a public intimation of how those present regard her unabashed flirting. As Frank carries on his assumed role of master of ceremonies and Emma's as queen of the occasion, her artificial gayety prompts a callous gibe at Miss Bates's habit of dull chatter.

The Eltons move away. Frank's comments on them and on hasty marriages in general, and Jane's reply, taken along with the fact of his having met her the day before when she walked home from Donwell, are evidently the upshot of a lovers' quarrel. Resuming his lively air, Frank says that when, after a couple of years abroad, he will be in want of a wife, he will ask Emma to choose one for him: "She must be very lively, and have hazle eyes." Emma thinks to herself that, apart from hazel eyes, Harriet will suit him perfectly; she apparently does not think of her own hazel eyes (Harriet's are blue), nor would anyone consider Harriet "very lively." At this point Jane, having borne enough, takes her aunt to join the Eltons, Mr. Knightley soon follows, and Emma, growing tired of Frank's "flattery and merriment," rejoices in the break-up of the "ill-assorted" party.

Mr. Knightley, escorting her to her carriage, rebukes her severely for her unfeeling cruelty to a woman of Miss Bates's "character, age, and situation," and tells of her victim's magnanimous words about it. At first Emma tries to laugh it off, but she is soon overcome by deep concern and self-condemnation. "Never had she felt so agitated, mortified, grieved, at any circumstance in her life." In her carriage, with the depressed and silent Harriet, "Emma felt the tears running down her cheeks almost all the way home, without being at any trouble to check them, extraordinary as they were." The tears, of course, are partly for her wounding of Miss Bates, but perhaps no less for her having degraded herself in Mr. Knightley's eyes and her own. This, the first keen distress the great Miss Woodhouse has ever experienced, is a real turning point in her life; her conscience has carried her some way toward self-knowledge.

The whole evening spent at backgammon with her father is an immediate reminder of Emma's most unfailing virtue; and, with "the warmth of true contrition" (a word that has religious overtones), she resolves to call on Miss Bates the next morning and begin "a regular, equal, kindly intercourse." Miss Bates is at first less at ease than usual but she becomes her cordial self when Emma inquires about Jane Fairfax, who has a bad headache after writing letters all morning; she has accepted the situation Mrs. Elton had found for her. Emma learns also that Frank Churchill had been summoned by Mr. Churchill to return early the next morning but had left that evening, after the picnic. Both facts are to have consequences.

Getting home, Emma finds Mr. Knightley, not in his normal mood: he is going to London to see his brother and his family— we suppose that Emma's flirtation with Frank, on top of earlier things, has been too much for him. Her father remarks that Emma has been to call on the Bateses:[2] "She is always so attentive to them!" Emma blushes at this "unjust praise" and smiles at Mr. Knightley with a disclaiming shake of the head. There follows one of those quietly, powerfully suggestive scenes which Jane Austen can create, even through description only (xlv):

It seemed as if there were an instantaneous impression in her favour, as if his eyes received the truth from her's, and all that had passed of good in her feelings were at once caught and honoured.—He looked at her with a glow of regard. She was warmly gratified—and in another moment still more so, by a little movement of more than common friendliness on his part.—He took her hand;—whether she

2 There seems to be a small awkwardness here. Mr. Woodhouse says "as I told you before"; he would of course have explained Emma's absence on Mr. Knightley's arrival. But now Mr. Knightley acts as if he heard this for the first time—as he must for the sake of what follows.

had not herself made the first motion, she could not say—she might, perhaps, have rather offered it—but he took her hand, pressed it, and certainly was on the point of carrying it to his lips—when, from some fancy or other, he suddenly let it go.—Why he should feel such a scruple, why he should change his mind when it was all but done, she could not perceive.—He would have judged better, she thought, if he had not stopped.—The intention, however, was indubitable; and whether it was that his manners had in general so little gallantry, or however else it happened, but she thought nothing became him more. —It was with him, of so simple, yet so dignified a nature.—She could not but recall the attempt with great satisfaction. It spoke such perfect amity.—He left them immediately afterwards—gone in a moment. He always moved with the alertness of a mind which could neither be undecided nor dilatory, but now he seemed more sudden than usual in his disappearance.

We view the situation through Emma's eyes and mind, but we understand what puzzles her, Mr. Knightley's divided feelings. His spontaneous response to her act of penitence attests his happy recognition of the Emma he loves. But we know, as she does not, that he believes her to be in love with Frank Churchill, a conviction forced on him earlier (the end of xli) and to be avowed later (xlix), and that he has little or no hope for himself. We know, too, that his conviction is mistaken, and, remembering that brief exchange at the ball—"Brother and sister! no, indeed" (xxxviii)— we see how much closer together, in spite of his lack of hope, Emma's misdemeanor and penitence have brought them. The whole episode of Box Hill and its aftermath has reached a pitch of seriousness above the normal level of comedy. That picnic was the last general gathering of the characters; from now on there are only dialogues, some of them highly dramatic, between individuals.

There follows immediately an event which prepares the way for the denouement: "The great Mrs. Churchill was no more." Her many illnesses, so often used to control her husband and especially their adopted son, had not all been imaginary. Now, thinks Emma, there will be no obstacle between Frank and Harriet; but the news does not betray Harriet into any expression of joyful hope, which seems to Emma proof of a strengthened character. To Jane Fairfax, "whose prospects were closing, while Harriet's opened" (the reverse of the truth), Emma tries to make belated amends, but all her overtures are declined, less, it appears, from ill health than from Jane's resolve to accept no kindness from her.

Some ten days after Mrs. Churchill's death comes the explanation of the mystery which has so long enveloped Jane and Frank (xlvi); this is the "violent" action or revelation that regularly starts the final movement of an Austen novel, and nowhere has it been so carefully prepared for as in *Emma*. The Westons, because of their cherished hope—and the belief they share with Mr. Knightley—are at pains to break gently to Emma the news that Frank and Jane have been secretly engaged for months, since before they came to Highbury. The astonished Emma's mind is divided between two ideas: her talk to Frank about Jane and Mr. Dixon and her concern for "poor Harriet." She quickly relieves Mrs. Weston's anxiety about her own heart; she had quite got over a temporary attachment. But she strongly condemns Frank for his deceiving them all and for his special attentions to herself; and how could Jane endure that? She proceeds to measure Frank by criteria which might stand as a description of Mr. Knightley. And then she thinks of Jane's having just accepted a post as governess. It was that, Mrs. Weston explains, that moved Frank to reveal all to Mr. Churchill, whose consent to the engagement was readily won.

At home alone (xlvii), Emma understands Jane's repulsing of a supposed rival, but she is tormented by thoughts of Harriet, "a second time the dupe of her misconceptions and flattery." Harriet, however, has already heard the news and, to Emma's great surprise, only thinks it very odd. The reason soon comes out, and it gives Emma a shock which it takes all her self-command to hide: Frank Churchill is a nobody in comparison with Mr. Knightley, and his saving her from the gypsies was nothing in comparison with Mr. Knightley's chivalry at the ball. To Emma's question whether she has any idea of Mr. Knightley's returning her affection, " 'Yes,' replied Harriet modestly, but not fearfully —'I must say that I have.' " Emma sits in silence for a few minutes. "A few minutes were sufficient for making her acquainted with her own heart. . . . It darted through her, with the speed of an arrow, that Mr. Knightley must marry no one but herself!"[3]

"Her own cónduct, as well as her own heart, was before her in the same few minutes." But her blind misguiding of Harriet in the past cannot permit injustice to her in the present, however much pain she herself must endure (in this most severe trial Emma's conscience asserts itself). She kindly invites further confidences. Harriet recalls that Mr. Knightley, after the ball, had shown increasingly cordial interest in her—as Emma herself had observed. Emma ventures to ask if he could have had Mr. Martin in mind (as we learn later he had), but Harriet has absorbed Emma's lessons too well to retain any interest in him. She would never have presumed to think of Mr. Knightley but for Emma's encouragement, and asks whether she has not good ground for hope. Emma, with great difficulty, contrives an answer that satisfies Harriet and contains an honest escape clause for Mr. Knightley and herself.

The rest of the chapter is given to Emma's self-lacerating thoughts: "Oh God! that I had never seen her!" "To understand, thoroughly understand her own heart was the first endeavour." "How long had Mr. Knightley been so dear to her, as every feeling declared him now to be?" Her fancied affection for the infinitely inferior Frank Churchill had been a complete delusion. "This was the knowledge of herself, on the first question of inquiry, which she reached. . . . She was . . . ashamed of every sensation but the one revealed to her—her affection for Mr. Knightley." A related train of thought has to do with her understanding of others. "With insufferable vanity[4] had she believed herself in the secret of everybody's feelings; with unpardonable arrogance proposed to arrange everybody's destiny." She had been wrong in everything, and "had brought evil on Harriet, on herself, and she too much feared, on Mr. Knightley." For it was not impossible that the best of men might be captivated by inferiors; and how he would be debased! If only she had allowed

[3] We know Jane Austen's dislike of "novel slang" and excessively figurative language, and, because of her own relatively plain style, the most commonplace of images here achieves a really startling effect.
[4] These words embody far more meaning and intensity than they had when used long before by Kitty in *Catharine* (*M. W.*, 236).

Harriet to accept Robert Martin! How could Harriet forget her own quality and look so high? But, Emma confessed to herself, it was she who had made the once humble girl so vain. In the anguish of these thoughts Emma does not recall her suggestion to Mr. Knightley that Harriet would be a perfect wife for him.

Much of the next chapter (xlviii) is given to more quietly rational but still agonizing and conflicting reflections. "Till now that she was threatened with its loss, Emma had never known how much of her happiness depended on being *first* with Mr. Knightley, first in interest and affection." She had taken him for granted. "In spite of all her faults, she knew she was dear to him; might she not say, very dear?" Yet his shocked rebuke of her behavior to Miss Bates had seemed too strong to carry love with it. If he did not marry Harriet or anyone else but would remain single, "she believed she should be perfectly satisfied"; the words give a hint of another self-delusion—and perhaps also of a shrinking, akin to her father's, from any kind of change. She would not, must not, desert her father; "She would not marry, even if she were asked by Mr. Knightley." We know such ideas will not hold, but they are natural enough in Emma's situation. These pages constitute the fullest and severest self-examination pursued by any Austen heroine except Anne Elliot, whose case is quite different. The nearest approach is Elizabeth Bennet's recognition, with study of Darcy's letter, of her lack of the discernment on which she had prided herself; but Emma has deeper and wider grounds for self-analysis and self-condemnation than Elizabeth had. The result is not only to establish her more firmly in our respect and liking but to compel us once again to acknowledge her capacity for strong emotion, here ardent love; indeed ardent love, however unconscious, had a good share in her suffering on the way home from Box Hill.

Emma's condemnation of herself is enlarged by Mrs. Weston's account of Jane Fairfax, who has avowed that, since she entered into a secret engagement, she had "never known the blessing of one tranquil hour"; and her afflicted conscience had made her irritable with Frank and Emma and others. Emma grieves all the more for her neglect of Jane, who would have been a far better friend than Harriet, and for her suspicions of Jane and Mr. Dixon, for all the ways in which she had stabbed her peace.

At this point we have some symbolic scene-painting of a kind
that appears in the later Jane Austen; it is too right and too
effective to be merely labelled the pathetic fallacy. Although it is
July, a cold stormy rain adds to Emma's inward gloom and makes
her father exceptionally difficult. She recalls their forlorn evening
after Miss Taylor's wedding, when Mr. Knightley had walked in
(the recollection, brief as it is, makes a sort of frame for the
whole story). She thinks of the coming months and the general
emptiness of Hartfield: Frank and Jane will be elsewhere, the
Westons will be kept at home by an expected baby, Mr. Knightley will not be dropping in as of old but perhaps be at Donwell
with Harriet. Emma has lost all hope of a happy marriage, and
through her own fault, but she is now capable of pure, disinterested resolution; she can only hope that "every future winter of
her life," however bleak and drab, will "find her more rational,
more acquainted with herself, and leave her less to regret. . . ."

But solace is nearer than she knows (xlix). The next afternoon
clouds give way to the sun and Emma goes out to enjoy the
freshness of the garden after the rain. Mr. Knightley appears,
having returned from London, and walks with her in silence.
Emma broaches the news of Frank and Jane, which he had already heard by letter, and he proceeds to offer tender balm to a
supposedly bruised heart. Emma manages to convince him that
she has suffered no wound, although she confesses that her vanity
had been flattered for a time by Frank's attentions. Mr. Knightley
sees Frank as a favorite of fortune: in spite of what he is and has
done, everything has turned out well for him, and at twenty-
three he has gained a perfect wife. He speaks, says Emma, as if he
envied Frank. He does, in one respect. Emma, fearful that they
are "within half a sentence of Harriet," refuses to be curious and
tries to shut him off. But then, feeling that he is hurt, she resolves
to face whatever he has to say: if he wishes to ask her opinion
about anything, "as a friend" she is at his command. Though
taken aback by the phrase, he accepts it, and asks, most earnestly:
"Tell me, then, have I no chance of ever succeeding?" At that
totally unexpected question Emma feels dread of being awakened
from what seems the happiest dream. Mr. Knightley goes on to
say that he cannot make speeches, as he might if he loved her less.
"I have blamed you, and lectured you, and you have borne it as

no other woman in England would have borne it." She must, she
does, understand his feelings, and will return them if she can.

While he spoke, Emma's mind was most busy, and, with all the
wonderful velocity of thought, had been able . . . to catch and
comprehend the exact truth of the whole; . . . that Harriet was
nothing; that she was every thing herself; that what she had been
saying relative to Harriet had all been taken as the language of her
own feelings.

She rejoiced that she had not mentioned Harriet, for whose coming disappointment she felt pain. But the author, infusing among
Emma's thoughts the only direct comment on fiction she makes
in the book, says that Emma was no heroine of sentimental romance, ready to sacrifice her love for the sake of another; Harriet
would be an impossible wife for such a man. "She spoke then, on
being so entreated.—What did she say?—Just what she ought, of
course. A lady always does."

This brief and jocular statement has sometimes been seen as a
shirking of the novelist's duty. But we know Jane Austen's
general—and wise—unwillingness to stage in full a hero's proposal and a heroine's acceptance, and the momentary flippancy
signals, not lack of feeling in Emma or the author, but the end of
a supreme crisis and the return to comedy. We have had ample
proof of Emma's emotional intensity and integrity in her drive
home from Box Hill, in her response to Harriet's revelation, and
in her present behavior with Mr. Knightley. "Seldom, very seldom," says the author, "does complete truth belong to any
human disclosure," but we gladly accept her evidence that a
thoroughly worthy couple are wholly united. The scene is a
fresh, subtle, and moving version of a standard motif, a proposal
brought on by the clearing away of a supposed attachment.

The author blends explanation of Mr. Knightley's recent feelings with summary of his present talk with Emma. Long jealous
of Frank Churchill, he had been driven to London by the Box
Hill picnic, but, learning of Frank's engagement, "He had ridden
home through the rain; and had walked up directly after dinner,
to see how this sweetest and best of all creatures, faultless in spite
of all her faults, bore the discovery." He had come to console,
not to propose; then, hearing that the villainous Frank did not

count, he had hoped only to be allowed to try to win her affection, and had found it already won. "She was his own Emma, by hand and word, when they returned into the house; and if he could have thought of Frank Churchill then, he might have deemed him a very good sort of fellow." Emma had lately felt a corresponding jealousy of Harriet, and "*Her* change was equal," from despair to "the same precious certainty of being beloved."

When alone, Emma faces two problems, her father and Harriet. She knows at once that she must not marry while her father is alive; the more difficult question inspires the idea of a temporary distraction for Harriet in a visit with her sister in London. Then she reads a long letter from Frank which Mrs. Weston has sent over. It confirms what we had partly guessed and explains what we had not. The letter—as a novelistic device quite legitimate in Frank's situation—convinces Emma that, while blamable, Frank had been less so than she had thought, and that he had suffered and repented and was truly and worshipfully in love with Jane. Frank's past conduct and present account of it fall far below Mr. Knightley's—and Jane Austen's—ideal, "the beauty of truth and sincerity in all our dealings with each other," but even he admits that the letter puts Frank in a better light.

In the last chapters (li–lv) the various threads are happily wound up. For the problem of Emma's father, Mr. Knightley has a solution, though it involves a great sacrifice for him which he does not mention but which Emma fully recognizes: that he should reside at Hartfield as long as Mr. Woodhouse is alive. Mr. Woodhouse, who always sees marriage as a calamity, is shocked by such a stroke blighting his own hearth, but he is eventually won over by the robbing of a nearby poultry-house and the reassuring idea of a son-in-law under his roof. In all her thoughts of marriage Emma is not at all concerned about depriving her nephew Henry of the inheritance of Donwell Abbey, though she does recall with a smile the jealousy of Jane Fairfax which had kindled her defense of little Henry's rights.

The other great problem remains: "It really was too much to hope even of Harriet, that she could be in love with more than *three* men in one year." But—a final irony—Mr. Knightley proves himself a far more astute matchmaker than Emma had ever been: he had taken pains to become acquainted with Harriet, he had recognized her good qualities, and he has contrived to reunite her with Robert Martin. Emma confesses that she had been a fool in that affair; she can now think that it would be a great pleasure to know Robert Martin. And she found it was; though it was inevitable that her close friendship with Harriet should "change into a calmer sort of good-will." That is only sensible, not cruel.

As for Emma and Mr. Knightley, while the Eltons content themselves with sneers, the Westons and others applaud the match. Mr. Knightley playfully predicts that the Westons' baby daughter will be thoroughly spoiled, but he is losing all his bitterness against spoiled children: because of Emma's faults and his thinking so much about her, he—another Mirabell—has been in love with her ever since she was thirteen at least. (In spite of Emma's reformation, it had crossed her mind that the Weston baby should be a girl, a possible wife for one of her nephews.) Emma establishes cordial relations with the now warm and open Jane Fairfax. Emma herself has been secretive in regard to Harriet's fantasy and thinks continued reticence on that subject desirable; but she looks forward with heartfelt felicity to giving her husband full and perfect confidence. We may feel ourselves among "the small band of true friends" at the wedding whose wishes and expectations "were fully answered in the perfect happiness of the union." It is quite fitting that, after her attainment of self-knowledge and her realization of love, the author should abandon the ironical presentation of Emma for straightforward seriousness—which does not forbid some light touches. One of the concluding scenes is a gay reconciliation with Frank Churchill: there is, she tells him, a little likeness between them, at least in their destiny, "the destiny which bids fair to connect us with two characters so much superior to our own."

In the unregenerate Emma's unbalanced blend of romantic feeling (directed chiefly upon others) and rational judgment, she—and also Jane Fairfax and Harriet Smith—can be recognized, critics have shown, as subdued modifications, realistic, ironic, or sympathetic, of both antiromantic and romantic types in the fiction of Jane Austen's age. Yet *Emma* is not a bookish novel. Emma's fancies are not—apart from a few vague hints—presented as the product of romantic reading or of a conventional romantic sensibility, like those of the young and naive Catherine

Morland and the young and inflammable Marianne Dashwood. The more mature and sensible Elizabeth Bennet is nearer Emma (though not very near) in being for a time misled by pride in her discernment. Emma, far more than Elizabeth, is proud of her discernment, but her repeated delusions spring from a combination of her fundamental qualities and circumstances. Her efforts to arrange other people's destinies—including the invention of an illicit bond between Jane Fairfax and Mr. Dixon—grow out of her irresponsible fancy and will (and, in the Martin–Elton case, snobbery), her exalted view of herself and her position, her boredom with humdrum life, her lack of serious interests, and her enjoyment of assumed power. And, along with such readily definable motives, conscious and unconscious, we see a young woman who can be said to exist only on the fringe of experience, who achieves a vicarious sense of adventurous involvement by managing another person's life. Critics often link Emma Woodhouse with Emma Bovary. If *Emma* remains a comedy and has not given birth to such a word as *Bovarysme*, we may still think that Jane Austen has at least as much insight as Flaubert into the workings of human nature. Moreover, although the comedy is abundantly amusing, it often touches on feelings and situations which could have been given a tragic turn.

Emma's prime fault, operating within the small circle of genteel village people, may seem correspondingly small (however mischievous or injurious to those concerned), and a few sour readers have seen the novel as a chronicle of trivia. "There are those," Louis Kronenberger remarks, "who think Jane Austen teatablish, as there are those who think that Mozart tinkles."[5] Yet Emma's is the same fault which, in people of the great world, politicians for instance, can be disastrous: it would not be absurd to connect Emma's managerial vanity and arrogance with a powerful government's belief in its right and duty to interfere with small nations—and Emma is not self-seeking. Although Jane Austen takes in no such large horizons, her simple paradigms have another kind of largeness: Emma and the people around her, while vivid individuals, are also representatives of what Dr. Johnson called "general nature," the typical and universal. That is one

[5] *Pride and Prejudice* (New York: Harper, 1950), xi.

central reason for our seeing Jane Austen as a "classical" author. And it helps to explain why, in spite of lapse of time and enormous changes, we so readily become inhabitants of her small world, knowing her characters as we know our friends—or rather better, since we have a creator and guide who knows them inside out and records their thoughts, words, and acts in an almost unerring moral cardiograph, yet with the relaxed ease of a humorous observer of the commonplace, fascinating spectacle.

While *Emma* is dominated (apart from her errors) by a heroine very conscious of class, she differs from her friends in that respect, and the novel is unique in the fact that so many of its characters have or have had a place in the workaday world: George Knightley, the active gentleman-farmer, his brother the London lawyer, Mr. Elton the parish clergyman, Mr. Weston the retired businessman, his wife the ex-governess, Jane Fairfax the prospective governess. (Mr. Woodhouse clearly inherited his fortune; he could never have made a penny.) *Emma* differs from the other novels also in that the principals are surrounded by a goodly number of semi-genteel, sub-genteel, and lower-class characters, some of whom evoke a display of Emma's snobbery. There are the Coles, who give a dinner, and the Coxes; Mrs. Goddard, who conducts a school, and her underbred teachers and her parlour boarder, Harriet Smith, who of course counts as an important character though socially inferior; and Mr. Perry the physician, who lives chiefly on the lips of his most devoted patient. There is the agricultural interest, represented by Robert Martin—whom Emma calls a yeoman and Mr. Knightley a gentleman-farmer—and his mother and sisters, and by Mr. Knightley's faithful steward, William Larkins. And whereas in the other novels servants are mostly nameless as well as invisible and inaudible (one exception is Mrs. Price's Rebecca in *Mansfield Park*), in *Emma* we hear of Mr. Woodhouse's cook, the peerless Serle, his coachman James, and James's daughter Hannah, one of the Westons' maids; Mrs. Elton's cook and Mr. Knightley's housekeeper; and the Bateses' maid-of-all-work, Patty. Beyond and below these are such poor families as the one Emma visits on a charitable mission.

The focal center of village life is Ford's shop, where Frank Churchill establishes his citizenship by buying gloves, and where

Mrs. Ford patiently endures Harriet's indecision. While Emma waits for Harriet, what she looks out on is given a description almost unique in Jane Austen, the everyday busyness of a village street. (*Persuasion* has a small picture of Bath streets in chapter xiv; and *Sanditon* has much about its seaside village.) This collective scene goes along with the individuals just catalogued and with an unusual amount of domestic detail to make Highbury, despite the author's restricted focus, by far the most substantial community in the novels; Bath and Portsmouth and London are of course a different matter. In this connection it is significant that, as the story and Emma's "education" advance, she becomes less and less the isolated great lady and more and more a member of the community, so that in the end, as we have seen, she is glad to become acquainted with the Robert Martin she had scorned as uncouth. That is the literal objectification of her being drawn out of her private world of romantic fancy into the world of actuality.

Readers have sometimes echoed the mild complaint made by Sir Walter Scott in his review of *Emma*: that Miss Bates and Mr. Woodhouse, in performing their roles as comic bores, are in danger of becoming real bores. But, if once in a while we incline to that feeling, it counts as nothing when we think of the positive value of the two characters in themselves, especially Miss Bates, and in their contributions to our sense of Emma's background and the Highbury community. Besides, Miss Bates's talk—always kept intelligible through its elliptical chain of associations—reveals important bits of information about Jane Fairfax. And Mr. Woodhouse gives us strong evidence of Emma's filial—we might say maternal—devotion; we are more tolerant of her fantasies when we think of her endless evenings spent in the entertainment of his friends or at backgammon with him. Miss Bates and Mr. Woodhouse, like the worthy Westons and the vulgar Eltons, conform to the general rule that Jane Austen's simple characters do not change. Harriet Smith, though unquestionably simple, is an exception, since she does change from mousey humility to vain imaginings of herself as Mrs. Knightley; but this unique transformation was brought about by a persuasive teacher and it is not permanent. Marriage may change Mr. Elton for the worse, or perhaps only exposes his real self. He, like the much cruder

Mr. Collins, is an exception to the rule that Jane Austen's clergymen are gentlemen; and it is impossible to conceive of either as in
the least degree religious. Mrs. Elton has a special and continuing
value. One of the brightest strokes of the author's comic genius is
the way in which this affected vulgarian, whom we abhor as
Emma does, is unobtrusively built up as an exaggerated embodiment of the unregenerate Emma's faults without her virtues.
Both are snobs who have more or less spurious notions of gentility; both plume themselves on their really meager cultural resources; as a bride, Mrs. Elton, at least for the time, preempts
Emma's role as the first lady of Highbury; her patronage of Jane
Fairfax and Emma's patronage of Harriet Smith are inspired—
though in different proportions—by self-love as well as benevolence; and Emma unwittingly describes herself when she says that
Mrs. Elton "wants to be wiser and wittier than all the world."

As for "intricate" characters, the kind Elizabeth Bennet liked
to study, the principals in *Emma* as elsewhere come under that
head; and they, like the lesser characters, are new creations, not
remade from earlier successes. Frank Churchill, the "villain," is
doubtless in the line of Willoughby, Wickham, and Henry
Crawford, although a secret engagement, however reprehensible
in the period and however painful for his fiancée, is for us a
comparatively mild offense. We may note, though, that Frank's
reason for secrecy was the prudential need of not losing Mrs.
Churchill's favor and fortune, a fact not remarked on by Mrs.
Weston, Emma, or even, at least explicitly, by the critical Mr.
Knightley when they read Frank's extenuating letter; Jane Austen, while calling in Mr. Knightley as the moral judge of the
letter and its author, perhaps took such a motive in such a young
man as a matter of course. Like Emma, though more skillful and
for purely selfish reasons, Frank is a manipulator of people, and,
like her, he learns his lesson; but part of his deception had been
gratuitous as well as unpleasant, and that was more necessary for
the author's purposes with Emma than for his own. Frank is a
clever, charming, restless, irresponsible "actor" like Henry Crawford, a less mature man of the world, more shallow and less
intellectual; but he can, like Henry, love and honor a girl of
much stronger principles than he himself can claim. Although the
story's requirements keep Jane Fairfax mostly silent in the back-

ground, the author somehow gives us a sense of ample knowledge, so that we can endorse Mr. Knightley's, and finally
Emma's, high praise. But even Jane Austen can hardly convince
us of a datum the plot demands, that a young woman with Jane's
mind, integrity, and emotional intensity could fall and remain in
love with such a dubious lightweight as Frank Churchill. We
have partly similar doubts concerning George Eliot's Dorothea
Casaubon and Will Ladislaw.

Mr. Knightley, the oldest and wisest of the author's male men-
tors, is much more serious than Henry Tilney, immeasurably
more alive and real than Colonel Brandon, a much stronger and
more attractive counselor and lover than Edmund Bertram. He
is more successful, to be sure, in guiding readers than he is for the
most part in guiding Emma, although he kindles her first self-
illumination and can take much credit for the end-product. We
have had glimpses of the skill with which Jane Austen gradually
develops their relations, the long growth of his paternal and
brotherly affection, the newer growth of his half-unconscious
jealousy of Frank Churchill, and his final emergence as an ideal
lover and husband, tenderly devoted, unselfish, clear-sighted, and
honest. We have also observed that the author can bring even
him within her ironic vision, but in a way that only makes him
thoroughly human and never reflects on his downright good
sense and integrity. If, thinking of his wisdom, authority, and
general beneficence, we incline to call him a village Grandison, it
must be with the large reservations that he is completely credible,
likeable, sometimes humorous, and even fallible.

Our response to Jane Austen's village comedy, our sense of the
depth and vibrations of her imagination and art, needs no external
quickening, but, if we wanted respectable contrasts, we might
think of the gulf between *Emma* and, say, Miss Mitford's *Our
Village* or Mrs. Gaskell's *Cranford*. To compare *Emma* with Jane
Austen's own earlier work is much more difficult. We took some
account of the strongly opposed estimates of *Mansfield Park*, a
mainly sober treatment of a serious moral and social theme which
some modern critics have considered her profoundest work and
some others her one great failure. The best or the only novel that
can be compared with *Emma* is *Pride and Prejudice*, and on that

pair Reginald Farrer long ago made a well-known pronouncement, that

while twelve readings of 'Pride and Prejudice' give you twelve periods of pleasure repeated, as many readings of 'Emma' give you that pleasure, not repeated only, but squared and squared again with each perusal, till at every fresh reading you feel anew that you never understood anything like the widening sum of its delights.[6]

This somewhat exaggerated contrast (which would apply to *Mansfield Park* and, as Farrer said, to *Persuasion* as well as to *Emma*) points to a real difference, to the richer subtlety of the design and texture of *Emma*, to the penetration and validity of a definable and coherent theme which embraces far more than a love story, fine and enthralling as that is. While many or most readers have always been happily satisfied with *Pride and Prejudice*, some others have seen more or less grave flaws, but *Emma* raises no comparable questions in the most captious mind. It is not a Cinderella romance but a completely realistic, consistent, and searching novel of character and personal relations, in which the heroine marries an old and familiar friend, her equal in station. It is not a social parable, though it says or implies much about the life of society. The heroine's attainment of clear knowledge of herself and other people is more complex and serious than it had been in *Pride and Prejudice*, and she becomes in the process a decidedly better and more likeable person. With all the bright comedy, the novel keeps moral values before us, but these incur no risk of becoming obtrusive as in *Mansfield Park*. As Lionel Trilling was able to say in 1957 (before women had risen in their might), "The extraordinary thing about Emma is that she has a moral life as a man has a moral life"; "A consciousness is always at work in her, a sense of what she ought to be and do."[7] Finally, *Emma* is, especially through its sustained irony, a masterpiece of development, of organic unity of form and tone.

[6] "Jane Austen," *Quarterly Review* 228 (1917), 23–24.
[7] "Emma and the Legend of Jane Austen," *Beyond Culture: Essays on Literature and Learning* (New York: Viking Press, 1965), 38, 44.

10

Persuasion

JANE AUSTEN'S LAST COMPLETED NOVEL was begun in August 1815 and finished, during a time of failing health, in August 1816, eleven months before she died; it was published by her brother Henry in December 1817, along with *Northanger Abbey*. If we knew nothing of dates we might well be disposed to place it last because of what critics so often call its autumnal tone, a quality created by the heroine's being not the usual seventeen or twenty but twenty-seven (an age at which, Marianne Dashwood affirmed, a woman could "never hope to feel or inspire affection again"),[1] and also by the symbolic autumn scenes on which her eyes and mind dwell with melancholy pleasure. On the other hand, a conventional and simplistic view of *Persuasion* might make it seem a work of youth: Anne Elliot, persuaded at nineteen to break with Frederick Wentworth, a brilliant and ambitious young naval officer with no means and with his way to make, and at twenty-seven cherishing an apparently hopeless memory, had long before

---

[1] To venture for a moment into shadowy data, it seems to have been at the age of twenty-five or twenty-six, in 1801 or 1802, that Jane Austen experienced the one serious love of her life (chapter 2 above). But, though a number of readers have been tempted to see some autobiography in *Persuasion*, there is no evidence for such a fancy.

come to believe in the primacy of youthful love over the prudential policy on which society operates. However, Jane Austen does
not think of Anne as having been clearly wrong and Wentworth
clearly right. In the contemporary division between romantic-
revolutionary and conservative novelists, *Persuasion*, as Kenneth
Moler has shown, is much closer to conservative views: Wentworth, with his impetuous trust in feeling, had things to learn as
well as Anne. Although, as we shall see, Anne's later judgments
on her early behavior may appear rather hard to reconcile, the
novel as a whole is quite consistent with the previous works of an
author who had always held that sensibility must be attended by
sense and had contrasted true love and marriage with the way of
the world.

In this short book everything must be reduced from the scale
of *Emma* and its predecessors, and much more use is made of
narrative summary of events and feelings than of dramatic dialogue, though summary can be given dramatic force. Besides,
Persuasion has more speaking characters than the other short
novel, *Northanger Abbey*, and these have to be presented with
relative brevity, although most of them (except Lady Russell)
are brought to life and rarely give an impression of meager treatment. Yet even the hero, up to the last moment when he puts his
vehement appeal into a hasty note, utters only a little more than
two thousand words, two thirds of these not addressed to the
heroine.

The first two chapters, with descriptive and narrative economy, set the stage and introduce the members of the Elliot family: the widower Sir Walter, a mindless baronet obsessed with
pride in his rank and good looks; his oldest daughter Elizabeth, a
female replica of her father who has long ruled the household and
neighboring society and is now, at twenty-nine, quite anxious
about matrimony; Anne, the second daughter, whose "elegance
of mind and sweetness of character" make her a nobody in the
eyes of her self-centered, insensitive father and sister; and Mary,
the youngest, the selfish and peevish wife of Charles Musgrove,
son and heir of the affluent squire of Uppercross. We hear of
several other persons of more or less account: Sir Walter's heir, a
Mr. William Elliot, whom Sir Walter and Elizabeth had intended
to be her husband but who had avoided the family and married

"a rich woman of inferior birth," and has lately become a widower; Lady Russell, a widow and neighbor of the Elliots, a female counterpart of Sir Thomas Bertram, who had been a close friend of Lady Elliot and has maintained affectionate intimacy with Anne, her god-daughter; and Mrs. Clay, the wily daughter of Sir Walter's lawyer, Mr. Shepherd, who might be called a sister of Lucy Steele and whose friendship with Elizabeth holds dangers for Sir Walter's security—as Anne vainly points out. This novel is, by the way, the most precise of all in its vital statistics and chronology, thanks partly to the author, partly to Sir Walter's constant perusal of "the book of books," the *Baronetage*: Anne was born in 1787; her mother had died in 1800; the story begins in 1814; and so on.

We are led into Anne's personal history by way of the immediate family problem, the necessity of extricating Sir Walter from the results of his lavish way of life. The solution arrived at by Lady Russell and Anne, and adroitly presented by Mr. Shepherd, is to rent Kellynch Hall to one of the rich naval officers whom the end of the war is bringing home. It is decided that Sir Walter and Elizabeth (and Mrs. Clay) will move to Bath and that Anne will spend a couple of months with her sister Mary Musgrove's family and then visit Lady Russell before going to Bath. Anne's first direct utterance in the book, in the course of a family council, is a general defense of the navy (for which her father has an elegant lounger's total contempt); her second is an identification of the proposed tenant, Admiral Croft, as a "rear admiral of the white" who "was in the Trafalgar action, and has been in the East Indies since." Only Jane Austen perhaps could use such formal particulars to suggest the emotional effect, in Frank O'Connor's phrase, of Anne's "years of brooding" and poring over navy lists. Mrs. Croft is the sister of a former curate of the district and hence, as Anne knows, of the Captain Wentworth to whom she had been briefly engaged eight years ago. And now she thinks of his being soon at Kellynch Hall and yet in spirit far from her.

The engagement had been broken because Lady Russell, moved by concern for Anne and by strong faith in worldly wisdom, had "deprecated the connexion in every light" (Sir Walter being coldly opposed for the second reason). Among Jane

Austen's "mentor" characters Lady Russell is much the oldest and, though well-meaning, is the least wise one; she cannot see beyond the social code of her class. In "the misery of a parting" Anne had got her chief consolation from the belief that her sacrifice was "principally for *his* advantage." "Her attachment and regrets had, for a long time, clouded every enjoyment of youth; and an early loss of bloom and spirits had been their lasting effect." She had met no man who approached Frederick Wentworth. When she was about twenty-two she had—to Lady Russell's sorrow—refused Charles Musgrove, an amiable sportsman of position and prospective wealth. She and Lady Russell never spoke of the earlier affair; but Anne, at twenty-seven, although she does not blame Lady Russell or herself for having been guided by her, knows that the decision had been wrong, no matter what the uncertainties ahead. Besides, such fears had proved groundless; her suitor had risen in his profession and made a handsome fortune. "She had been forced into prudence in her youth, she learned romance as she grew older—the natural sequel of an unnatural beginning." More than any other of the novels *Persuasion* is concerned with time and change and continuity, with the heroine's thoughts of the past, a past composed of short-lived happiness and eight years of unhappiness, and of the very unhopeful present and future.

We can hardly fail to guess at the start how the story will end, but in our journey through it we share to the full the isolated heroine's largely painful experience. Her journey is not, like that of the earlier heroines, from illusion or delusion to reality; Anne had passed that stage before the novel begins. And at no time has she had a confidante. Jane Austen's sympathetic interest (to pass by the novel's satirical strain) and ours are fixed on Anne's consciousness, although most of the action and conversation is reported by the omniscient author. Captain Wentworth soon arrives at Kellynch Hall, becomes a frequent visitor with the Musgroves, and enchants the young Louisa and Henrietta (who, unlike the Bertram sisters, are quite amicable rivals). Anne dreads her first meeting with him, and when it comes, in the midst of a group, it is limited to a bow and a curtsey. His first impression of herself Anne cannot forget, though in a way its finality becomes calming: Mary Musgrove reports his saying that Anne is so altered that he would not have known her. He, she knows, has not changed at all; "the years which had destroyed her youth and bloom had only given him a more glowing, manly, open look. . . ."

At this point (the end of vii), the author shifts from Anne's consciousness and gives a page to explanation of Wentworth's feelings, which we must have in mind if we are to follow the central story of Anne's fears and eventual hopes. He had thought her "wretchedly altered," though he had not expected his spontaneous words to be repeated. He had not forgiven her for weakly yielding to persuasion and deserting him. He had never since met her equal, but, except for some curiosity, he had no desire to meet her again. "Her power with him was gone for ever." Now, he can say jocosely to his sister, Mrs. Croft, he is ready to marry any pretty girl between fifteen and thirty who will have him—except (here the author goes inside his mind) Anne Elliot; but—says the author also—"Anne Elliot was not out of his thoughts" when he seriously described his ideal, "A strong mind, with sweetness of manner."

We observed the frequent and skillful use of this mixed method of presentation in *Emma*; in *Persuasion*, this is the only significant time we are taken outside Anne's observation or consciousness until, at the end, she and we are given Wentworth's account of his gradual change of heart; and the last short chapter is the author's valedictory comment on the happy marriage and the fortunes of other characters. But, allowing for a desirable degree of uncertainty and suspense, we are kept aware of the stages in the renewal of Wentworth's love through Anne's anxious efforts to interpret his every act and look and word. She is not only much the oldest but—on a level very different from that of the adolescent Marianne Dashwood—the most enduringly passionate of Jane Austen's heroines.

After that first meeting, Wentworth speaks to Anne seldom and with distant civility. He seems to get on so well with the Musgroves that there is speculation about whether he favors Louisa or Henrietta (who has been almost engaged to the curate and cousin, Charles Hayter); Anne doubts his being in love with either. She fastens on every sign, propitious or adverse, of his feeling toward herself, as when he silently pulls a boisterous Musgrove child off her back but apparently has no wish for speech.

The bulk of evidence seems to be unfavorable, notably some afforded by a country walk. Louisa warmly declares that, if she loved a man as Mrs. Croft loves the Admiral, she would let nothing separate them, and Wentworth says, "I honour you!" He soon elaborates his idea of constancy. Anne sits down to rest and overhears further talk between the pair, now in the hedgerow behind her (the use of overhearing, not an ideal technical device, is part of the author's effort to bring everything within Anne's consciousness). Wentworth contrasts Louisa's decision and firmness with Henrietta's pliability: "It is the worst evil of too yielding and indecisive a character, that no influence over it can be depended on. . . . let those who would be happy be firm." Then— an object-lesson of a kind unexpected in Jane Austen—he plucks a hazel nut from a bough and in a little lecture, more than half serious, praises its happy survival as an example of firmness—the quality in which, Anne knows, he had once found her so sadly lacking. There follows a scrap of talk which has mixed results for her assessment of his feelings. Louisa interests him when she speaks of Anne's having refused a proposal from her brother Charles; she adds that her parents thought the refusal due to Lady Russell's persuasion (as we noticed earlier, Anne had gone against Lady Russell's desire). Further, it is soon evident that this long walk to the Hayters' place has reunited Charles Hayter and Henrietta, so that Louisa is now marked out for Wentworth. But there is a bright moment when the Crofts, coming along in their gig, invite the tired Anne to ride home, and Wentworth silently helps her into the carriage. "He could not forgive her,—but he could not be unfeeling."

In the course of the famous visit to Lyme (xi–xii) Anne and Wentworth are carried a little beyond "common civilities." When, leaving the beach, the party encounter a strange gentleman, about thirty, his admiring look at Anne's face, flushed and brightened by the wind, is, she sees, observed and apparently seconded by Wentworth. She cannot make an assured judgment of his feelings when they are all suddenly involved in the chief "event" of the novel, Louisa's fall on the Cobb which knocks her unconscious: Henrietta faints and everyone is distracted, Wentworth hardly less than the others. (The author's account of the incident includes a salutary comic item.) Anne alone shows pres-

ence of mind and efficiency.[2] Wentworth, who feels needless
guilt for having given way to Louisa's desire for a second jump,
exclaims: "But so eager and so resolute! Dear, sweet Louisa!"
Anne, whose perfection does not extinguish jealousy in love or
critical intelligence, wonders whether he now holds his "previous
opinion as to the universal felicity and advantage of firmness of
character; and whether it might not strike him, that, like all other
qualities of the mind, it should not have its proportions and limits" (a very "classical" and Austenian principle). Only at the end
of the book do she and we learn that Wentworth had indeed
absorbed that lesson; at the time, although he consults her about
"what we had best do," Anne has no doubt that when Louisa
recovers she and Wentworth will become engaged.

The expedition to Lyme sows seeds of later developments for
Anne, Wentworth, and others. They are all curious about the
stranger (whom Anne had met again in the inn); he proves to be
almost certainly the William Elliot who is Sir Walter's heir (one
of the author's useful, economical, and harmless coincidences).
They make the acquaintance of Wentworth's old friends (who
"would have been all my friends," Anne thinks), the excellent
Captain Harville and his wife, who take Louisa into their small
house to nurse her, and Captain Benwick, whose engagement to
Harville's sister had been ended by her recent death. Anne alone
can talk with him about the poetry of Scott and Byron, who help
to nourish his half-real, half-sentimental melancholy, and she suggests more reading of prose, such as the moralists and writers of
letters and memoirs, as more fortifying in their precepts and

---

[2] We might once more cite Fanny Burney's *Camilla*, a novel Jane Austen
knew well. When a group of people are thrown into a panic by an angry
bull the hero says to Camilla, "with an approving smile": "You alone . . .
have remained thus quiet, while all else have been scampering apart, making
confusion worse confounded. . . . You can listen, then, even when you are
alarmed, . . . to the voice of reason!" (1, bk. ii, c. vii).

The excursion to Lyme Regis takes place in November. Jane Austen was
there in November 1803 and September 1804 (Chapman, *Jane Austen*,
"Chronology," and Letter 39, September 14, 1804). Her personal knowledge
informs the description of "the immediate environs of Lyme" (xi), in
which guidebook rotundities are redeemed by the author's sense of temporal
continuity—as if "romantic" scenery and Lyme were Tintern Abbey. Cf.
Karl Kroeber, *Styles in Fictional Structure: The Art of Jane Austen,
Charlotte Brontë, George Eliot* (Princeton, 1971), 84; N. Page, 11-12.

examples of "moral and religious endurances." Even if such counsel sounded priggish, as it does not, it would be disinfected by
Anne's realization that, like some of those writers, she herself is
better at preaching than at practice. Her affinity with Wentworth in both kindness and discernment has appeared in her
being able to distinguish between the genuine and the false in
Benwick's feelings, as Wentworth had been in regard to Mrs.
Musgrove's illusions about her dead son (viii).

The latter half of the novel (xv–xxiv) is set in Bath, an appropriate scene for the workings of social pretension and snobbery
which author and heroine both dislike. Anne finds that her father
and sister are basking in "the elegant stupidity of private parties"
and that William Elliot, having undergone a complete meta-
morphosis, has effected a cordial reconciliation with the family
he had scorned and shunned. Mr. Elliot is happy to find that
Anne is the young woman he had seen at Lyme. His attentions to
her become so marked that there is soon general expectation of a
match. Lady Russell approves of the idea and draws a briefly
alluring picture of her as the future Lady Elliot of Kellynch Hall;
but Anne, though admitting that in many respects she thinks
highly of him, says they would not suit each other. It is not only
that her heart is fixed elsewhere but that Mr. Elliot, while intelligent and agreeable, inspires distrust of his sincerity and integrity. Her suspicions of dubious or discreditable conduct in the
past include what appears to us as an odd Evangelical item:
"Sunday-travelling had been a common thing"—which some critics would doubtless prefer to assign to Fanny Price (or leave to
Mrs. Proudie); the idea that the author is laughing at Anne is
inconceivable.

A letter from Mary Musgrove brings the astonishing news that
Louisa and Captain Benwick are engaged. Anne's chief reaction is
the thought that Wentworth is now "unshackled and free"; her
"feelings were too much like joy, senseless joy!" And Wentworth, who had long ago left the convalescent Louisa to visit his
brother, soon arrives in Bath. At his first encounter with Anne he
displays mainly embarrassment. At the next meeting, in the public rooms, he is about to pass by with a bow when Anne—ready,
like other Austen heroines, to take the initiative—holds him in
what becomes friendly talk. He does not comprehend how the

intellectual and supposedly inconsolable Benwick could become engaged to a girl who, though very amiable, is so inferior to Fanny Harville:

"A man does not recover from such a devotion of the heart to such a woman!—He ought not—he does not."
Either from the consciousness, however, that his friend had recovered, or from some other consciousness, he went no farther. . . .

Anne feels "an hundred things in a moment." (The words "or from some other consciousness" are not the only hint in this scene left to the reader to fill out.) A little later, when separated from Wentworth, she is blissfully aware of having learned "more of his feelings towards Louisa, more of all his feelings, than she dared to think of!" All that he had said, "all, all declared that he had a heart returning to her at least," that old resentments have been "succeeded, not merely by friendship and regard, but by the tenderness of the past. . . . He must love her."

Mr. Elliot's attentions have been growing warmer (he even approaches a proposal), and are now of course distressingly unwelcome. As one of the family group at a concert, he sticks so closely to Anne that Wentworth finally goes off with "there is nothing worth my staying for." Meanwhile we have entered upon a sequence which occupies more or less of four chapters (xvii, xix, xxi, xxii) and is perhaps the most laboriously contrived device in all of Jane Austen; it is a disappointing surprise in an artist whose apt invention and delicate proportioning of means to ends we take for granted. This is the series of calls Anne makes on a former schoolfellow, a Mrs. Smith, now an impoverished widow and invalid—not the kind of person Anne's family seek out. Through her nurse Mrs. Smith is kept up with Bath gossip and takes a keen interest in Anne's affairs, especially her coming marriage to Mr. Elliot. When Anne denies that, Mrs. Smith feels it is now right to tell her the truth about Mr. Elliot: he is a specious, cold-blooded, black-hearted villain, who married for money; ruined her husband, his friend; refused to help her regain control of some West Indian property which might relieve her straits; has come to value highly the baronetcy he had once despised, and hence has been on guard against Mrs. Clay's scheming to win Sir Walter. The author evidently felt the temporary need of an apparent rival to Wentworth (he had never been that in Anne's mind) and, when his usefulness was over, the need of getting rid of him; and she fell back upon eighteenth-century melodrama (with some corresponding language) akin to Colonel Brandon's story of Willoughby. Like Brandon's, Mrs. Smith's evidence is supplied rather late in the day; her not very good explanation of her previous silence is that she had understood the engagement—in which she had a self-serving interest—to be an accomplished fact. Besides, the whole business was hardly needed; Anne had already decided against Mr. Elliot with sufficient finality. One would like to think that the author, if she had had time and health and energy for her usual full revision, would have replaced the episode with something more worthy of herself and the main body of the novel.

At any rate she recovers and carries the story to a dramatic climax which is surely the most beautiful and deeply moving scene in all her work. (It is, as we shall see, a radical revision of a first attempt.) The Charles Musgroves, the Crofts, and Captain Harville, who have come to Bath, are together at their inn, where Anne joins them. Wentworth sits down to write a letter on Harville's behalf (about a miniature he soon produces). In response to the elder Mrs. Musgrove's talk of Henrietta's immediate wedding, Mrs. Croft—who herself had risked early and rapid marriage—speaks her disapproval of long engagements based on uncertain prospects; Anne, listening with special interest, observes that Wentworth suspends writing and turns "to give a look—one quick, conscious look at her." Captain Harville shows Anne the miniature of his friend Benwick, originally done for his sister and now to be reset for Louisa: his sister, he says, would not have forgotten Benwick so soon. They go on talking of male and female constancy, each championing his or her own sex. Men, says Anne, " 'are always labouring and toiling, exposed to every risk and hardship. . . . It would be too hard indeed' (with a faltering voice) 'if woman's feelings were to be added to all this.' " Wentworth's pen falls on the floor, as if "he had been occupied by them, striving to catch sounds, which yet she did not think he could have caught."

To a question from Harville, Wentworth replies that he will be done in five minutes, and the other two resume their discus-

sion. The normally reserved Anne speaks out fervently in praise
of men's constancy, so long as

"the woman you love lives, and lives for you. All the privilege I claim
for my own sex (it is not a very enviable one, you need not covet it)
is that of loving longest, when existence or when hope is gone."
　She could not immediately have uttered another sentence; her
heart was too full, her breath too much oppressed.
　"You are a good soul," cried Captain Harville, putting his hand on
her arm quite affectionately. "There is no quarrelling with you. . . ."

　Wentworth, having folded and sealed a letter, in a hurried,
agitated way, goes out with Harville, giving no word or look to
Anne, but at once returns, apologizes for forgetting his gloves,
draws a letter from under the papers on the table, places it before
her, "with eyes of glowing entreaty fixed on her for a moment,"
and quickly goes out again. "On the contents of that letter depended all which this world could do for her!" It does all. Wentworth had overheard her impassioned assertion of constancy in
both men and women, and had written impetuously to assert his
own, which had survived and surmounted all resentment. He had
come to Bath solely on her account, and he would not have
waited ten days to speak if he could have read her feelings as she
must have penetrated his.
　Anne longs to escape from people and be alone, but Charles
Musgrove amiably insists on escorting her homeward. They meet
Wentworth, and Charles leaves the pair to move, heedless of
passers-by, toward a retired walk, where—though no speeches
are given—

the power of conversation would make the present hour a blessing
indeed; and prepare for it all the immortality which the happiest
recollections of their own future lives could bestow. There they ex-
changed again those feelings and those promises which had once
before seemed to secure every thing, but which had been followed by
so many, many years of division and estrangement. There they returned again into the past, more exquisitely happy, perhaps, in their
re-union, than when it had been first projected; more tender, more
tried, more fixed in a knowledge of each other's character, truth, and
attachment; more equal to act, more justified in acting.

As they recall both the recent and the remote past, they confirm or enlarge what we had more or less surmised. In Bath, "Jealousy of Mr. Elliot had been the retarding weight, the doubt, the torment," but it had been yielding to encouraging signs and had been vanquished at last by Anne's speech to Captain Harville, which had led Wentworth to seize a sheet of paper and pour out his feelings. "Her character," he says, in the author's summary of his talk, "was now fixed on his mind as perfection itself, maintaining the loveliest medium of fortitude and gentleness." After the years of unforgiveness, he had learned only at Uppercross to do her justice, and although, in "angry pride," he had attempted to attach himself to Louisa, at Lyme he "had learnt to distinguish between the steadiness of principle and the obstinacy of self-will." But—from here onward we have dialogue—Wentworth found that he was regarded as virtually engaged to Louisa and he felt (like Edward Ferrars) that he "was hers in honour if she wished it." So he had gone away to visit his brother "and act as circumstances might require." On the news of Louisa's engagement he had hastened to Bath with the hope of finding Anne unchanged, but there he had found the double danger of Mr. Elliot and Lady Russell.

The last dialogue occurs at a party given by Sir Walter and Elizabeth, a party which for once, in Anne's present happy state, does not seem dull. We can understand the author's desire to register a final judgment on the question of romance versus prudence, yet a central part of it may leave us somewhat puzzled. Anne says, as she had said much earlier (iv), that she was right in being guided by a quasi-maternal friend, even though the advice was wrong, and that in a similar situation she herself would never have given it (xxiii): "But I mean, that I was right in submitting to her, and that if I had done otherwise, I should have suffered more in continuing the engagement than I did even in giving it up, because I should have suffered in my conscience." This, and the whole context of earnest assertion, come from a person of the finest moral sensitivity and integrity, yet it seems to be directly opposed to what had also been an earlier conviction, that, while defending Lady Russell and herself, "she should yet have been a happier woman in maintaining the engagement, than she had been in the sacrifice of it" (iv). Indeed she had been ready to reject

her elder's advice two years after she had taken it: in this last
dialogue, when Wentworth, replying to the speech quoted from,
says that he had perhaps been a worse enemy to himself than
Lady Russell, and asks whether, when he returned to England in
1808 with a few thousand pounds, she would have renewed the
engagement then, " 'Would I!' was all her answer; but the accent
was decisive enough." He exclaims over the hurt pride which had
kept him from such a move and takes the blame on himself.

This chapter has been outlined at some length partly for its
own sake, partly because it was an immediate recast of the only
surviving draft of a section of any novel, so that comparison illustrates Jane Austen's aims and methods. Just after finishing the
book she found the climactic chapter "tame and flat" (*Memoir*, c.
xi, p. 166), and, in spite of her failing health, she replaced it with
two chapters, one of which we have gone through.[3] In the first
version Anne, having just heard Mrs. Smith's revelation concerning Mr. Elliot, walks homeward thinking about its various consequences, and falls in with Admiral Croft near his own door. He
persuades her, against her will, to go in and see his wife, saying at
first that she is alone with her mantua-maker and then—to Anne's
consternation—that nobody is there except Wentworth. The
Admiral engages Wentworth in conversation in the next room
and Anne hears repeated mention of herself and Kellynch. Wentworth returns to her and, in great embarrassment, gives a message
from the Admiral, who had just been told that Anne and Mr.
Elliot are to marry and live at the Hall: while disbelieving the
report, he is ready to cancel the lease if that is "the *wish* of the
parties." Anne, also much embarrassed, assures Wentworth that
there is no truth in the report. After "a silent but a very powerful dialogue" between their eyes, he takes her hand, exclaiming
"Anne, my own dear Anne!" There followed, in the author's
summary, Wentworth's account of the renewal and deepening of

[3] The cancelled chapter (originally x) was replaced by the mainly new
x and xi (xxii and xxiii in most modern editions). The cancelled chapter,
first printed in the *Memoir* (1871 edition), is reprinted in Chapman's edition
of the *Memoir* (1926) and printed from the MS., with the original last
chapter, in his *Two Chapters of Persuasion* (Oxford, 1926); this text is
reproduced in the editions of *Northanger Abbey* and *Persuasion* by Chapman (1933) and J. Kinsley and J. Davie (Oxford, 1971) and of *Persuasion*
by A. H. Wright (Boston, 1965).

his love. This part (a good deal of it changed into direct speech) and ensuing exchanges between the two were retained, more or less exactly, at the end of the new chapter.

This first version begins, and continues after the reunion, in a vein of comedy—with the straightforward Admiral and Mrs. Croft in the contrived role of matchmakers—which is awkwardly managed and very jarring and inadequate as a prelude to the climax; and the climax itself is inadequate. The lovers are suddenly thrust upon each other by outside manipulation instead of coming together as the mature and high-souled beings they are. A further point is that the first account of the reunion followed directly after Mrs. Smith's revelation, when neither Anne nor the reader was prepared for it. In the revision a new chapter was written and inserted between the two events, a chapter which, with Anne present, brings in the unpleasant Elizabeth, Mrs. Clay, and Mr. Elliot, then the pleasant Musgroves and talk of Henrietta's wedding, and finally a glimpse of the supposed enemies, Mrs. Clay and Mr. Elliot, walking together—a slice of mainly ordinary life which slackens the pace and allows the climax to come with unimpaired force. In the finely built setting of the inn, in the next (and also new) chapter, the speeches which declare Anne's faith in the constancy of men and the superior, hopeless constancy of women, speeches followed at once by Wentworth's impassioned letter—this scene shows the lovers drawn together by their own deepest needs, on the deepest or highest plane of drama that Jane Austen ever reached. This was, as Mr. Southam says, her first attempt to end a novel with a scene of climactic emotional intensity, and it is no wonder that she did not at first succeed; the wonder is that she could achieve such a triumph of rewriting.

In a letter to Fanny Knight four months before her death Jane Austen, in a general comment on novels and heroines, said that "pictures of perfection as you know make me sick & wicked"; and a few lines further on she spoke of Anne Elliot: "You may *perhaps* like the Heroine, as she is almost too good for me" (Letter 142: March 23, 1817). Anne is undoubtedly good, a martyr, in large and small ways, to her sense of duty, but no one could be turned off by her goodness as many people are by that of the other isolated heroine, Fanny Price—to whom, though, of all the heroines Anne is nearest in some essential qualities. She is signally unselfish (always a prime virtue for Jane Austen), and bears patiently with that signally selfish and querulous hypochondriac, her sister Mary Musgrove, and with her odious father (of whom she has a clearer understanding than she wishes she had) and her equally cold-hearted and snobbish sister Elizabeth. She remains magnanimously attached to Lady Russell, whose advice had cost her so much; and her refusal of Wentworth had been based partly on unselfish concern for his career. If we censure her for weakness in yielding to advice, we must allow for the inexperience of nineteen, for Lady Russell's special authority, and for the want of any other counselor. And, like most of Jane Austen's other thoughtful and complex characters, Anne is capable of change, not of course in her love for Wentworth (except in its deepening) but in the developed strength which enabled her, long before he became a man acceptable by worldly standards, to recognize the rightful claims of love when she could have no hope of its fulfillment. At the same time it is that love which keeps her human and lovable in her unceasing watch for signs of change in her alienated lover and in her jealousy of Louisa—though she always maintains her dignity. Anne does not have by nature, and in her situation could not be expected to have, the gayety and wit of Elizabeth Bennet or Emma Woodhouse; but she has more mature insight, wisdom, and intensity in love than either. She also has more intellectual and reflective cultivation than they, and her contemplation of autumn scenes evokes, along with recollections of poetry, far more mature emotions than the youthful raptures of Marianne Dashwood. Even in Bath, a proof of Wentworth's jealousy of Mr. Elliot can inspire "musings of high-wrought love and eternal constancy" which give a poetic glow to city streets: "It was almost enough to spread purification and perfume all the way" (xxi). Here the author includes a touch of protective mockery, but in general Anne's character and experience do not invite, indeed almost wholly forbid, the usual play of irony. Jane Austen's friend, Mrs. Barrett, a witness we have heard before, declared that Anne Elliot "was herself; her enthusiasm for the navy and her perfect unselfishness, reflect her completely." These incomplete and somewhat incongruous virtues were certainly in Jane Austen, and we might add many others, more or less shared by other heroines; there are also obvious differences between Anne and her creator.

Captain Wentworth is given the confidence, energy, and forthright decisiveness to be expected of a naval officer. It should not be held against him that at Lyme—mainly because he blames himself, unjustly, for Louisa's accident—he falls short of Anne in controlling his overwrought feelings and coping with the emergency. He is not merely an able and ambitious man of action; he has sensitive perceptions and can analyze his own emotions and motives and other people's (though he understands his friend Benwick less well than Anne). He is loving enough, and magnanimous enough, to let his injured pride and prolonged resentment against Anne be overcome by renewed and increasing recognition of her rare quality. Unlike Edmund Bertram and George Knightley (the latter he resembles in some respects), Wentworth is not cast as the heroine's mentor; rather, she might almost be called his, though only through the effect of her character as it reveals itself. But he is a spirited and attractive hero of a new kind, and, though he is distinguished enough in appearance and manner to be welcomed in Sir Walter's and Elizabeth's drawing-room, he is as much as Anne an enemy of society's scale of values. Even as a happy fiancé, he cannot promise immediate forgiveness and affection for Lady Russell.

Persuasion keeps us aware of three groups of people: Sir Walter and Elizabeth Elliot, Lady Russell, and the recent recruit, William Elliot, representing the world of status and fashion, its fringe at least; the Musgroves, whose family affection, solidarity, and general decency represent much that is good in the squirearchy (though Mary Musgrove remains an Elliot) as well as an interest in property (they "had their own game to guard, and to destroy"); and, thirdly, the world of the navy, which, though an arena for individual ambition, is also a world free from the stagnation, pretentious or unpretentious, of the other two worlds. All these individual characters have their own identity, but most of them can be classified in one way related to the theme of the novel, that is, according to their views of love and marriage (although there is no trace of artificial schematization). In the upper-class orthodoxy of the first group, marriage is only or mainly a matter of family and financial standing, love being perhaps the nought in the ten; Lady Russell has a heart, though it is overlaid by the prejudices of her class. The easygoing squire's family (Mary again excepted) allow room for love while preferring love with land. On the side of wholly disinterested love, warm, stable, and self-justifying, are the free, sincere, unspoiled naval people, the hero and heroine, the Crofts and the Harvilles. Louisa and Henrietta can perhaps be put with these, since Henrietta is happy to accept her curate (whose future property commands Charles Musgrove's respect), and since Louisa, to everyone's surprise, is won by Captain Benwick (whose addiction to books, especially romantic poetry, is offset, in Charles Musgrove's opinion, by his enjoyment of rat-hunting in the barn). Benwick's ability to forget his grief for Fanny Harville in a speedy and very different love puzzles and distresses such believers in constancy as his friends the Harvilles and Wentworth.

In *Mansfield Park* the navy had been represented, from the professional and moral ends of the spectrum, by the Crawfords' admiral-uncle and young William Price (not to mention his dubious father). In *Persuasion* the naval officers, and the hardy and genial Mrs. Croft and the hospitable Mrs. Harville, make a natural, wholesome, and perhaps—if Jane Austen's naval brothers are our standard—not over-idealized group. Francis Austen, by the way, deprecated the idea of his being a model for Wentworth but said that Captain Harville's domestic habits, tastes, and occupations had a considerable resemblance to his own. Harville, an intellectually unsophisticated man but a thoughtful and sound-hearted one, is a worthy recipient of Anne's bleak and eloquent claim for women's constancy in love. All these officers, except perhaps Benwick (though his professional competence is vouched for) give a new nautical flavor to *Persuasion*—especially the bluff, hearty, greatly likeable Admiral Croft and his wife. Their reminiscences go along with the shorter span of Wentworth's, and with the Admiral's greetings of old friends in Bath, to call up the whole naval service. While he cannot pass a picture in a shop window of a quite unseaworthy ship, he frequently overturns the gig in which he and Mrs. Croft survey the countryside. His main function in the novel is his exposure, both unconscious and conscious, of such a simulacrum of a man as Sir Walter Elliot—whose many mirrors in Kellynch Hall he puts out of sight. The bringing of the Crofts and Harvilles and of course Wentworth to Bath underlines the contrast between the two worlds.

For all its concentration on attitudes toward love and marriage, *Persuasion* has a vein of sharp satire. Sir Walter's speech and behavior are realistic enough to keep him from becoming a caricature. His mind has room for only two ideas, his rank and his well-preserved good looks. His contempt for those beneath him is matched only by his servility toward those above, his cousins the Viscountess Dalrymple and her daughter, whose mental vacancy is on a level with his own. Elizabeth Elliot is her father's counterpart in snobbery of both the haughty and the servile kind.

In *Persuasion*, as in *Sense and Sensibility* and other novels, Jane Austen's satirical instinct seems at moments to carry her beyond her customary amused and imperturbable poise. Some tough-minded as well as tender-minded critics have fallen upon one bit of satire as reprehensible hardness and bad taste—as some have upon bits of the letters. The elder Mrs. Musgrove, who is in general presented as a worthy person, remembers that her son Dick had served a while under Wentworth and, getting out his few letters, gives herself up to melancholy musing, although, says the author, Dick was a young man (as Wentworth evidently recalls) whose death had been more of a relief than a loss to his family (viii). Wentworth goes to sit with her and shows "the kindest consideration for all that was real and unabsurd in the parent's feelings," and he is further praised by the author for the self-command with which he attends to the "large fat sighings" the mother pours out over her worthless son. It is characteristic of Jane Austen that she should distinguish, and have her hero distinguish, between sincere and insincere grief as exhibited by the same person; and a writer of unblinking candor would be surprised by the charge of callousness here. The offensive item, by the way, might perhaps be called, simply as a combination of words, the most modern phrase in Jane Austen.

A number of critics have considered *Persuasion* the finest of all the novels. But ranking the six in order of merit, though it has always been indulged in (if not much by austere modern analysts), is an idle pastime. All the novels have some qualities in common and some that are uncommon or unique, and in all the theme is bound up with, or exists in, the development of the heroine. The central uniqueness of *Persuasion* is that the sad, rich experience and character of the isolated Anne Elliot enable her, in more conspicuously decisive terms than the other novels use, to break loose from an outworn, half-spurious social pattern and achieve freedom and fulfillment in a different world which she and her worthy lover help to create.

Sanditon

T HE FRAGMENT KNOWN AS *Sanditon* (*M. W.*, 363–427) is remarkable in several ways. Jane Austen's health had been failing through the larger part of 1816 and she died on July 18, 1817, yet she found the spirit and energy to write a substantial part of a new novel between January 27 and March 18—perhaps partly in an effort to combat illness and depression. Secondly, *Sanditon* is not at all the beginning of a typical Austen novel but a quite new departure. A third point, which does not really contradict the second, is that much of the substance and manner recalls the author's early burlesque and parodies.

The setting is the seaside village of Sanditon in Sussex. The promoting of Sanditon as "a small, fashionable Bathing Place" is the all-absorbing business and religion of Mr. Parker, a man of about thirty-five, who is "a complete Enthusiast." Sanditon is, among various images, "his Hobby Horse"—a suggestive hint of Laurence Sterne's Shandys. In the first five chapters Mr. Parker is the buoyant dispenser of information about the village and the persons we are to meet. We have noticed Jane Austen's increasing consciousness and use of place in her later novels, and Sanditon, more than the very different Mansfield Park or Highbury, has a solid physical existence; indeed it might be called a main character, thanks partly to the promoter's zeal, partly to descriptions of a concrete fullness unprecedented in Jane Austen. (Mr. Parker's innocuous crusade, by the way, might make us wonder how Jane Austen would view the modern destruction of so much of Georgian Bath in the name of development—not that she liked living there.)

The tale opens with a less fatal calamity than one in *Love and Friendship*: Mr. Parker and his wife, on a misguided journey in quest of a surgeon for Sanditon, are overturned in their carriage and his foot is sprained. Having received prolonged hospitality from a nearby farmer (a quiet conservative, the opposite of his guest), the Parkers take home with them for a visit the farmer's daughter, Charlotte Heywood, aged twenty-two. On the way Mr. Parker, for her benefit, talks about the great lady of Sanditon, Lady Denham, who is a vigorous seventy but, as his "Colleague in Speculation," is too cautious. She has long fought off three groups of relatives who are eager for her money, though she has made some concessions. Two young members of the favored group, Sir Edward Denham and his unmarried sister, have lately lost ground. Lady Denham has taken in from another family group the young Clara Brereton, who, along with beauty, has an excellence of mind and character which has won the strong goodwill of her patroness. If the reader, now or later, suspects Clara of artful designs, an idea which could not enter Mr. Parker's mind, the author gives no support to it.

The fourth chapter brings the Parkers and Charlotte into Sanditon. The promoter expatiates on the many virtues of the place and rejoices in any signs that the village is growing. He has given up his ancestral home for a new one with a fine view of the sea; he rather wishes he had not named it Trafalgar House, "for Waterloo is more the thing now." We hear of his brother Sidney, a clever but unsettled young man who pretends to laugh at "Improvements" and at his sisters' imaginary ailments. Charlotte, established in her room, looks out "over the miscellaneous foreground of unfinished Buildings, waving Linen, & tops of Houses, to the Sea, dancing & sparkling in Sunshine & Freshness." We may infer that the sea is not open to improvements.

Charlotte and the reader are given advance information about three other persons, Mr. Parker's sisters Diana and Susan and his

younger brother Arthur, when he reads aloud a letter from Diana
(v). It is clear, in spite of Mr. Parker's benevolent commentary,
that all three are extreme hypochondriacs, much worse than Mr.
Woodhouse. Arthur, a little over twenty, is too delicate to en-
gage in any profession, but Diana and Susan are too strong-
minded to let continual physical ills impede their beneficent activities. (The topic of illness, in these cases imaginary, may have
been occasioned by Jane Austen's own condition—not that she
was in any sense a hypochondriac, though her mother may have
been inclined that way.) Diana is, according to Mr. Parker, "the
most active, friendly, warm hearted Being in existence," and her
letter supplies proof: she has, with prodigious efforts, secured
two large groups for the Sanditon season, a family and a girls'
school. She would like to come herself, but "in my present state,
the Sea air w^d probably be the death of me."

From now on, as Charlotte meets the various people, we see
and hear them through her eyes and ears, and Mr. Parker's accounts are more or less altered by a more judicious and discriminating observer who has no connection with him or his relatives
or Sanditon. There is, as before, more specific description of
scenes and persons than we are accustomed to in Jane Austen. A
visit to the lending library even yields a list of subscribers—
headed of course by Lady Denham; Mr. Parker wishes the list
were longer and more distinguished but comforts himself with
the thought that it is only July. They meet Lady Denham and
Miss Brereton and invite them home for tea. Miss Brereton,
lovely, poor, and dependent, Charlotte can see only as "the most
perfect representation of whatever Heroine might be most beautiful & bewitching" in all the volumes of the library. The sober-
minded Charlotte, however, is no romantic: her imagination is
amused by novels, but she is "not at all unreasonably influenced
by them." And Clara Brereton, far from being a persecuted heroine, seems to be on very comfortable terms with her benefactor.
That lady, a talker almost as voluble as Miss Bates but more
coherent, and as thrifty as Mrs. Norris, shows the fear of rising
prices and financial losses that disturbs and hampers the optimistic
Mr. Parker.

The prosaic, middle-class commercialized atmosphere of Sanditon receives a jet of romantic flamboyance when Sir Edward and

his sister call on the Parkers. Charlotte likes his appearance and manner and relishes his apparent liking for her, but these first impressions are soon cooled by his evident devotion to Miss Brereton and later by his extravagant sensibility. When they are all together on the terrace, Sir Edward leaves Clara for Charlotte, much to the latter's surprise. He launches into such a rhetorical glorification of the sea that she cannot but think him "a Man of Feeling." From that he soars into a still more fervent and florid rhapsody on love and the poetry of love, going far beyond Captain Benwick's sighs over Scott and Byron: Burns has far more passion than Montgomery, Wordsworth, Campbell, or Scott. Charlotte avows that she is "not poetic enough to separate a Man's Poetry entirely from his Character," so that she doubts Burns's truth and sincerity. This sets Sir Edward off on a defense of "the sovereign impulses of illimitable Ardour," and Charlotte begins to think him "downright silly" as well as morally wanting; and she has realized that he had chosen to walk with her only to pique Miss Brereton.

Charlotte is glad to exchange Sir Edward's gushing sentimentalism for Lady Denham's talk about her more practical concerns. She imparts to Charlotte an unnecessary warning that both her nephew and her niece must marry money. The latter has just been trying to wangle a week's visit at Sanditon House, but, though they are very good young people, Lady Denham has never been overreached in her life and will not be now; she cannot make her house a hotel. Charlotte, unable to sympathize, says nothing, but thinks her "very, very mean"; "And she makes every body mean about her."

Sir Edward's next rhapsody to Charlotte, on novels, is given mainly through the author's summary and critical comments. He is of course much more sophisticated than the young Catherine Morland. "His fancy had been early caught by all the impassioned, & most exceptionable parts" of Richardson and his sentimental successors. To him a lover's villainy is "Genius, Fire & Feeling"; and he feels himself "formed to be a dangerous Man—quite in the line of the Lovelaces." While he practises on any pretty girl, his one serious aim is to seduce Clara: "Her Situation in every way called for it." "Clara saw through him, & had not the least intention of being seduced—but she bore with him patiently enough to confirm the sort of attachment which her personal Charms had raised." Sir Edward has debated whether, if persuasion failed, he could carry off his prey to "Tombuctoo," but want of cash "obliged him to prefer the quietest sort of ruin & disgrace for the object of his Affections, to the more renowned." Such antisentimental satire, despite the serio-comic idea of seduction (a new note in Jane Austen), inevitably calls up some of the juvenilia; Sir Edward is far from Henry Crawford or Wickham or Willoughby.

The remaining four chapters are given almost wholly to Diana, Susan, and Arthur Parker, who, braving the hazards of travel and sea air, come to Sanditon in order that Diana may pursue her good works: she must procure accommodations and servants for the two groups she succeeded in luring to the resort. Her breathless story astonishes Charlotte, as Diana perceives; Charlotte has in fact been thinking "Unaccountable Officiousness!—Activity run mad!" Diana sweeps on, proclaiming that charitable labors are the best remedy for invalidism. Charlotte suspects that, as Mr. Parker worked off "his superfluity of sensation as a Projector, the Sisters were perhaps driven to dissipate theirs in the invention of odd complaints"; apart from minor ailments, nourished by quack medicine, "the rest of their sufferings was from Fancy, the love of Distinction & the Love of the Wonderful." And in their charitable exertions vanity went along with benevolence. Charlotte, being curious about the fragile Arthur, was surprised to find a stout young man sitting by the fire making and munching heavily buttered toast and drinking cocoa; he is very ready with particulars about the delicacy of his constitution. Diana is temporarily confounded by a message which indicates that her two groups of people are actually only one; she must hurry away and deal with the problems she has created—but she can parcel out the blame among the many persons she had enlisted to help, so that not much remains for herself.

Mrs. Parker takes Charlotte to call on Lady Denham and on their way they meet Sidney Parker, a well-bred young man who has just arrived and whose coming will bring joy to Mr. Parker and credit to Sanditon. As they enter the grounds of Sanditon House Charlotte catches through the morning mist a glimpse of "something White & Womanish" on the other side of a fence. A closer view proves that it is Clara Brereton, sitting "apparently very composedly" beside Sir Edward, both enjoying furtive privacy. "It could not but strike her rather unfavourably with regard to Clara;—but hers was a situation which must not be judged with severity." Since the author has already vouched for Clara's moral security, we may doubt whether Charlotte's visual progression is intended to reinforce the idea of Clara's physical and mental situation as equivocal, though we are left with a small puzzle.

The fragment breaks off with a clear return to satire. The callers are shown into a sitting room where Mrs. Parker points out a large portrait of Sir Henry Denham over the mantel and elsewhere, "one among many Miniatures," Lady Denham's first husband.

In its general structure *Sanditon* reminds us of *The Watsons*, the fragment of a dozen years earlier: the late work, while looser in the proportions and connections of its parts, also reads somewhat like a scenario in which the author sketches scenes she expects to amplify and organize. In matter and manner *Sanditon* is radically different from its predecessors. Its plot or theme is an enigma, since the fragment contains so many possibilities of restricted or complex development. Presumably the background would remain—the character and atmosphere of the village in the process of forced growth and of the multifarious activities of its middle-class and lower-class inhabitants. There is a possible germ of a normal Austen story in Clara Brereton, although we have only a few moments with her, and in Charlotte Heywood, the well-balanced and perceptive observer; both young women might have appeared in the earlier novels. On the other hand, these two are almost lost in a broad, amusing satire almost wholly populated by eccentric, exaggerated "humor" characters, some of them, as we have seen, farcical enough to have figured in Jane Austen's youthful burlesques. According to family tradition, she called the tale *The Brothers*; but we cannot begin to guess what story might have been created out of the three Parker brothers and their possible relations with other characters.

That the author was working seriously is shown by the numerous changes she made in the manuscript, which was evidently a first draft. In general, in the midst of all the variety of speech, action, and description, there are bits and phrases which have the Austen touch; the predominant texture, though, is lively but rarely subtle satire directed at rootless, restless, mainly shallow people. The shift to a new world and new methods—or the mature handling of youthful methods—might, if the author had regained her health, have led to a very significant rebirth; and some critics see in *Sanditon* not merely remarkable promise of a new vein but a positive achievement.[1] Others—with high respect for the author's courage and mental energy—may be unable to discern much more than brisk and brittle cleverness.

[1] Notably Mr. Southam in his acute critique (100–35), the fullest there is. Manuscript changes are recorded in R. W. Chapman's edition, *Fragment of a Novel Written by Jane Austen* (Oxford, 1925), and discussed by Southam.

Conclusion

I N MY YOUTH, a remote period, it was not uncommon to meet ordinary educated people who assumed that Jane Austen was nice reading for girls, a sort of feminine equivalent of G. A. Henty. In our time Lionel Trilling can say (in his essay on *Mansfield Park*):

Once we have comprehended her mode of judgment, the moral and spiritual lessons of contemporary literature are easy—the metaphysics of "sincerity" and "vulgarity" once mastered, the modern teachers, Lawrence and Joyce, Yeats and Eliot, Proust and Gide, have but little to add save in the way of contemporary and abstruse examples.

Whether or not we see most of these "teachers" in the line of Jane Austen, such a pronouncement is an arresting testimony to her stature and enduring significance as far more than a humorist and satirist and artist in filigree. Of course we read and reread her mainly because she is irresistibly entertaining, but it may be permissible to emphasize again the ideas and attitudes which we absorb while being entertained.

Jane Austen might have anticipated Robert Frost's avowal (in her own translation) that he had had a lover's quarrel with the world. She would surely, in sober mood, have agreed with Elizabeth Bennet in one of her sober moods (xxiv):

[194]

There are few people whom I really love, and still fewer of whom I think well. The more I see of the world, the more am I dissatisfied with it; and every day confirms my belief of the inconsistency of all human characters, and of the little dependence that can be placed on the appearance of either merit or sense.

No simple label can be attached to a writer whose humor, moral judgment, and religious faith secured her against both optimism and pessimism. In spite of various trials, of which she had her full share, she manifestly enjoyed life and enjoyed writing about it; but she was too intelligent, too wise, to hold any extreme or one-sided view of mankind.

Jane Austen's instinct for order and proportion is both ethical and artistic; the two strains are complementary and inseparable. Her much-praised poise and sanity, her unassuming, impersonal air of authority, are sometimes discounted, or even damned, on the ground that she stands firmly on a narrow, rigid, and obsolete code of values, whereas modern novelists, realistic, skeptical, and courageous, face actuality in all its bewildering complexity and confusion. Common premises seem to be that moral complexity has been conditioned by and grown along with technological complexity, that there are no moral absolutes, that skeptical honesty can confront confusion only by reproducing it; and a frequent "moral" is that reality, truth, exists only in the instinctual self, that the rule of life is obedience to that self. This kind of flattering unction may be thought a far more fatal delusion than any of Emma's or Jane Austen's. It would seem clear that moral values and problems in their essence, apart from changing practical applications, are much the same as they always have been, that most people, like their forebears, live more or less by the traditional principles which intellectual or emotional rebels can dismiss or denounce as pinched, warped, and obsolete (although they themselves may live with quite conventional decorum). If the rebellious notion were true, all great literature of the past would have died long ago.

In her social satire Jane Austen is not merely reprehending behavior she happens to dislike; as an individual voice of a central tradition, she exposes violations of the standards of morality, manners, and taste achieved by at least an enlightened minority over many centuries. Deviations from accepted norms are of course the staple material of social comedy, but they have not often been handled with Jane Austen's blend of fundamental seriousness and silvery or astringent laughter. She has a sharp eye for false values, cancers which have developed within the social organism. These are ineradicable elements of human nature which can and must be opposed. But Jane Austen's satire is not merely negative. She always keeps right values before us; these support, and are supported by, the right choices of individual characters, for, as Milton said, reason is but choosing.

Thus the moral fabric of Jane Austen's novels has a much larger context and foundation than the author's individual outlook or that of her age and class. She adds her own strong, pungent, and discriminating conviction to a scale of values which had age-old experience and authority behind it. For her that means a fusion of Christian virtues and principles and eighteenth-century reason, the latter being in large part an active inheritance from Christian-classical tradition, and the whole being sensitized and fired by controlled feeling. Whether or not Jane Austen had read a word of Burke, her pictures of village life embodied Burkeian principles of traditional wisdom, stability, and order. And her heroes and heroines, through self-discipline and integrity, must at once accept and transcend the tried rules and values of society, which, however far from ideal, still constitutes the only framework and nursery of virtue, reason, civility, and community.

Suggestions for Further Reading

THE BEST BIBLIOGRAPHY (by B. C. Southam) is in *The New Cambridge Bibliography of English Literature*, ed. G. Watson, 3 (1969), 692–700. A special work is *An Annotated Bibliography of Jane Austen Studies, 1952–1972*, by Barry Roth and J. Weinsheimer (1973).

Besides R. W. Chapman's edition of the works, which is used for this book, J. Kinsley and various critics have done a scholarly edition (1970–71). Editions of single novels, with introductions, are innumerable.

Biographical works are cited above under "Abbreviations" and in chapter 2, n. 1. Chapman's *Jane Austen: Facts and Problems* (1948; slightly revised, 1949, 1950) is a compendious survey of the life, works, and related topics.

The history of Jane Austen's reputation is set forth by C. B. Hogan, "Jane Austen and Her Early Public" (*Review of English Studies* 1, 1950); Chapman, *Jane Austen: A Critical Bibliography* (1953, 1955), a collection of brief comments and excerpts, 1811–1954; J. Cady and I. Watt, "Jane Austen's Critics" (*Critical Quarterly* 5, 1963); B. C. Southam, *Jane Austen: The Critical Heritage* (1968), which, with an introductory survey, collects reviews, essays, and comments of the years 1812–70.

To come to modern critical studies (omitting titles for authors cited and indexed in this book), that of Mary Lascelles (1939, 1963) remains distinctive. F. R. Leavis emphasized Jane Austen's "intense moral preoccupation" (*The Great Tradition*, 1948). Some critics who deal more or less closely with the individual novels are: M. Mudrick (1952, 1968), whose acuteness can be blunted by wrongheadedness; Andrew H. Wright (*Jane Austen's Novels: A Study in Structure*, 1953; revised, 1961); W. A. Craik (*Jane Austen: The Six Novels*, 1965); A. W. Litz (1965), who is scholarly, succinct, and suggestive; Y. Gooneratne (*Jane Austen*, 1970). Among anthologies of essays are those of W. Heath (1961), I. Watt (1963), B. C. Southam (1968), Judith O'Neill (1970), and, on *Pride and Prejudice*, E. Rubinstein (1969). Some of the essayists cited in this book are A. C. Bradley, R. A. Brower, Lord David Cecil, R. Farrer, Q. D. Leavis, C. S. Lewis, Edwin Muir, Lionel Trilling; numerous others are in the anthologies and in periodicals, especially *Nineteenth-Century Fiction*. Some comprehensive special studies which have more or less interest for general readers are those of H. S. Babb, A. M. Duckworth, K. Kroeber, D. Mansell (*The Novels of Jane Austen*, 1973, a spirited if "rather single-minded interpretation"), N. Page, K. C. Phillipps, B. C. Southam, S. M. Tave (whose book I did not see in time to use). Four critics especially concerned with eighteenth-century influences have likewise more or less general interest: F. W. Bradbrook (*Jane Austen and Her Predecessors*, 1966), L. W. Brown, K. L. Moler, and H. Ten Harmsel.

Many novelists have expressed opinions, from the laudatory Scott and the hostile Charlotte Brontë (in Southam) to those of our own time (for names without a reference see the index), e.g.: Henry James; Virginia Woolf; D. H. Lawrence (*Apropos of Lady Chatterley's Lover*, 1930); E. M. Forster; Elizabeth Bowen (*Saturday Review of Literature*, August 15, 1936; *London Magazine* 4, iv, 1957); S. Kaye-Smith and G. B. Stern (*Talking [Speaking] of Jane Austen*, 1943–44; *More Talk of [More About] Jane Austen* 1949–50); Margaret Kennedy (*Jane Austen*, 1950); Frank O'Connor (1955: in Heath); K. Amis (1957: in Heath and Watt); Malcolm Bradbury; Angus Wilson; David Lodge; L. P. Hartley (*Essays by Divers Hands* 35, 1969); Eudora Welty (*Shenandoah* 20, iii, 1969).

Among the many background books are: J. M. S. Tompkins, *The Popular Novel in England 1770–1800* (1932); Walter Allen, *The English Novel* (1954); Ian Watt, *The Rise of the Novel* (1957); R. J. Kiely, *The Romantic Novel in England* (1972).

Index

Index